Foreword

by
Councillor Ed
Chairman of Grassing

When I read Ian Goldthorpe's book I realised that it contains an enormous amount of information in a very small volume, being essentially a history book as well as a concise walkers' guide – perhaps, in effect, 'A History Lesson on the Hoof'.

In the many walks Ian so accurately and meticulously describes, either through this beautiful countryside or around the many fascinating little towns and villages, he goes to great pains to point out a number of interesting features and items of historical importance that may otherwise be missed. His excellent photographs admirably illustrate the great beauty of this small corner of the Yorkshire Dales and his absorbing little drawings depict, in particular, the great charm of many of the older buildings.

So this book is not only for people who are now able to walk the Dales footpaths, but also for those who once did and have now, in effect, reached their 'sell-by' date! It will I am sure, as it has for me, revive many happy memories even activating dormant leg muscles and rusty knees, possibly also causing many readers to reach for their boots and take to the hills again to discover many points of interest that were missed on previous visits.

Contents

Acknowledgements

Whilst carrying out the research and actually writing this book I have been most impressed, and greatly encouraged, with the tremendous enthusiasm for the project by the many local people, together with much fascinating information, advice and help which they have all so freely given. Before I started to write this book I thought that I was reasonably knowledgeable about the area, but now I realise how little I really did know!

Of course, there will be many who live in the area and have contributed a great deal to the community in various ways who haven't even got a mention and I apologise to them, most sincerely, since in deciding what to include I have had to concentrate upon those aspects that will most appeal and interest the many people who come here from all parts of the world.

However, the following I feel deserve a special mention and again I apologise for any omissions since there are many whom I have met during my research, and on the various walks who have shown me around their fascinating homes often making me cups of tea, at the same time giving me little bits of interesting information much of which has been included.

DAVID AND FREDA HELM in the first place for inviting me to write this book, at the same time giving me an entirely free hand regarding its format and what to include. We had a long debate upon the title and hope that we might have got it right, since making a mistake in this field can often doom a publication to failure and we don't want to have to store thousands of unsold copies for many years to come! However, writing this book and meeting many interesting new people has been a great therapy for me at a time of increasing anxiety due to my dear wife Mary's long and serious illness. Mary gave me great encouragement when writing my previous books and typed so beautifully all my manuscripts. Now I have to do them myself using my one finger!

HEATHER BEAUMONT for much valuable information relating to Hebden Village and the nearby countryside.

MEG BLOOMFIELD for information relating to the period during the Roman occupation of Upper Wharfedale.

JEAN BOOTH for helping me with dating some of the older walls in the Grassington area.

MONICA CHADWICK for correcting my initial text relating to both Cracoe Cairn and Rylstone Cross.

TOM CHALMERS for much help in connection with the Grass Wood Nature Reserve.

EDWINA CLEMENTS for information on Kilnsey Village.

EDGAR DARWIN for many interesting bits of information relating to Grassington in years gone by.

ANTHONY (Tant) DEAN for much fascinating information relating to Threshfield Village.

PETER FETHNEY for kindly showing me all the old photographs in the Upper Wharfedale Museum and for letting me have photocopies of a number from which certain of my drawings were made. Also for agreeing to read all my manuscripts, especially checking my grammar and attempting to remove at least some of my many commas!

ROBIN GAMBLE for information on Thorpe Village.

The late TED GOWER, who hearing about this project when I invited him to coffee one morning asked me if I would be willing to include some of his drawings. The next morning he arrived with a great armful of his delightful sketches some of which I am most pleased to include; my drawings will never be in his class and, of course, he could draw trees most beautifully – I can't!

CLAIRE GREAVES for information relating to the recent restoration and improvements to the Methodist Church in Grassington.

ROBIN HALL for information on Thorpe Village.

THELMA HALL for help in connection with the history of the buildings in Conistone Village.

The RAP Team, for being so patient with me and so readily making further alterations to the text after the initial typesetting had been carried out.

STELLA KEMP for much information about the former Grassington Hospital.

MARTHA KNEALE for help in connection with the many wild flowers to be found in this area and kindly identifying several specimens.

KENNETH LEAVER for kindly giving me the names of many properties in Burnsall Village and approximate dates of new buildings, conversions and alterations.

ANNE LISTER for information relating to The Rookery in Thorpe Village.

BRIAN METCALFE for much information about Linton Village and the Linton Residential School.

JOSIE METCALFE for information relating to Kilnsey Village.

SUSAN MITTON for giving me a lot of information about the buildings of Hawkswick Village.

BRIAN MOXHAM for kindly loaning me certain reports on some of the older buildings in the area prepared by members of the Upper Wharfedale Field Society Vernacular Buildings Study Group, and also for permission to reproduce his excellent drawing of the interior of Fold Farm in Kettlewell as it may have appeared in Medieval times.

WENDY PAGE for some interesting information about the Burnsall Grammar School.

LUCY PROCTOR for information about Threshfield Village.

JEAN REINSCH with her great knowledge of the area over many years, for giving me many historical details in connection with the whole section of Upper Wharfedale covered by this book.

ANTHONY AND VANESSA ROBERTS for many interesting items in connection with Kilnsey Village and Ramble No 9.

KEITH AND PAT SIMMONDS for much useful information in connection with Conistone Village.

IAN SIMPSON for information relating to the fine line of horsechestnut trees alongside the river at Hebden.

JOE SMITH for much information about Linton Mill and the nearby cottages known as 'Botany'.

MARY SMITH for telling me all about the founding of the Upper Wharfedale Field Society almost fifty years ago, and also for giving me much information about Threshfield Village.

JOHN SPENCER for information relating to the Wharfedale Rugby Union Football Club.

ALAN STOCKDALE for some very interesting information relevant to my chapter on Burnsall Village.

JANET TAYLOR for much help in connection with my chapter on Arncliffe Village.

ERIC THOMPSON for some very interesting information relating to the history of Rylstone Cross.

JOHN TOWNEND for information relating to the Manor House in Thorpe Village.

SARAH WHITFIELD for kindly loaning me her photograph of Ellesmere House in Grassington before alterations early in the 20th century, enabling me to make a drawing of this building as it appeared at that time.

MARK WILLIAMS of the Yorkshire Dales National Park, for providing me with extracts from the Ordnance Survey maps of the various villages to enable me to identify individual buildings.

DAVID AND JOAN WILSON for so kindly allowing me to inspect some of the details in their home designed by Sir Edward Maufe and loaning me the photograph of Far Scar showing the now demolished dovecotes from which my drawing was made.

COLIN & DAVID WRIGHT, of Gatelands Printers, for so obligingly printing photocopies of my draft texts for comments, whilst I waited, each time I called.

JOHN WRIGHT MBE for his great and unending help with many chapters in this book, more especially those relating to Grassington and its immediate surroundings, which has been invaluable.

MIRIAM WRIGHT for kindly doing the final proof reading.

FINALLY I must thank John & Eleanor Ford, Thelma Hall, Donald & Nancy Heffer, David Helm, Mary & Dennis Hurst and Jean Reinsch for each accompanying me on some of the many walks.

I was indeed most touched when David and Freda Helm the proprietors of the Dales Book Centre asked me if I would like to write a book about Grassington and the surrounding area, which they proposed to publish. I myself, like so many others, am a comparative newcomer having lived here for only twelve years! Incidentally, the indigenous members of the community have a most delightful name for those of us who were not born here, which is 'offcumden'.

Really, I have no special claim to fame except, perhaps, that I invented the Rossendale Way in Lancashire, now a designated middle distance footpath which is marked upon the Ordnance Survey maps. Also I helped, in a very small way, to rid Rossendale of almost all of its unfortunate legacy of unsightly derelict land together with the initiation of a massive tree planting programme involving the planting of thousands of native species, which has now been going on for over twenty years making parts of the Borough almost as attractive as the Yorkshire Dales National Park. In addition, together with a friend, I tramped the Ribble Way the whole of its seventy, or so, miles from the Dolphin Inn in Longton, below Preston, to Gavel Gap high up in the Pennines close to the source of the River Ribble, at the same time writing the text for the Official Guide to this fascinating and most beautiful walk which follows short sections of both the Pennine Way and the Dales Way along its route.

At the outset I decided that this book should be a local effort and I am especially grateful to Edgar Darwin, the Chairman of Grassington Parish Council, for so readily agreeing to write the lovely Foreword. Also I am much indebted to the many local people, already acknowledged, who have so kindly read my initial scripts making helpful comments and giving me much additional information.

For very many years now I have been coming to Grassington and the Dales and so I am commencing, in the first chapter, by describing something of my childhood memories. Also I am including a little about the fascinating history of Grassington and the surrounding villages and, more especially, mentioning the important buildings both old and new together with other features, which we shall see not only in the various settlements but also upon some of the walks, mostly short and suitable for beginners, which I shall describe and which are also amongst my best-loved.

But few visitors to the area will really know what it is like to live here! You will be aware of our wonderful range of shops and the great many delightful places in which to eat. Some of you will have stayed in our hotels and ancient inns, or our guest houses and holiday cottages, even on nearby caravan or camping sites, but I am sure that you are not aware of the many other facilities and events of which the casual visitor, especially, will not know about. Did you know, for instance, that there are over sixty different organisations in the Grassington area covering all age groups and all sorts of activities? For not only is this community a very caring one, but there are many people living here with outstanding talents and expertise, who are very willing to give a lot of their time and effort for the benefit of others.

So, in addition to telling you some of the things that most guide books talk about, but hopefully in a much more exciting way, I am going to say a little about the many attractions and activities that take place here, and also something about the great characters who work so hard running our shops and other facilities, together with all the other events that make the Grassington area such a dynamic and satisfying place in which to live attracting people from all over the world, many coming over and over again.

Ian Goldthorpe, Grassington,
North Yorkshire.

January, 1998.

My Early Recollections of Grassington and the Dales

I was born on Guy Fawkes Day 1931 into what, at the time I suppose, was a fairly privileged family. A few years earlier my father having studied at Guys Hospital set up what was to become a very well respected and successful dental practice on the west side of Hull which my only brother, Keith, was later to take over. My mother was a professional musician.

From as far back as I can remember we always had a car, initially a little Austin Seven, and frequently at weekends we all went for a ride usually as far as the southern edge of the North Yorkshire Moors where on almost every occasion I was very sick, possibly due to the much less well surfaced roads and the petrol fumes which seemed to invade even the best of cars at the time!

After my brother was born a regular holiday pattern was established whereby my brother and I were taken each year for a weeks holiday to Whitby; my parents having a separate holiday in the Dales taking with them an uncle and aunt. Whilst they were on holiday, usually in Wharfedale, we were looked after by a nurse who had helped my mother considerably after the birth of my brother. Nurse Bursall came and stayed with us and took us out each day in her little car when we had a really exciting time with picnics, etc. I think that the Dales were considered too advanced for us at the time, more especially since there was no sand to dig! However, I always found the North Yorkshire Moors with its dales and delightful little towns and villages much more exciting than sitting on the beach; nevertheless I was especially fascinated with Robin Hood's Bay, where there was no sand at all but the rocks were covered with seaweed, limpets and lots of other marine life!

As regards Whitby we always stayed with Mrs Marwood in a spotlessly clean cottage, located in a little courtyard of small houses entered through a narrow archway, halfway down the hill on the right of Flowergate. I especially liked to go through Woolworth's in those days with its distinctive smell and narrow wooden strip floors, going in on the upper floor and emerging at a lower level overlooking the fine harbour. Almost every day, after breakfast, Mrs Marwood's daughter June would take my brother and I into the nearby Pannett Park, where we would spend a long time watching the large goldfish swimming around. Whitby has changed hardly at all since those days in the mid 1930s, apart from the introduction of the fine new bypass road and bridge, from which there is a superb view of the Old Town and the new marina.

My grandparents had been visiting Grassington for many years, long before I was born, travelling by train and staying at the Manor House in The Square, at that time run by two sisters Maud and Liz Simpson.

From an early age I started painting pictures and was most impressed by a colour postcard that our parents sent to us from the Dales, reproduced from a watercolour of the famous view of Bolton Abbey with the stepping stones in the foreground. This painting was very similar in character to a series of postcards, including the Bolton Abbey view, that have appeared in Grassington in the last three years, or so, depicting rather nice scenes in the Dales again reproduced from watercolours. I kept this postcard for many years and had about three attempts at copying it, but I am sure that my efforts were in no way as good as the original painting!

It was in the very early 1940s, during the Second World War, when my brother and I were first brought to Grassington and I well remember instantly falling in love with the place! When the war started my father gave up his car and, instead, cycled to the surgery a distance of between two and three miles on a rather solid and old fashioned bicycle that he had acquired. Our doctor, who still had two cars I suppose in case of emergencies, kindly lent us a car to travel to the Dales for this holiday. It was in the days of red petrol and petrol coupons and so I seem to recall that we didn't go far afield once we arrived here, having travelled up Wharfedale via Collingham and Harewood.

We stayed at Grassington House, which at that time was run by the two Miss Crabtrees. This beautiful building greatly impressed me, for there was no conservatory at the front and the fine railings and entrance gateway and gates were intact and hadn't even been taken away for the war effort! Where the car park now stands was a most beautiful walled garden which gave me great pleasure. I was most impressed by the vivid green of the, almost weedfree, lawn and the similar greenness of the other lawns in the area due, I suppose, to the much greater rainfall than we were used to in Hull.

The Pump and Grassington House in the 1920s showing the railings and gateway

The uneven cobbled square fascinated me and I well remember my father telling me that Garrs Lane, which was also cobbled and very uneven and rutted outside the present Grassington Pharmacy, was a Roman road. He wasn't far wrong since although it is doubtful whether this part of Garrs Lane was ever a Roman road, Scar Street and possibly also the rough partly cobbled lane running past Pletts Barn, known as 'Water Street', are thought to date back to Roman times.

The Pump, or Fountain, was not in its present location and the paved area with seats in the centre of The Square was

occupied by the underground public toilets, which were not to be visited if you could possibly avoid it, since as I remember the gents it would only have merited about a quarter of one star by present day standards! A local resident recently recalled to me how when she was young she frequently played in The Square with her friends. A favourite game was to wait until someone went into the toilets and then jump onto the flat roof, that was little over two feet above the level of the cobbles, and tap-dance on the glass brick lighting panels set into the concrete slab. Main Street was surfaced about as far up as The Dales Kitchen and on its left-hand side were located the large metal pylons which appeared to dominate the adjacent buildings. There were four main corner metal angle supports, which almost joined at the top and in between on each side was a lattice work of metal strips to give strength to these ugly green painted structures, which through their thick drooping wires carried the electricity generated by the river. I vaguely recall the Town Hall, keeping guard over the top of Main Street which at that time, as far as both visitors and locals were concerned, provided mainly cinema type entertainment in the evenings.

The Black Horse

I remember being taken into the Black Horse when Mr Stubbs, a very large and robust man, was the landlord. A local artist, Reginald Brundrit who normally painted landscapes, did a portrait of

Mr Stubbs which required many sittings in order to get the likeness correct. The picture was called 'Fresh Air' Stubbs and thus this is what he was known as thereafter! This painting was accepted and later purchased by the Royal Academy. However, a photograph of the painting can be seen in the Upper Wharfedale Museum in The Square. At this time the bar was a fairly small room extending from the present front door to the wall of the building adjoining Garrs Lane. Externally the front of the building was very much as it is today, but the most notable internal feature was the parrot, sitting in its cage on the bar, which frequently used very bad language, indeed many words that I had never heard before due to my innocent childhood!

The most dominant feature in The Square at the time was the Café Royal located in the 'Liverpool Warehouse' building in the section presently occupied by Country Concept. This tearoom had a huge sign painted in black with the name in large gold Roman lettering. It was very much a place for hikers and cyclists and I don't remember any other cafés, or restaurants, of any significance at the time.

My grandfather's favourite walk, and also that of my father, was to struggle up Moor Lane to Yarnbury. The top of the first steep rise used to be called 'Hungry Laugh Hill' by the lead miners because at this point on their way home from work they could smell their dinner cooking and gave a great hungry laugh! On reaching Yarnbury we turned right on to the unsurfaced lead mine road, then cutting across on a footpath into Hebden Gill through Hebden Village and back along the river to Grassington. This ramble was a picnic job which took us all day and had to be done, I soon learnt, every time we came to the Dales. Mercifully, even in those days there was a seat on the first steep section leading up to Spring House Farm where the Royal Oak Furniture Company is now located. Occasionally, and especially if it was fine, extra mileage was added in order to visit the chimney and after the war to see the little industry which had sprung up to obtain barytes and other valuable minerals from the old spoil heaps. The picnic lunch was always

eaten in Hebden Gill, in the bleak upper section which is treeless and where the effect of the lead mining era is very much in evidence. I well remember the pretty wooded lower section of this little valley, before the main village is reached, with its cottages and little waterfall. The next point of note was the suspension bridge over the River Wharfe; here my brother liked to coax me into the centre where the handrail is very low and then cause the bridge to vibrate and shake! The nearby avenue of chestnut trees along the riverside always impressed me, and also signalled that the major part of the walk was over and, at last, we were on the homeward stretch!

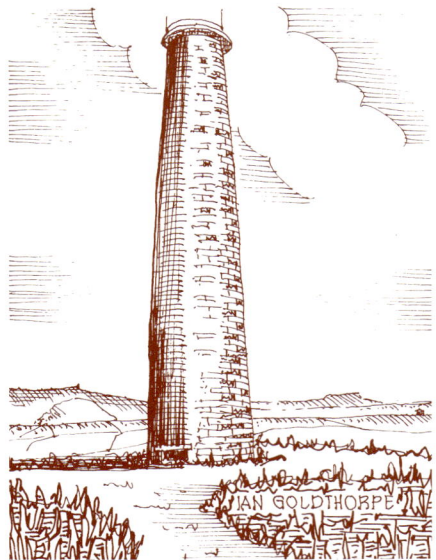

Lead Mines Chimney

My next fascination was the ram pump below Lythe House, which was there then and still looks just the same today; you can still hear it pumping intermittently once every ten seconds or so! We always stopped to look at the stepping stones, but I don't think that we ever managed to go across since in those days, there were a few stones missing and if I recall correctly they were both where the flow of water was greatest and the river at its deepest.

Low mill was in a derelict state and had a very large crack in its upstream gable wall;

its walls were also partly covered with ivy. In each successive year we had another look at this building and always marvelled that it still hadn't fallen into the river! Happily now it has been beautifully restored.

On our way back to Grassington we usually had a look at the Linton Falls, walking along the 'Tin Bridge' in order to get a better view. The metal bridge, which was erected in 1904, was still in operation when we came to live here; it had the same latticed metal balustrade detailing as the electricity pylons had in Main Street, and both were made by Glasgow firms.

A walk to Linton Village was always on the agenda. Our route each time was the same, proceeding from The Square along Hebden Road where there was only a small amount of development, turning right down the 'Snake Walk' which at that time was a narrow walled and mostly flagged footpath all the way from its start at the main road. From the Linton Falls we walked straight up to Linton along the road, usually pausing to have a look at Little Emily's Bridge. At this time Linton Mill was in full operation but it was not a pretty building following its rebuilding, being entirely single storey with a series of northlight roofs. The Fountaine's Hospital building impressed me very much and seemed much larger in scale than it does today; my brother and I enjoyed walking over the old bridges. Our return to Grassington was always by the same route.

The following year we were brought to Grassington House again and in the main the holiday followed a similar pattern, except for the fact that some friends joined us and I very well remember going into Grass Wood with them for a picnic. We also saw the Strid and walked through Bolton Woods. However, the most memorable feature of this holiday, for me, was that I was violently sick and Dr Cameron, who lived at Grassington Old Hall in those days, soon arrived on the scene. This is probably why, in the following year, we were taken to stay at the Devonshire Hotel on the other side of The Square. Of course, we still had food rationing and I well remember Mr Cowan, the landlord, saying each morning 'I don't

know what I am going to give you all for dinner this evening'. However, he always had a very nice meal ready for us and I especially remember having salmon one evening which, of course, was a very special delicacy in those days!

For the next few years we went to stay at Arncliffe in Littondale for our annual holiday. For me one of the great joys of the Yorkshire Dales is that the little towns and villages are still, for the most part, as I remember them in my early youth and so is the countryside with its outstanding scenery, ancient woodlands, stone barns and great network of stone walls, still on the whole well maintained.

Of course there have been changes and many probably for the better, for instance the coming of electricity to the area and the subsidies to hill farmers, that have enabled the pattern of farming that has gone on for centuries to continue.

November 1997 marked the 50th anniversary of the passing of the 1947 Town and Country Planning Act, which made it obligatory for local authorities to set up planning departments and for the general public to submit planning applications for changes of land use, new development, etc. This great pioneering piece of legislation which has now been copied around the world, together with other legislation such as, for instance, the scheduling of sites and structures as ancient monuments, the listing of buildings as being of special architectural or historic interest, the designation of outstanding groups of buildings as conservation areas, the protection of important trees by the making of tree preservation orders and, of course, the National Parks and Access to the Countryside Act to name but a few, have done much to preserve and enhance Britain's rich heritage from the past.

In the very early 1950s, when mains electricity came to the Dales, before the National Park was designated the CPRE (Council for Protection of Rural England) did a major job in negotiating to get the new overhead power lines sited so that they would not spoil the famous views. This applied within the various towns and villages, as well as in the countryside along the roads and footpaths since it proved impossible to get the electricity authority to put the cables underground as, for instance, in the case of certain parts of the Lake District.

It is interesting to speculate upon what might have happened to the Yorkshire Dales especially with the advent of the motor car, if we hadn't had the planning and associated legislation, together with the endless efforts of the CPRE and other interested amenity organisations such as, in more recent times, the Yorkshire Dales Society.

Certainly the famous reef knolls in the vicinity of Thorpe and Cracoe villages would by this time have virtually disappeared at the hands of the large quarrying firms, since they contain an extremely pure type of limestone. Many farmers would have sold off bits of their fields, the parts with the best views, to town dwellers for the erection of holiday cottages these usually being constructed with the cheapest materials, probably with corrugated iron roofs and all quite alien to the character of the area. Many of the fine trees would have been removed to sell for their timber, and most of the key trees in the villages and towns would have either been 'butchered', or removed usually upon the pretext of endangering buildings or cutting out daylight. Many of our beautiful old buildings, with traditionally small windows, would by this time have had large picture windows inserted to let in more light and afford a better view.

The above is only a very small indication of the considerable and irreversible damage that might have been done and, so, we should all be eternally grateful for the wonderful work which the National Park Authority has carried out since its inception in 1954 possibly, as far as the buildings are concerned, their control being as outstanding as that of any other national park in the country. Now that the National Park is an independent authority headed by a young and dynamic National Park Officer, Heather Hancock, we should all give her, her colleagues and committee our full support in connection with the many difficult decisions which they will have to make in the years that lie ahead, in order to be able to preserve and further enhance our very rich heritage from the

past but still making it relevant to the future. Incidentally, Heather was brought up in Kelbrook when it was still part of Yorkshire; now it is part of the great and historic County of Lancashire where I spent many very happy years during my working life and my wife Mary and I have many good friends.

The setting up of the Yorkshire Dales Millennium Trust together with a substantial grant from the Millennium Commission, will enable a lot of valuable work to be carried out within the next few years including the restoration of many historic field barns, the rebuilding of many miles of dry stone walls, new tree planting in ancient woodlands together with the planting of new woodlands using native trees, to mention but a few items.

Returning to our holidays in Arncliffe, this village despite being used for many years for the filming of the ITV serial 'Emmerdale' might well be described as one of the Yorkshire Dales' 'time warp' villages, since it is still virtually as I remember it as a child. For three or four years we stayed at the Falcon Hotel when Marmaduke Miller was the landlord. He was a kindly man, although very lame, and a very excellent watercolour artist; but I think that nearly all his pictures were painted in Littondale! At that time Freddy

The Falcon

Grisewood, the famous BBC presenter, was a frequent guest but he was never there at the same time as we were staying. Bridge End House with its large fireplace that inspired Charles Kingsley to write his famous book 'The Water Babies', was used as an annexe and was usually fully booked; it is now the home of Mrs Miller, Marmaduke's widow, who did the marvellous cooking in those days. On one occasion I recall that my brother and I had to stay with Mrs Gill at the post office which is still run by a member of the same family, Annis Gill. It is the cottage behind the telephone box and had a whitewashed front wall in those days. At the end of the green, abreast of the telephone box, was a very large tree which was obviously near the end of its life. Nearby were some very small saplings which had recently been planted; they are the three large trees we now see today.

The Falcon has changed little since we stayed there and has the same grained front door, which always seems to be firmly closed whenever I go there. Nearby is the unaltered gents toilet, which nevertheless can be very useful and surely by this time ought to be listed! The Village Green is still exactly as I first remember it, the only new developments being the very recent installation of kerbstones to the edges of the grassed areas and some new stained windows to a cottage, on the opposite side of the green to the Falcon,

which appear to me to be slightly out of character. Beyond the Village Green are only three other major changes, namely the beautiful conversion of a barn into a house, a small unfortunate flat roofed extension to the lovely Victorian school and the fairly new Village Hall which, I understand, is very well used by the residents of Littondale as a whole.

From Arncliffe we went on to stay for our holidays for one or two years with Mr and Mrs Coates at the delightful 17th century Croft House in Litton, which still looks much the same today. I remember going to Arncliffe with their son Laidler, to help to ring the three bells for service one Sunday. The vicar's wife at the time was also a farmer, having a fine herd of Guernsey cows and living in the nearby large Georgian vicarage, which has now been split into two private houses. On one occasion in Litton it rained solidly from our arrival on the Saturday and so, on the Thursday, we decided to have a drive to Aysgarth to see the falls. As soon as we reached the top of Kidstones Pass we

Arncliffe
Village Green

were bathed in sunshine, the falls were in flood; once back in Wharfedale it was still raining heavily and so it continued until we returned home on the following Saturday.

The holidays with my parents were followed by a number of cycling holidays, usually with friends, staying at youth hostels. The most memorable event of this period was pushing our bicycles from Kettlewell up Park Rash, which at that time was covered with huge limestone boulders. Once we reached the summit, which was the boundary between the old West Riding and North Riding counties, the road down Coverdale was beautifully surfaced.

After I went to Manchester, in 1960, I spent many happy weekends staying at youth hostels and walking with friends in the Peak District, Lake District, Yorkshire Dales, the Bowland Fells and Pendle. Initially when we visited the Dales we travelled by express bus to Skipton, then taking the local bus to Linton where we usually stayed at the youth hostel, the former Linton Rectory which is reputed to be haunted! We usually had time for at least one pint in the Fountaine Inn before 'lights out' at the hostel. At this time the Inn had not been extended 'up the steps at the back', and the bar was opposite the entrance. The 'snug', on the right inside the door, is still much as it was in the early 1960s.

I especially remember one occasion at Linton when we had a violent and lengthy thunderstorm during the Friday night. The following day was perfect and so we decided to walk along the river to Bolton Abbey and then get the bus back in the late afternoon. The river was fairly low, everything was very peaceful, and just before Loup Scar I decided to go to the edge of the water to take a photograph looking back towards Hebden. Fortunately, I took my eye away from the viewfinder before taking the picture; for without any warning a wave of muddy water the best part of three feet in height came sweeping down the river carrying with it tree branches and other debris. I had only just stepped back in time! So do beware, for the River Wharfe, although possibly one of the most beautiful rivers in Britain is also one of the most treacherous! It is renowned for rising and falling several feet in a matter of minutes. Recently when it was not in flood, it claimed the lives of three victims in the space of three days and in the summer of this year very sadly the honeymoon couple from Hampshire. It looks beautiful and innocent, especially when the flow of water is minimal, but even then it has many lethal and dangerous stretches, often with cold fast undercurrents. Incidentally this river takes its name from the Saxon word 'guerf' which means 'swift'.

Croft House

When you come out of the car park at Colvend in Grassington, you will see a nicely carved oak sign pointing leftwards inscribed 'To the Village', and usually a fair number of people wending their way on foot the two hundred or so yards along Hebden Road to the famous cobbled square.

Grassington is really a small town not only on account of the very urban character of its central area, but more especially because it was granted a Charter for a market and fair in 1282, which continued to be held until about 1860. As recently as the late 1970s the annual Patronal Feast was still taking place on the cobbled square. Of course it also has its famous Town Hall about which more will be said later.

Mention also should be made here of Edgar Darwin, the very well respected Chairman of Grassington Parish Council. He has lived here all his life, when he was young working for his father who was a farmer. He later had his own farm which is now carried on with the help of one of his sons. Nowadays Edgar most diligently carries out many important civic duties such as after-dinner speaking, laying the odd foundation stone and unveiling the occasional brass plaque. For such an important post I, personally, feel that he should rightly be styled 'The Mayor of Grassington'. He tells me that we didn't have any civic regalia until fairly recently when he managed to obtain a somewhat suitable chain from a local jumble sale!

And so Grassington is, perhaps, the smallest of Yorkshire's rich heritage of fine and historic market towns. It also has probably one of the best and most compact shopping centres with some famous names! Of course, people come from all corners of Britain to sit on Helen Midgley's famous easy chairs and try on her almost endless supply of delightful shoes, many of the customers being ladies whose husbands frequently fall asleep on the other chair! In addition there are many fine and unusual dresses to be had, together with the distinctive handbags and umbrellas which really make you wish you had an endless supply of money. But beware of the prominent sign that reads 'Changes of mind cannot be exchanged'.

Nearby is Robert Bunney, the well-known gentlemen's outfitter, where all the local men are attracted in order to try on garments and other items in the elegant interior of his shop, having almost the appearance and atmosphere of a miniature stately home! It reminds me of one very well respected member of our community who met one of our 'offcumdens' outside this shop when the old 'local' said to the comparative newcomer 'Be careful you don't lose out, because Mr Bunney is going to have a sale and I have started saving up so that I can afford to look in the window!'.

Our third well established and famous shop, which is well signposted from The Square and tucked away in Pletts Barn one of Grassington's most historic buildings, is The Mountaineer. Here you can buy every piece of equipment that you are ever likely to need in order to prepare for any eventuality when exploring the spectacular countryside of the Yorkshire Dales.

Of course to walk through any of the Dales towns and villages with the distinctive plastic bags from any of these traders carries almost as much credibility as walking through London advertising the fact that you have been shopping in Harrods!

There is a number of other outstanding shops which contribute greatly to the prosperity of Grassington. If you are looking for a nice gift to take home for your children, friends or relations a look around Woodware, The Gallery and The Nook really is a must.

Woodware, with its many floors at different levels and maze of small rooms is, in effect, 'Grassington's Departmental Store'. The Gallery is packed from end to end, and almost from floor to ceiling, with

Location of the principal uses in the centre of Grassington in February 1998

1 The Country Gardener — Garden Centre,
Gift Shop, Home Improvement Centre

2 WYMAS — West Yorkshire Metropolitan Ambulance
Service Grassington Station

3 Pride of The Dales via Horseless Carriage Services

4 Springroyd House — Bed and Breakfast

5 John Spencer — Solicitors
Wilman & Lodge — Chartered Surveyors,
Estate Agents and Valuers

6 Grassington Service Station

7 Town End Garage

8 Earls Emporium of Fine Foods

9 Dales Newsagent — National Lottery, Greeting Cards

10 Dales Toffee Shop — Homemade Toffee and Fudge,
Dairy Icecream, Delicious Gifts, Cold Drinks

11 The Gallery

12 Harkers of Grassington

13 Spar Supermarket

14 Halifax

15 Church House

16 The Wine Shop

17 Robinsons Country Collection

18 Robert Bunney — Quality Clothes for Gentlemen

19 Stork Exchange — Children's Second Hand Agency
Some New, Hire Service Available, also Video Hire

20 Woodware

21 Devonshire Hotel

22 J W Hodkinson — TV, Video, Electrical

23 Country Concept

24 Peter Walbank Fabrics

25 Ashfield House Private Hotel

26 Helen Midgley — Ladies Fashions, Shoes
The Green Room — Organic Hairdressing
Eves The New Woman — Beauty Therapy

27 Picnics — Sandwich Bar and Takeaway

28 Christine — Hair Design

29 Bubbles of Grassington — A Licensed Restaurant

30 The Dales Book Centre

31 J H Herd — Television Rental

32 Country Fresh — Flowers and Greengrocery

33 The Foresters Arms

34 Martyn Fretwell — Shenstone Gallery

35 Bill Stockdale — Quality Family Butcher
(Colin M Robinson)

36 Grassington Surgery

37 Grassington Post Office
— Quality Greetings Cards, Stationery & Gifts

38 Number 47 Licensed Restaurant
— Bed and Breakfast

39 The Dales Kitchen Licensed Tearooms and Brasserie

40 Gemini Studios — Handmade Jewellery,
Local Art & Crafts, Curios

41 Craven Cottage Licensed Restaurant & Tea Rooms
— Bed and Breakfast

42 North Yorkshire County Library
— Grassington Library

43 The Royal Oak Furniture Company
— Acorns to Oak Furniture Showroom

44 Chapel Antiques — Kitchenalia, Victoriana,
Farmhouse Furnishings

45 Junk & Disorderly

46 Grove House — Bed and Breakfast

47 Grassington Town Hall and Devonshire Institute

48 Town Head Guest House
— Bed and Breakfast, En-suite Facilities

49 The Mountaineer

50 Grassington Congregational Church

51 Fish & Chips — Traditional & Tasty

52 Lucy Fold Tea Rooms

53 The Black Horse Residential Hotel & Restaurant

54 Grassington Volunteer Fire Station

55 Grassington Antiques

56 Slater Marchant — Insurance Brokers

57 Grassington Pharmacy

58 Manor House Holiday Flats

59 Folk Museum — Upper Wharfedale Museum Society

60 Grassington House Hotel
— Hotel & Restaurant with Public Bar

61 Moore's China Shop — Spode Blue Room Collection

62 Cobblestones Café

63 Dales Country Trading

64 The Craft Shop

65 The Nook — Tax Free Shop for Overseas Visitors

66 The Smithy

67 Midland Bank

68 Barclays Bank

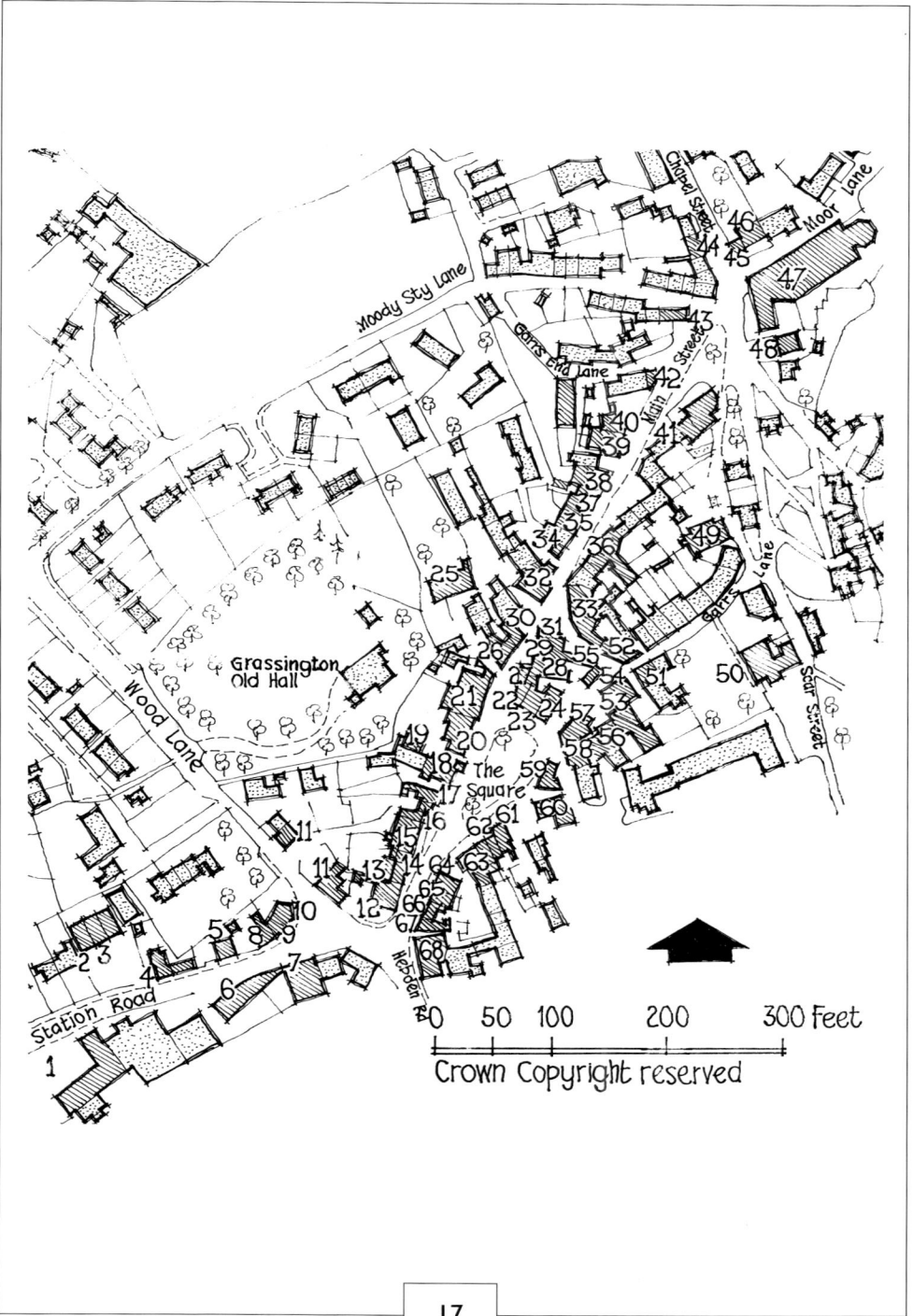

Moody Sty Lane

Chapel Street

Moor Lane

Gair's End Lane

Main Street

Garrs Lane

Star Street

Grassington Old Hall

Wood Lane

The Square

Hebden Road

Station Road

0 50 100   200   300 Feet

Crown Copyright reserved

17

exciting things but beware of the very low and very hard beams if you go upstairs! However Jan, who runs it, can always find in a matter of seconds, or so it seems, any item you might ask for if she has it in stock! The Nook is really for the very discerning shopper and really needs a full exploration including the rooms upstairs.

Mention, of course, should be made of the Smithy on the right just as you enter The Square. Originally there were four smithies in the town of which only this survives. There has been a smithy on, or near, this site for about 400 years since it is mentioned in Pierse's survey of 1603. In the 1930s it was the meeting place of many of the old men of Grassington, where all the gossip went on and the blacksmith at the time called it a 'reet kall 'ole'. The local men now tend to sit on the seats at the end of Garrs End Lane, adjacent to Main Street and those in front of the Town Hall, the former being known as 'The House of Commons' and the latter as 'The House of Lords'. However the end of the seat nearest to Main Street is now left empty, since in recent years the person making a habit of sitting there has always been first to die! The present blacksmith, Basil Keep, doesn't do any shoeing of horses but is a superb craftsman and makes a lot of delightful items in metal ranging from lamps to footscrapers! He has also made spiral staircases for a number of houses in the Dales. Many of the items he makes are on sale nearby at Woodware, but if his light is on call in to see him and have a chat. Basil has improved the first floor of this building for the use of his son Robert, who is a talented artist and very adept at framing pictures.

The Smithy

On the food side Harkers of Grassington, on the left as you enter The Square, has been our local bakery for very many years but has had some changes of ownership. Jeremy is especially well known for his excellent bread, a large selection of homemade biscuits, Yorkshire curd cheesecakes, delicious fruit pies and outstanding sandwiches.

Nearby on Station Road is Earl's Emporium for Fine Foods run by Peter and Lyndsey Earl. They both make many different quiche recipes and usually a sweet – their lemon one is excellent – before they open the shop each morning; in addition over sixty cheeses are generally in stock.

Picnics on the right in Main Street just above The Square, also deserves a mention for its excellent homemade sandwiches, which are ideal for taking on walks and come in neat plastic packs reminiscent of sandwiches from Marks & Spencer! The Spar supermarket is open for long hours and most useful for those in rented cottages, as also is the Fish & Chip shop.

Peter Walbank and Barrie Hodkinson are two well established businesses located in the old 'Liverpool Warehouse' building at the top of The Square. Their shops are both well worth inspection for the surprisingly comprehensive ranges of both fabrics and electrical goods. Don't omit to have a look at Grassington Antiques tucked away in a little fold behind Peter Walbank's.

In addition we have an excellent Wine Shop in The Square boasting as good a selection of beers, wines and spirits as you will find in many of the supermarkets. Bill Stockdale, our butcher, has a very high reputation over a wide area and Country Fresh run by David Lockyer and Julia Lambert sells good quality fruit and vegetables as well as flowers. Their delightfully arranged baskets of fruit, complete with an attractive card for you to write, make a lovely and inexpensive present to take to a loved one!

The Upper Wharfedale Museum also located in The Square, occupying what was originally two lead miners' cottages, is well worth visiting if you want to know more about the fascinating history of this area since it contains many interesting artifacts. The museum is open every afternoon during the summer months and during the afternoons at weekends throughout the remainder of the year. The Museum Society are, however, willing to open by prior arrangement at other times for interested groups and they especially like to welcome school parties. To arrange for a party visit please telephone Peter Fethney on 01756 753059.

Country Concept and Moore's China Shop are comparative newcomers. The China Shop contains a wide range of Spode Blue Ware and many items of white china much sought after by china painting clubs, but it was the delightful range of historic shop buildings in the Nation of Shopkeepers series based upon examples to be found in England's great wealth of old market towns that caught my attention and so, for a mere few pounds, you can buy your own 'listed building'. Nearby, Dales Country Trading is located in a building that has its origins in a 17th century corn mill, later used as farm buildings and then as cottages. Its interior is fascinating with many different levels, today being neat and tidy and offering for sale many items of clothing.

For a wide range of newspapers and magazines try the Dales Newsagent. David Helm's family have had a shop in Grassington for nearly sixty years and his Dales Book Centre is very well stocked, having an excellent range of books especially about the Dales, other parts of Yorkshire, Lancashire and the other national parks in the north. However, don't omit to go upstairs to see the many lovely paintings by local artists and mainly of the Dales, also the selection of books largely of local interest on sale at half price!

Further up Main Street on the left is Shenstone Gallery run by Martyn Fretwell in the former smithy said to have been owned by the notorious murderer, Tom Lee in the 1760s. Beyond is Gemini Studios where Katie Denby, who is the Exhibitions Silversmith for the Jorvik Museum in York, makes fine jewellery and sells work by other local craftsmen; again don't omit to visit the upstairs gallery with many more pictures of the Dales painted by local artists.

Beyond is the Acorns to Oak furniture showroom displaying only a small number of the many items made at Spring House Farm on Moor Lane on the way up to the lead mines. Here Paul and Janet Kent established their traditional oak furniture business in 1985, now known as the Royal Oak Furniture Company today employing nearly forty people. Their beautiful furniture is sold in Harrods and their extensive showroom at Spring House Farm is well worth a visit.

If you have the misfortune to be taken ill, or have an accident, our two talented and well respected doctors, Ian Kinnish and Andrew Jackson and their dedicated staff, will be only too willing to help and in dire emergencies their Immediate Care Scheme will quickly swing into action. Of course we also have a resident ambulance as well as a fire engine, both with devoted local crews, together with a Fell Rescue Team started by Len Huff and Ken Smallpage in 1948. Their new headquarters building was officially opened in 1977 by HRH The Prince of Wales, who arrived by helicopter. After the opening ceremony Prince Charles spoke to a number of people gathered outside the perimeter fence including an elderly cyclist. The Prince asked him how far he had come to which the man replied 'I've come from Bradford especially to see you' to which Charles quickly replied 'You must be mad'.

Our chemist, Peter Redhead, located at the top of The Square will process your colour films in just one hour! If you want a really attractive present at a very reasonable price try the Dales Toffee Shop, known locally as 'Toffee Smith's', near the entrance to The Square, where locally produced shortbreads, fudges and toffee are available in attractive boxes with a delightful drawing of The Square and other local Dales views drawn by Ted Gower, a local artist.

At present we have four banks, Barclays now with a cash machine, Midland, the Halifax which is also an estate agency – probably the smallest in England which sadly may have closed by the time this book is published – and the Girobank at the Post Office. In addition, Wilman & Lodge also have an estate agency, John Spencer, our solicitor located in Station

Road, is a Rugby Union Internationalist and former Captain of England, having been President of Wharfedale RUFC for twenty years. He is also Vice-Chairman of the Governors of the historic and academically excellent Ermysted's Grammar School in Skipton. John Spencer is also an agent for the Skipton Building Society. Just off The Square, tucked away in a little fold off Garrs Lane is located Slater Marchant, our insurance brokers.

In Station Road on the left on the way down to the bridge, complete with car park, is The Rustic Rabbit and the Country Gardener garden centre together with a 'do it yourself' section well worth careful inspection!

Mention should be made here, I feel, of the demise of two very well-known local shops, first Grassington Hardware in Chapel Street, now Chapel Antiques, which was always known locally as 'The Shop with the Bath Outside'. The bath which was prominently displayed on the wall outside had an additional note attached which read 'Back scrubbing extra'. Secondly, Miss Cooper's Wool Shop, where The Craft Shop is now located. She had a dog which detested men; as soon as a man entered the shop it would suddenly appear from the room behind and jump over the counter! It would usually try to bite the man's ankle as he left the shop. Miss Cooper was a familiar figure each morning as she trudged from her home in Chapel Street, down Garrs Lane and across The Square in her famous wellington boots, accompanied by the dog. After retiring she became happily settled in Threshfield Court, but sadly died in March 1998.

Should you unfortunately be stricken with toothache, then we have our own dentist, Philip Bode, whose surgery is located on Station Road towards the bridge.

Of course, the locals go out shopping before the visitors arrive, when the various food shops are very busy and there is a continuous stream of people going in and out of the newsagents. Shopping in Grassington is both a pleasant and time consuming occupation on account of all the people you meet who want to have a chat.

Regarding social activities in Grassington and Upper Wharfedale the Grassington Festival which was started sixteen years ago by Peter Walbank, Colin and Fleur Speakman and was then carried on by Ken Marsden followed by Dennis Dodge and Judith Joy, is one of the most important events in our annual calendar. Thanks to the enthusiastic and very dedicated Festival Committee and its influential Artistic Director, Rowena (Bunty) Leder, many of the great and famous have appeared on the stage of our Town Hall. For instance over the years these have included Julian Lloyd Webber, Lord Healey, Richard Stilgoe, Kit and the Widow, Ian Wallace, Pam Ayres, Sir Ranulph Fiennes, Tony Benn MP, John Briggs and Lord Harwood to mention but a few. The Festival lasts for a fortnight taking place at the end of June and the beginning of July. Recently on meeting Bunty I asked her how she managed to get such famous people to come to such a small place as Grassington, to which I got the usual somewhat straightforward and blunt reply 'Because we pay them'. On reflection she quickly added that 'Artists like to work and now that the Grassington Festival is well established many more famous names are anxious to come here'.

Ken Dodd opened the Grassington Festival in 1998, bringing his latest show to mark the completion of the extension and refurbishment of Grassington Town Hall, a most important building in the everyday life of the residents of Grassington and Upper Wharfedale.

The Grassington Town Hall Millennium Project was the brainchild of Dr Andrew Jackson and Paula Vickers, who are both much involved with the Grassington Players and also the Grassington Pantaloons. As a result, a Millennium Project Committee was set up under the auspices of Grassington Parish Council. Terry Woodhead was appointed the Project Manager and it is a great credit to this committee as a whole to note that well over £600,000 was raised or promised in just over nine months. Over £300,000 was granted by the Millennium Commission and other generous donations were received from North Yorkshire and East Riding Community

Development Fund, Rural Development Commission, English Partnership, Foundation for Sport and the Arts, Craven District Council, North Yorkshire County Council, Yorkshire Dales National Park Authority, Halifax, Yorkshire Care Group, The Duke of Devonshire's Charitable Trust and Barclays. In addition, donations were received from many local people and the names of all the donors to this project are to be put into a Commemorative Book to be kept in the Town Hall. At the time of writing the Committee are still some £2,000, or so, short of the overall target and various fundraising events and other small projects are being arranged. This project has been honoured by the award of a Charter for Community Initiative inaugurated and personally signed by HRH The Duke of York. The award took place in January 1998.

When visiting the Town Hall be sure to have a peep at the enormous kitchen, once a billiard room, which can easily be viewed through the hatch in the Games Room. It is larger than many of the village halls in the Dales and at the specific request of the local ladies who do the catering for the many events that take place here, it has been left largely unaltered!

On the aspect of churchgoing, I would think that the people of Grassington and the immediate area are more godly and the percentage church attendance considerably higher than in the country as a whole. For not only have we the ancient Parish Church of St Michael and All Angels, Linton-in-Craven located on a delightful site down by the River Wharfe serving Grassington and the villages of Linton, Threshfield and originally Hebden, but also the Congregational Church in Garrs Lane, the Methodist Church in Chapel Street and, more recently, the Roman Catholic Church of St Margaret Clitherow in Threshfield.

IAN GOLDTHORPE

The Methodist Church

21

Whilst I can only speak personally about Linton Church, I understand that the other three churches are well supported. It is a most moving experience to take part in a service in this 12th century Anglican Church, where local people have worshipped within its walls continually, Sunday on Sunday, from about 1150 up to the present time, although of course over the years the building has been altered and extended many times. Our Rector the Rev'd Canon Christopher Hayward, is a very well respected man, ably assisted by the Rev'd William Wheeldon, who was once a monk at Mirfield and more recently the Principal of the College of the Resurrection at Mirfield. The Rev'd Al Hodge, who lives in Burnsall has recently joined Christopher and William, all three being extremely popular! In addition, we have three Readers and a great army of retired clergy and their wives who live in Threshfield, and all of whom take a very active part in the life of the church. Ever since my wife Mary and I came to live in Grassington, Linton Church has been very well attended and now is frequently almost packed to capacity for the 10.30 am service, usually with a number of visitors often from far corners of the world!

This ancient church, which is open daily, is obviously a great source of comfort for the many visitors who come within its hallowed walls, finding time for a few minutes of quiet reflection in such a beautiful place, so often leaving poignant messages on our Prayer Board to pray for loved ones and those in need.

Of course funerals are very important social occasions in the Dales and no more so than in the part of Upper Wharfedale covered by this book. In whichever church or chapel such an event takes place will almost certainly guarantee a 'full house' since the dales folk attach great importance to giving the departed a good send off! Such an event is usually followed by a repast in one of our hotels or ancient inns.

The churches of all denominations in Upper Wharfedale work very well together for twice a year we have a joint service in the Town Hall, in which the clergy and ministers from the various churches take part. Needless to say, the Town Hall is always packed to capacity on such occasions and it is necessary to arrive there very early in order to get a good seat. Also we have an Annual Joint Churches Walk through some of Upper Wharfedale's beautiful countryside. Usually about two dozen people take part representing all denominations; we take a picnic lunch and stop for a short service at each church or chapel along the route. Mention should also be made of the now very popular Ecumenical Carol Service which is held in the Roman Catholic Church of St Margaret Clitherow.

Ann our Rector's wife, is a part-time Sister along with Judith Kinnish our doctor's wife at Threshfield Court a most caring nursing home. The original nursing home building was formerly the Wilson Arms Hotel, which was built about the turn of the century when the railway from Skipton to Grassington was opened. It has recently, in 1997, been extensively redeveloped and refurbished by the Yorkshire Care Group its very considerate owners, to provide, in addition to the nursing home ten independent dwelling units known as 'The Stables' having optional nursing home facilities. The Matron, Valerie Gains, and her Deputy, Liz Bedford, together with their most dedicated staff are doing a wonderful job in what must now surely be one of the finest establishments of its kind within the whole of North Yorkshire. Many of our friends and also my dear wife Mary, who only a few years ago were doing long walks and taking part in many other activities, now live there.

The Grassington Art and Crafts Exhibition came about as a result of a meeting called thirty one years ago by Major Bob Allen of Grassington, the object being to raise money to repair the cobbles in The Square. This has now become the highly esteemed annual event which takes place in the Town Hall towards the end of August each year. On the first weekend a Flower Festival is held, in rotation, in one of our four churches. Before each festival our talented army of flower arrangers, who are mainly drawn from the membership of the combined churches, descend upon the respective church to arrange a spectacular display raising money for the particular church in question. In order to exhibit in the Art and Crafts Exhibition participants have to be resident within a fifty mile radius of Grassington. The overall standard is extremely high and, as far as the pictures are concerned, there are many delightful examples which well portray the beauty of the Yorkshire Dales. Of course the cost of relaying the cobbles in The Square was paid for many years ago and surplus funds from this event are used for the benefit of both residents and visitors in the Grassington area.

Some sixteen years ago, at the suggestion of Peter Walbank the Chairman, the Grassington Chamber of Trade decided to organise a series of Dickensian events on the three Saturdays before Christmas, since hitherto trade at this time of the year had been very slack due to people instead spending their time shopping in the larger cities and towns. On these occasions all the traders and many visitors are dressed in Victorian costume and the town is most attractively decorated with a little Christmas tree and lights over each property in the centre. The Square, Main Street and Garrs Lane are all closed to vehicular traffic and there is a programme of events throughout each day and either the Grassington Players or the Grassington Singers perform in the Town Hall in the evening. For weeks before the ladies in the area are busy making thousands of mince pies, many of which are sold with coffee in Church House in The Square and at both the Congregational and Methodist churches. Overall the churches and other local people with stalls in the streets raise thousands of pounds for charities. The Morris Dancers from Burnsall, the Grassington Handbell Ringers and the Choir of Bradford Cathedral all usually perform on each occasion. It is estimated that in excess of 10,000 people visit Grassington on each of these Saturdays, many coming long distances by coach. On account of the ever increasing popularity of this event and all the detailed arrangements that have to be made beforehand, Mary Wilkinson was appointed to co-ordinate these occasions three years ago and this has resulted in their smooth running ever since.

One of the most flourishing organisations is the Upper Wharfedale Field Society which was started in 1949 following a meeting attended by Dr Arthur Raistrick and a number of other interested local people. Although starting from small beginnings, the Society now organises walks between six and nine miles in length, usually within the National Park on the third Saturday of each month, and shorter Monday evening walks during the summer months. During the winter months a series of lectures and members' evenings is held in the Town Hall, again about every three weeks on a Monday. Often a visiting lecturer will come to talk upon a subject of particular interest to the members and, even on a snowy night, we have sometimes had as many as eighty people present. Over the years the Society has grown and there are now six groups, each of which members interested in particular aspect can join. These cover ornithology, botany, archæology, geology, vernacular buildings and local history. Each group has its own chairman and meetings usually take place in members' houses; separate walks and outings also being organised.

The Upper Wharfedale Concert Club was started over eight years ago by Hugh Roundhill, ably assisted by David Mann. A private fifty seater coach is always easily filled and on some occasions two buses are hired. The venues for concerts, ballets and plays include the Town Hall, Grand Theatre and West Yorkshire Playhouse in Leeds, the Alhambra Theatre and St George's Hall in Bradford, the Victoria Theatre in Halifax and the Bridgewater Hall and Opera House in Manchester. Hugh and David seem to be adept in choosing really outstanding performances. Members participating can request whom they would like to sit next to, and only on one occasion has a member requested not to be seated next to a certain other person; this shows how well we all get on with each other, I suppose!

Since 1988 Bob Skipworth has been organising three outings a year to Opera North Leeds which always prove popular, with a fifty seater coach again easily being filled on each occasion.

Also worthy of special mention are the winter music evenings arranged by Edwin Page, a most talented retired local teacher and pianist. These originally started in the Red Lion in Burnsall in 1978 followed by the Wilson Arms Hotel in Threshfield, then on to Gills Top in Grassington and are now held at Aynham Close, a local sheltered housing scheme. A small charge per person is made on each evening, which is put into a fund, and at the end of the season given to the local venue to be used for charitable purposes. Edwin has a particular theme each meeting, covering classical music in general and telling something of the life of the composer, whose work he is about to play. He also plays certain items on the grand piano and at the interval Wendy, his wife, provides delicious coffee and biscuits with the help of some of the other ladies present.

For those interested in carrying out research into social and family history the Wharfedale Family History Group will be of special interest; this group meets monthly at Aynham Close. The members are dedicated to carrying out a programme of recording and indexing all memorial inscriptions in the Wharfedale area.

The Grassington & District Horticultural Society is another popular organisation providing a series of winter lectures in the Town Hall. In addition Len Lang, the Honorary Secretary, arranges two outings a year, two shows in the Town Hall and an Open Garden Day in Grassington and Threshfield each alternate year.

The Grassington Players are another very active organisation with many members, who stage at least two plays a year in the Town Hall to almost professional standards. Their producers are Dr Andrew Jackson, Beryl Bamforth and John Armitstead. The Grassington Pantaloons produce a pantomime in the Town Hall in February each year and Dr Andrew Jackson writes the script.

Again performing well-nigh to professional standards are the Grassington Singers, who give their concerts in the Town Hall ably conducted by Terry Bamforth. There are many other activities which take place in the area of which perhaps the

Embroiderers Guild, the Friendship Club, the Women's Institute and the Grassington Handbell Ringers deserve a special mention.

Regarding sporting activities there is a number of clubs covering angling, badminton, bowling, morris dancing, cricket, football, swimming and, of course, the well-known Wharfedale Rugby Union Football Club which was founded as far back as 1923. In addition there are several organisations and activities for the younger members of our community.

All new residents coming into the area are given a Directory giving very full details of the many facilities in the area delightfully compiled by four local people with a most attractive cover drawn by Brian Moxham. They took over the concept from a former Methodist Minister, the Rev'd Barrie Hirst whose intitial guide was both out of date and out of print!

As far as places to eat are concerned in Grassington itself, there are many to choose from and it would, I feel, be unfair to single out specific ones. However, most are of a very high standard and between them cater adequately for most tastes.

For this reason many of our guest houses do not provide an evening meal. However, there are many different types of accommodation available in Grassington and its very immediate environs ranging from a 17th century farmhouse by the river, 17th century houses within Grassington itself often with fine 'Tudor styled' fireplaces and in some instances beautiful gardens often tucked away in the ancient 'folds', old coaching inns, converted barns, Victorian and Edwardian houses. Four poster beds are also on offer and, in addition, there are many cottages available to let, some of which are very quaint, dating back to the 1600s.

So you will now know that Grassington is not exactly a sleepy little place, and in any case I haven't mentioned any of the activities that go on in the neighbouring villages, all of which have well used village halls.

A Short History of Grassington

First, I think it is worth noting the origin of the name 'Grassington' which is derived from the old English word 'gaersing' which means grazing and the word 'tun' which means farmstead, or hamlet.

The Grassington we know today is comparatively new when we consider that in much earlier times the local people all lived upon the moors less than half a mile to the north of the present town, in a large open area known as 'Lea Green' above Grass and Bastow woods. These earlier settlers would have initially picked this area since at the time this would be less densely forested and, being on higher ground with outcrops of rock, the woodland would comprise thin scrub with ashes rather than oaks which would be easier to clear and also to use for the construction of dwellings. There was also more early development on the west side of the river, just to the north of Threshfield. From research that has been carried out, and numerous artifacts that have been found over the years, these settlements date back as far as the Bronze Age, namely around 2,000BC. Two Celtic villages were also located between Grassington and Bastow Wood. In order to see evidence of some of these early settlements, preferably in late evening sunlight, go up Main Street turning left along Chapel Street to the left of the Town Hall, and then right up the steep Bank Lane, at the end of a long row of lead miners' cottages. After passing some stables on the right, go through the gate ahead and proceed along a nice grassy walled lane. On the left, some hundred yards or so from the gate at the end you will clearly see the sites of some of the houses, together with the remains of some Celtic field enclosures. These primitive dwellings would comprise a low dry stone wall on top of which would be erected a crude timber framed hut, with a pitched roof covered with bracken and heather.

The Romans arrived in Upper Wharfedale during the 50sAD, departing sometime in the 5th century. It is worth noting that they quickly developed the area of Upper Wharfedale around Grassington as an important grain growing area which was soon supplying Ilkley and Bainbridge, comprising hundreds of acres of Romano-British development being an extension of an earlier Celtic agricultural site. They were, of course, great road builders and by AD76 they had completed the road from Aldborough to Ilkley, up Wharfedale and beyond. They had started to mine lead at Greenhow and Scar Street, also possibly the rough and partly cobbled lane in Grassington known as 'Water Street' may be part of their road leading to Greenhow. Some years ago there was a sign at the beginning of Scar Street indicating that this was a Roman road. Hopefully this sign will be put back in the near future and I also feel that high priority should be given to carefully repairing Water Street, together with the repaving of the pleasant fold adjacent to Pletts Barn.

There was a Roman villa not far away in Gargrave. The Roman name 'villa' referred to a farm complex. From Buckden the Romans built their road along the line of Buckden Rake, then over Kidstones Pass to their Fort at Bainbridge. In Wensleydale they built a number of villas and one of the most important roads they built from Bainbridge was that going south to Manchester. Much of the first section of this road survives as 'Cam High Road', then becoming for a time the route of both the Pennine Way and the Dales Way. Little is known of its route across the Forest of Bowland, but part of its route is evident where it crosses Longridge Fell near Ribchester. Here they had built another Fort in AD79, which lies partly below the Medieval Church and the adjacent Churchyard. The National Trust Museum in the village records Ribchester's ancient history and possesses many artifacts. Nearby is the White Bull, which is an inn with Roman columns gracing its front entrance. Beyond in Greenside, as a result of excavations carried out by the Lancashire County Museum experts in the 1970s the foundations of various rooms of the Bathhouse can be seen.

The White Bull

Here the Romans built a ford over the River Ribble, and through the West Pennine Moors much of the route of the next section of the road is well-known. Several miles of road near Darwen and through Affetside are built on top of the original Roman road terminating at the southern end of Deansgate, in Manchester. At the north end of Deansgate Manchester Cathedral is located and at the other end excavations were carried out in the early 1980s, on the site of the Roman Fort in Castlefield. The reconstruction of the North Gate of the Fort at this time is an example of the final Fort built here around 200AD, the only one that would have been constructed in stone. The original Fort was made of timber and its walls of soil. Inside, the buildings included the Commander's

The reconstruction of the North Gate of the Fort in Castlefield

House, stables, a hospital, granary and barracks to house the soldiers.

As far as development within the bounds of present day Grassington is concerned this also goes back a very long way, since the Doomsday Book in the year 1087 recorded that at this time there was already 300 acres of arable and meadow land in its vicinity, upon which tax was paid to the king. It would appear, therefore, that Grassington had been founded several generations earlier and the late Susan Brooks, a local historian, thought that this would be sometime early in the 7th century. This site would have been chosen on account of it being located on a fairly level shelf above the more densely wooded slope leading down to the river.

One of the few streams in the area, though today hidden in a culvert under part of Main Street and The Square, also provided a ready water supply. Nearby was land that could be gradually cleared from the moraine covered slopes. Initially it would be difficult to plough, not only because of the contours but also on account of the great number of stones and boulders, even though the soil was fertile. These were removed and placed in lines about thirty feet apart and the land between ploughed. On account of the slope, in most instances the furrows had to be worked along the contours with the sods being turned downhill, eventually creating a series of steps separated by steep 'risers' which have survived intact, since for many centuries now the Dales have been a great sheep rearing area with very little arable land. These terraces, which today are much in evidence on the hillsides around Grassington are often known as 'strip lynchets'. Locally, they are commonly known as 'raines' and thus 'Raines Lane' which runs along one of these terraces. The first wooden huts to be erected made from nearby trees, surrounded a grassed open space, which until not long ago was known as the 'Market Place' and now 'The Square'.

When William of Normandy became king of England in 1066 the country was fairly well organised from a local government point of view. For in the time of Edward the Confessor, his predecessor, the country was divided into shires which in turn were divided into hundreds, or wapentakes, as they were locally known. Grassington was in the wapentake of Staincliffe. Most townships and villages had a thegn (or thane), a lesser nobleman, usually responsible to an overlord or in some instances directly to the king. The most important change that William made was, in most cases, to replace the thegn by a Norman Lord of the Manor. The last Anglo-Saxon thegn of Grassington was Gamelbar, a wealthy man who owned land in Linton and Threshfield. He became a king's thegn after the Conquest and was thus, in effect, the first Lord of the Manor under William. William divided out all the country, apart from the royal estates, amongst the comparatively few Norman barons who had helped him win the kingdom. These barons were able to grant out much smaller estates to their friends and relations, which were called manors. The first Lord of the Manor of Grassington was Nigel de Plumpton who by 1190 held the manor from the great Percy family, who in turn held it from the king.

A manor at the time was the smallest unit of local government and the king relied upon the Lord to keep it in order. To the Lord of the Manor it was a source of income and his prestige depended upon the number and condition of the manors that he held. Normally he would not have a lot of personal contact with his manors, this being the responsibility of his bailiffs and stewards. However, in the Grassington Manor the Lord reserved for himself some of the best arable land as well as Grass Wood. The local people had strips of arable land and pasture rights on the common pasture in return for working a stated number of days, usually as craftsmen, etc., according to their particular skills. In 1282 Robert de Plumpton gave the king ten pounds for the

IAN GOLDTHORPE

Grassington Old Hall

27

institution of a market and also a fair in Grassington. The market was held each Friday and the fair was held on the day before and the day after September 29th, the Feast of St Michael and All Angels, to which Linton Church is dedicated. In 1752 the calendar was changed losing eleven days which the local people refused to accept and, from then onwards, the Grassington feast was held on 10th October instead of September 29th.

The Lord of the Manor only paid occasional visits to his Manor House or Hall. Grassington Old Hall, as it is known today, was originally a timber framed building which was replaced by a single storey stone building forming part of the present structure. Fountains Abbey had a large estate at Kilnsey which extended up on to the moors to the west. About 1190, not so long after the abbey was founded, Nigel de Plumpton gave the Abbot and the Community right of passage through his land at Grassington avoiding the arable and meadow land. This went on until 1539 and the beasts, carts, horses and men during this period followed a route across the open common pasture, roughly on the line of High Lane. Incidentally, it is recorded that about 1400 Fountains Abbey received some lead from Grassington which came from the Lea Green area.

In 1597, George Clifford, 3rd Earl of Cumberland, inherited the Lordship of the Manor of Grassington. He quickly arranged mortgages with most of the tenants, as he was in debt at the time, whereby they received a lease of their holdings for a short term in return for a lump sum repayable at a fixed date. Many of these leases were already in place by 1603 and within five years most of the mortgages were paid off.

At the time George Clifford inherited the Manor nearly all the buildings, apart from Linton Church and Grassington Old Hall, would be constructed in timber, including the bridge over the river, which by this time was in a very dilapidated state. In 1603, the old timber bridge was dismantled and the downstream section of the present structure, originally known as 'Linton Bridge', was erected as a narrow stone humpbacked packhorse bridge,

similar in many ways to Barden Bridge and also possessing many masons marks. The older structure can be clearly seen today if you look at the stonework on the downstream side. It was repaired in 1661, widened in 1780 and raised to its present level in 1825. A cantilevered pedestrian footpath was added on the upstream side in 1984. Nearby, in 1600, would be the 'cruck' building today known as 'Lady Well Cottage' with a thatched roof and walls constructed of wattle and daub.

Lady Well Cottage would probably have been the last cruck building when going up the dale; some cruck buildings still survive in Drebley and lower down Wharfedale many of these buildings remained until early this century. It would appear that from Grassington updale most of the buildings would be of timber framed construction reusing, in many instances, timbers from the earlier huts, together with thatched roofs and wattle and daub infill between the framework. There were few individual field barns at this time since from the Medieval period onwards the produce and food for the animals was kept in tithe barns operated by the Lord of the Manor. The barns that did exist would be mainly of timber construction although a few stone ones would have already been built and Pletts Barn could well come into this category, perhaps dating from the latter part of the 16th century.

The new landowners who were known as 'freeholders', soon set about exchanging land with their neighbours in order to get together large enough areas to form reasonable sized fields and, once they had paid off their mortgages, set about rebuilding their farmhouses together with new farm buildings in stone. Soon afterwards land, and often whole farms, were sold to people from outside Grassington since investment in land was growing; this led to absentee landlords and thereby a new breed of tenant farmers.

I think that it would be appropriate here to just mention, very briefly, some of the other industries and events which have played an important part in the life of Grassington up to the present time, often leading to the subsequent arrival of new people into the area.

28

Church House and adjoining stable in 1910

Lead mining in the vicinity of Grassington has been carried out since, at least, as early as the 15th century, initially as mentioned earlier being on Lea Green in the form of shallow opencast pits which can still be seen alongside the Dales Way. When George Clifford, Earl of Cumberland, became Lord of the Manor the industry, which had been carried on intermittently over the years, took on a new lease of life. The Earl, who was familiar with lead mining brought skilled men from his Derbyshire mines to work in the mines on Grassington Moor. In addition, miners from Swaledale and Cornwall also settled here bringing with them valuable expertise relating to mining techniques. A few years later, the Earl built a smelt mill adjoining his corn mill on the River Wharfe.

A century or so later, in 1750, the Duke of Devonshire married one of the Clifford heiresses and came to be the Lord of the Manor of Grassington. He quickly began a great development plan for the industry including the construction of a water-course, the erection of a large new smelt mill together with a cupola, and the tall chimney which is still an important feature today. The Duke then greatly improved the road between Grassington and Gargrave, where he owned a wharf on the Leeds and Liverpool canal.

As a result of this great influx of new people into the area, many new properties were built in Grassington, mainly in the form of infilling between the buildings of the farming community, from the latter part of the 17th century up to the early part of the 19th century. Also a number of the existing larger properties were each split into two or three smaller dwelling

units, and thus the unique and quaint urban character of Grassington came into being, many of the little 'folds' being the original farmyards in more rural times.

But even though many people had moved here at times when the lead mines were prospering, life in Grassington must have been grim and very hard. The daily trek up Hungry Laugh Hill to Yarnbury in all sorts of weather must have been a nightmare and have taken its toll on the health of the miners. Life for their families would also be difficult living in very cramped conditions, in damp cottages and having to carry water from either Well Head or The Fountain in The Square, long before the advent of damp proof courses, electricity, mains drainage or mains gas, a prospect that would have enticed few of our present day offcumdens to settle here! How different things are today with the many carefully restored cottages, in the summer months adorned with numerous window boxes and hanging baskets together with wall creepers and very colourful little front gardens, such that a picture of the attractive cottages in Chamber End Fold with their great myriad of flowers together with the occasional hollyhocks and sunflowers may well soon compete with the thatched cottages of the South of England for a place on the front of greeting cards, chocolate boxes and biscuit tins of the leading brands of these lines of merchandise.

The late 1870s marked the start of the demise of the lead mining industry and many miners and their families gradually left the area. Shortly afterwards, Grassington House changed its use from a private house into a boarding house, thus heralding the birth of the tourist industry which is still so important to Grassington today. Towards the end of the 18th century a new textile industry had grown up with the establishment of Grassington and Linton mills, but compared with the lead mining industry, these both had a relatively short life. Grassington Mill had closed by 1894 and Linton Mill was closed in 1959.

Quarrying and the transportation of limestone is now quite an important industry employing a number of local people. When I first came to Grassington, Swinden Quarry was very small and, until not so long ago, the road to Skipton went between the various buildings connected with the processing plant. In more recent times the old quarry at Skirethorns has been considerably expanded, and a limited planning permission was granted some ten years ago for quarrying at Cool Scar near Kilnsey.

Going back in time again to the 18th century, there was a great need for some better roads. Therefore, in the late 1750s the road from Grassington to Pateley Bridge was turnpiked, the route as far as Hebden being sited much lower down, with a marked double bend where it goes around some old enclosures. In 1853 the Duke's improved road to Gargrave was joined by a new road from Cracoe to Skipton. The road up the dale from the bridge turned immediately left, avoiding the steep hill up into Grassington, joining the line of the present Grass Wood Lane near the barn just beyond Bull Ing Lane.

With the coming of the railway in 1902, many new people, mainly Bradford commuters, moved into the Grassington area and the long terraces at Bridge End and Brooklyn, looking almost as though they had been transported from Bradford, arrived shortly afterwards together with other properties to satisfy the new demand for housing.

Soon after the First World War, in 1919, Grassington Hospital on the road to Hebden was opened by Bradford as a TB sanatorium, having approximately two hundred beds together with living accommodation for staff and doctors. In 1966 the hospital ceased to be a sanatorium, becoming instead a Psycho-

Geriatric hospital and finally closing late in 1984. When the hospital changed its use there were twenty three Spaniards who were members of staff who continued to work there. At its peak there were, for a short time, as many as two hundred and eighty beds and about one hundred and fifty six staff, resulting in new people moving into the area, additional employment for local people and a number travelling daily from the Skipton area.

Early in 1939 the Linton Residential School site was developed as a camp to temporarily accommodate whole families who had lost their homes during the war, a number coming from the Brighton area. Soon after the end of the Second World War the camp buildings were bought by Bradford Corporation who established a residential school in the buildings for underpriviledged children, which again brought some new people into the area and provided additional employment for local people. The school finally closed in the early 1980s.

Again in the 1980s, a limited amount of new development was permitted by the National Park Authority and, together with the advent of early retirement, a number of people who had visited the Dales over the years and fallen in love with the area moved here, mainly from London, Lancashire and West Yorkshire at the same time initiating many of the newer activities which now take part in the Grassington district.. This growth in activities was further helped by the many new people who have been coming to live at Long Ashes since the early 1980s.

Since Mary and I came to live here, there has been virtually no unemployment; similarly there is a great wealth of very talented craftsmen, especially connected with the various aspects of the building industry about which more will be said in the next chapter. In this context we shouldn't forget the ancient craft of building and repairing dry stone walls. Of course farming is probably still the most important industry in the Yorkshire Dales as a whole, and we are frequently reminded of this as ever larger tractors and muck spreaders trundle their way through Main Street.

Follow the Country Code

- Enjoy the countryside and respect its life and work

- Guard against all risk of fire

- Fasten all gates

- Keep your dog under close control

- Keep to public paths across farmland

- Use gates and stiles to cross fences, hedges and walls

- Leave livestock, crops and machinery alone

- Take your litter home

- Help to keep all water clean

- Protect wildlife, plants and trees

- Take special care on country roads

- Make no unnecessary noise

Safety on the Moors and Fells

Anyone wishing to undertake the walks described in this book should bear in mind the variety of terrain and weather conditions which might be encountered. Stretches can be hazardous and ramblers are strongly recommended to take the following precautions:

Plan your route beforehand and leave details with someone.

Give yourself plenty of time; take some food and drink with you.

Use the proper equipment – stout boots, spare clothing, waterproofs – and take a map and compass with you.

In case you have difficulties take a torch, and a whistle. (The international distress signal is six long blasts or flashes at ten second intervals followed by a pause of one minute).

Exercise extra caution in wintertime as the weather can change rapidly. Colourful clothing can be very helpful for identification from a distance. In an emergency dial 999. Ask for Police who can contact the Upper Wharfedale Fell Rescue Team.

KEY TO SYMBOLS USED ON MAPS

————	Footpaths described
– – – –	Other footpaths mentioned
— — — —	Other footpaths not necessarily public rights of way
≈≈≈·≈≈≈	Line of dismantled railway
━━━━	Classified Road
═══════	Minor Road or Lane
═ ═ ═ ═	Unfenced Road or Track
⬤⬤⬤⬤	River or Beck
✳	Site of local, historical or archaeological interest
♧♧♣♧♣♧	Trees and Woodland
❘❩❘❩❘❘❘❘	Hillside
⌒⌒⌒⌒⌒	Crag, scar or quarry face
—64—	National Grid line reference number
▰	Building
✝	Church or Chapel
△	Hilltop
⩊	Viewpoint
LS	Ladder stile
S	Stile
Sg	Gated stile
G	Gate
GW	Gateway
FG	Field or Farm gate
KG	Kissing gate
CG	Cattlegrid
FB	Footbridge
T	Public Toilets

Where symbols are linked, for instance 'SG', indicates that the stile is to the left of the gate in direction of approach.

Before describing this walk I think that it would be appropriate here to say something about the nature of many buildings which we shall see on this, and all the remaining walks in the book, together with my special, or perhaps more to the point limited, knowledge of the many lesser buildings not designed by architects which come into the category now generally described as 'vernacular buildings', which can include the simpler dwellings, barns, etc.

During my architectural training in the field of architectural history I specialised more on Gothic and Victorian architecture. For instance, I spent almost one whole summer vacation helping a fellow student, who was writing a thesis upon the 'Churches of the East Riding of Yorkshire', by visiting and photographing all of these buildings on our bicycles which included an outstanding group located on the Yorkshire Wolds designed by a number of the leading Victorian architects.

But it was during the period from the late 1960s up to 1974, when I worked with Lancashire, that I was to learn much more about the simple vernacular buildings, and so I hope that you will feel it appropriate at this point for me to say a little about my experiences at that time. When I joined the Lancashire County Planning Department, it was at the time both one of the largest in the country and also one of the most respected by the planning profession, headed by Udolphus Aylmer Coates, its nationally famous and distinguished County Planning Officer. Two of my responsibilities in this vast county,

which embraced many different architectural styles and local building traditions, were listed buildings and conservation areas. These included such diverse groups of buildings as the Moravian Settlement, adjoining the boundary of the City of Manchester in the south and Little Langdale in the English Lakes in the north, which contains many unspoilt farmhouses and, of course, the well-known Slaters Bridge.

Looking back this was one of the most interesting periods during the whole of my working career, for I was able to inspect the interiors of many of the vernacular buildings throughout the County belonging to a variety of building traditions. The County also gave grants to help with the repair and maintenance of listed buildings and it was my responsibility to personally inspect them, assessing their suitability and prepare a report for the Planning Committee. One of my most interesting assignments in this respect was to meet Lord Clitheroe, and together with him climb up on to the roof of the South Aisle of Downham Church, which was leaking badly. Afterwards he kindly invited me to have lunch in Downham Hall, which was a most pleasant experience, especially being waited on by his butler. Needless to say, the Committee decided to give a grant to Downham Church! On a number of occasions I met Canon Whitsey, the Vicar of Downham, in connection with proposed alterations and restoration works to Whalley Abbey part of which serves as the Conference Centre for the Blackburn Diocese. A few months later Canon Whitsey left Downham to become the Bishop of Chester.

Old Lower
Hodder Bridge

My most memorable occasion dealing with listed buildings and ancient monuments was in connection with the Old Lower Hodder Bridge, which has three segmental arches and dates from the Medieval period. At this time, in the early 1970s, the centre of the river marked the boundary between Lancashire and the former West Riding of Yorkshire. The bridge was in a very bad state of repair, being well covered with plants and a number of trees on the top whose roots were making serious inroads into the stonework, thus endangering the stability of the fine arches. It had been agreed that the Lancashire County Surveyor's Department would carry out the necessary restoration work under the supervision of a representative of the Historic Buildings Section of the Department of the Environment now, of course, known as English Heritage. I, therefore, arranged a meeting with a representative from both the Department of the Environment and the County Surveyor's Department on the site. On arriving at the site, all three of us walked to the centre of the bridge, which of course has no parapets, to discuss what was to be done. Unfortunately, these two gentlemen, whose names I can't remember, seemed to take an instant dislike to each other and a dreadful row quickly developed as to exactly how the necessary repair work was to be carried out. In view of the rumpus I very quickly retreated from the bridge back on to dry land as I felt sure that one or both of them would soon land in the river! However, in the end, the meeting ended amicably and the bridge was duly restored looking very austere for many years afterwards, but happily the vegetation has now returned again making it a beautiful subject for a colour photograph or a painting. A particular feature of many 17th and early 18th century buildings in Lancashire, especially in or near the Pennines, was the large number of stone floors at first floor level comprising thin slabs of Haslingden Flag, often in sections up to six feet square being supported on oak beams; also the large number of the original internal stone staircases that had survived.

Whilst in some areas of the country many of the early timber framed buildings remain, sometimes dating back to Medieval times, in Upper Wharfedale these earlier buildings have all but disappeared, some of which would also have been of 'cruck' construction. And so most of the earliest buildings we see today date from the beginning of the 17th century, many being built by the first freeholders. Some of these people soon became prosperous farmers and those owning free land of a value of forty shillings, or more, became yeomen and as such were qualified to serve on juries and to vote. They soon began to build more elaborate houses which are frequently referred to as 'yeoman farmhouses'.

Ever since the 17th century this part of Upper Wharfedale has been well endowed with a great army of skilled craftsmen, which still applies today, who have always been able to skilfully adapt and alter the buildings, especially in more prosperous times and as fashions changed. In addition the Dissolution of the Monasteries meant that the monastic stone-masons' lodges were able to take on building work elsewhere and their great traditions are reflected in the quality of the stonework of many of these yeoman houses.

In 1982 the Vernacular Buildings Study Group was formed in Grassington and the aim is to survey and record the vernacular buildings for the national archives including the National Buildings Register. This Group is a section of the Upper Wharfedale Field Society and is affiliated to the Yorkshire Vernacular Buildings Study Group, both of which the author is a member. Over the years the Wharfedale group have surveyed many of the older buildings in the area covered by this book, but due to the skilful way in which adaptations and alterations have been carried out throughout the centuries it is both a fascinating and challenging occupation trying to determine the development and history of each building. How much simpler it would be if only the buildings could talk? If they were able to talk of much greater interest would be what they have to say about the people who lived in them; the intrigue and goings on of the residents would make a much more exciting and saleable book than this one, especially regarding centuries ago when

Far Scar

this part of Upper Wharfedale would be very remote and relatively inaccessible from the rest of the country.

So I am going to do my best to say something about the architectural history of some of the more important and interesting buildings which we shall see, both old and new, on the various walks and rambles. Also I shall mention the names of the architects and craftsmen in the case of some of the newer buildings, restorations, etc.

Returning now to the walk around Grassington, this starts at the National Park car park at Colvend. First a look inside the National Park Information Centre is well worthwhile if it is open at the time of your visit.

This building (1), which was designed by Richard J Eves Associates, architects, was opened in 1988 and is a good example of present day craftsmanship. The stonework is so excellent that it almost appears to have been a conversion from an existing building, but this is not so. Considerable care was taken to cantilever part of the foundations in order to avoid disturbing the roots of the nearby trees. This Centre is open daily during the summer months and at weekends and some weekdays during the winter period. There is an excellent exhibition explaining much about this part of the Yorkshire Dales National Park, with some excellent photographs and illustrations. Here all the information is available if you want accommodation, or other details, should you be proposing to stay in the area; a bed booking service is also offered.

The Centre is managed by David Rymer, Senior Information Assistant, who is a well-known local personality. For many years David, together with his brother Peter, ran a travelling greengrocery business in Upper Wharfedale and then for a further eight years The Fruit Shop in The Square, where Moore's China Shop is now located. David is also a celebrated local singer having a very fine baritone voice.

Turn left outside the entrance to the Information Centre, pass through one of the small gates following the sign marked 'To the Village', crossing Hebden Road on to the footpath. In a few yards on the left is Colvend.

This property (2), was built by Stephen Eddy who was the Mining Agent for the Duke of Devonshire. In the 1920s it was the home of Sir Arthur and Lady Godwin, who became the first Lord Mayor and Lady Mayoress of Bradford. In 1970 Colvend was purchased by the National Park and developed as a sub office. The Information Centre was formerly located in a single storey building attached to the main building and was demolished in 1989 to make way for Richard J Eves Associates carefully designed extension, which painstakingly matches the original building, and was completed in 1990.

On the right on the hilltop behind the Bus Station and the Post Office Sorting Office will be seen, in the trees, Far Scar.

This house (3), was built in 1920 to the designs of Sir Edward Maufe, the architect of Guildford Cathedral, for his brother Carl and Carl's wife Joyce. It is said to be a copy of a Sussex farmhouse and was never completed. Soon after building work commenced the cost of materials increased dramatically, due to inflation, and as a result the northern gable to the west elevation which should

35

National Park
Car Park (Colvend)

Start of Walk →

Garrs End Lane

Moody Sty Lane

Wood Lane

Station Road

Main Street

Beckett Road

Springfield Road

Moor Lane

Scar Street

Garrs Lane

Clibb Street

0   100   200   300   400   500 Feet

Crown Copyright reserved

have been identical to the south gable with a lean-to beyond, was reduced in width and a blank gable wall left to the north elevation. It was always intended that the scheme would be completed at a later date, but this was never carried out because the Maufe's felt that they already had enough accommodation.

Internally the woodwork was of a very poor quality, again due to the difficulty in obtaining good well-seasoned timber at the time, and much of it has been nicely replaced by the present owners. Maufe's pleasing and simple staircase remains together with a ground and a first floor fireplace which he designed. The first floor fireplace is of particular interest, since it is located across the corner of a bedroom, with a series of shelves above which diminish in length the higher up they go. Both fireplaces have simple rather chunky stone surrounds, with a raised squared moulding around the edge. The mullions to the windows again are square and chunky and the fallpipes likewise are square and of cast iron. Some of Maufe's original metal windows remain having characteristic casement fasteners with decorative arrow-head embellishments. A few years earlier an identical scheme, which was wholly completed, was carried out in Ilkley for another brother.

During the Second World War Mrs Maufe had the garden dug up to form allotments to help with the war effort. Carl died in 1942 and in 1947 Mrs Maufe sold the house to James Proctor who owned it until 1960, incidentally keeping ponies on the lawn! Shortly after acquiring the property James demolished the two dovecotes, shown on the drawing of the house, and used the stone to build a large garage at the rear.

Continue ahead crossing Springfield Road. A few yards further on, on the right, is St Michael's Rectory.

This new Rectory (4), was designed by Barry Rawson of Wales, Wales and Rawson, architects. The Rector moved here from a temporary residence in Station Road early in 1991. This building was erected in the vegetable garden of the Old Rectory next door. The Old Rectory dates from the 18th century and was much altered in the late 1920s, being used as the rectory from 1911 until it was damaged by fire in 1986.

Church House doorway

At Barclays Bank bear right into Main Street and the cobbled square.

On this walk I am only mentioning the buildings and other features which I feel are of outstanding importance. If you would like to know more about this fascinating little town, and embark upon a slightly longer perambulation, may I strongly commend to you a little booklet on sale throughout Grassington at the modest price of £1 entitled 'One Hundred Things to See on a Walk Through Grassington'. This publication, which has been produced by a local charity - Grassington One Hundred - has now sold well over thirty thousand copies and thus enabled many thousands of pounds to be given to local charities and good causes in Upper Wharfedale.

Here we join the Dales Way.

The lower part of Main Street including the first part of The Square is known locally as 'Town End'.

As Main Street starts to widen out Pletts

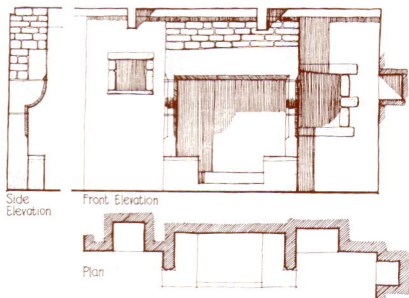

Fireplace at N°1 Rathmell Fold

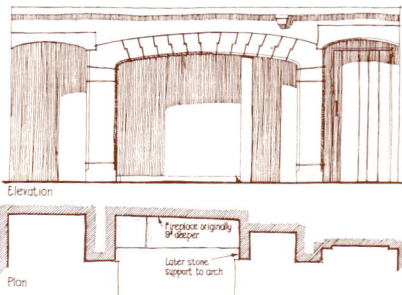

Fireplace at N° 2 Rathmell Fold

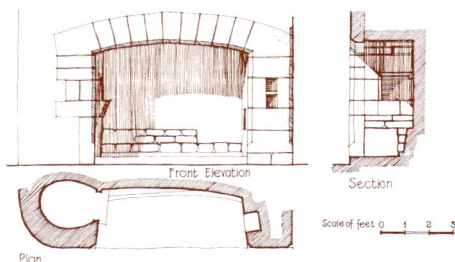

Fireplace at N° 53 Main Street

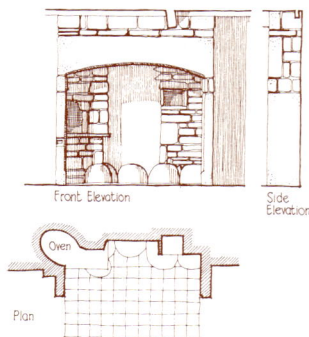

IAN GOLDTHORPE

Fireplace at Endicot, Chapel St

17th Century fireplaces in Grassington

Fold will be seen on the right and opposite is Church House.

Pletts Fold (5), is one of many ancient 'folds' in the town which may originally have been early farm yards.

Church House (6), possesses many 17th century features including some fine mullioned windows and a continuous drip moulding above the ground floor windows and entrance door. The Georgian window at first floor level is a later insertion. Above the door are the initials 'SAP 1694' which stand for Stephen and Alice Peart who built this property, which is a good example of a 'yeoman farmhouse'. The building contains many interesting features including a fine fireplace, a beehive oven and some beautiful panelling.

Grassington, and indeed the other villages included in this book have a great wealth of 17th century fireplaces. The importance of the fireplace

from Medieval times onwards cannot be over-stressed, since it was the only source of heating for cooking and warming. It needed to be large to accommodate a relatively large number of people; and to give more daylight, a window, known as a 'fire window', was often inserted. As soon as additional fireplaces were fitted it was seen as a good means of raising taxes, hence the 17th century fireplace tax. Up to the latter part of the 17th century all bread had to be baked in the local lord's communal oven; thus beehive bread ovens were not installed until relatively late. Oat cakes were baked on a bakestone, often built into the fireplace. The largest fireplaces were the smokehoods, but these were not very efficient in moving the smoke and soon were converted into the large inglenooks that we see today. The fact that so many of the stone fireplaces in Grassington are similar confirms that they were probably mass produced. There are at least four identical ones in Main Street - did they fall off the back of a cart?

Many of these fireplaces have been rediscovered during the last twenty years or so as a result of careful restoration work that has been carried out. During the late 18th and 19th centuries, with the advent of kitchen ranges and especially the Yorkshire range which represented a great step forward in the field of cooking and the supply of hot water from a side boiler, this new equipment was usually inserted within these fireplaces and the area around walled up and plastered over. Then with the introduction of the electric cooker these ranges were removed and the tiled fireplace came into vogue. The earlier fireplaces with a large span usually had separate stone voussoirs in the segmental arch, sometimes joggled. The later fireplaces often have a separate keystone and a single curved stone lintel on each side, usually carved to imitate a series of voussoirs. The narrower fireplaces always have a single stone lintel, often with a curvel soffit. A number of these fireplaces can be seen in buildings in Grassington which are open to the public.

After passing to the Airey family Church House later became Chapman's Temperance Hotel, before being purchased by Linton Church in 1925. A coffee morning is held here every Saturday morning throughout the year, each time for a local charity and every Wednesday morning at 10.00am a Communion Service is held.

The Birdsall family, who lived in Grassington, are thought to have presented the clock on the front of the building. James Birdsall, a descendant of this family came to live here a few years ago. He and Wendy, his wife, are both talented actors and take part in many of the productions staged by the Grassington Players. James also writes books and for many years painted the scenery for the annual pantomime produced by the Grassington Pantaloons.

Just beyond Robert Bunney's shop turn left into Jacob's Fold in order to get a glimpse of Grassington Old Hall over the wall.

Grassington Old Hall (7), is one of the oldest inhabited houses in the Yorkshire Dales. Originally a timber framed structure stood on this site, being replaced by a simple stone building forming part of the present dwelling, which at that time would be only single storey dating from the 13th century.

As mentioned in an earlier chapter, this was built by the de Plumptons as an occasional residence; they were the Lords of the Manor from the early 12th century until the end of the 16th century. The building has since been altered and extended many times, a major restoration taking place at the end of the 19th century. However, when the present owners took over the property the hall was again in a poor state of repair but they have very carefully carried out a full restoration.

Now return back to The Square and note The Pump which originally had three troughs.

The Pump, or The Fountain (8), as it was originally known, has been removed from its former position and served this part of the town until the 1890s when the Grassington Waterworks Company was formed. The Pump, however, continued to operate until the 1930s. The attractive structure probably dates from the latter part of the 18th century or early in the 19th century.

The Square was recobbled in 1973 with funds raised by the Grassington Chamber of Trade. The centre paved area with seats was occupied by the underground toilets from around 1925 until 1976.

The Square probably in the 1930s

Across The Square, Grassington House Hotel and the Upper Wharfedale Museum are located.

Grassington House (9), the finest Georgian building in the town, was built in 1760 by a Mr Brown who was one of the promoters of the

Grassington to Pateley Bridge turnpike road. The Allcock family, bankers in Skipton, lived here for many years. It has been used as a guest house and hotel since the 19th century. Whilst personally I regret the changes that have taken place in connection with this property, nevertheless the car park in place of the garden is a most useful asset since Grassington House is one of the few properties in the centre of the town with its own provision. The conservatory, likewise, also provides extra valuable accommodation in this hotel, and perhaps eventually it may be possible for it to be remodelled to make it more in keeping with this beautiful building! The second floor sliding sash windows have been replaced with casement windows in recent years which I feel are quite acceptable. Internally the dining room with its fine fireplace and recessed bookcase has remained intact, together with the fine staircase.

The Upper Wharfedale Museum (10), was converted from two former lead miners' cottages. Initially this museum was located for a number of years in a room at the back of the Black Horse Hotel. The present building was officially opened in 1979 by Robert Crowther of California, grandson of John Crowther (1858-1930) the Grassington Antiquary, Historian and Botanist.

At the top of The Square is the Liverpool Warehouse building.

This fine building (11), dates from the mid 18th century or perhaps even earlier, and stands on the site of a former tannery. Underneath the section occupied by Peter Walbank is a fine cellar with a vaulted roof which may have been part of the old tannery. In 1848 William Cockshott, of Linton Mill, was worried about the inadequate shopping facilities for his employees and so he decided to open a shop in this building. It was in the section occupied by Country Concept today and a large sign between the windows to the first and second floor soon appeared bearing the name 'Liverpool Warehouse.' This appears to have implied that the goods sold here came by canal to Gargrave from Liverpool and thence by road here but this is, in fact, not so. The name 'Liverpool Warehouse' was a term used extensively for similar stores, especially throughout the North of England, selling a wide range of goods catering mainly for everyday requirements. Many of the goods sold in these

shops would be imported through Liverpool, but the goods sold here would have mainly come by road from Skipton, Leeds and Bradford. The canal, at this time, would be largely used to transport heavier more bulky materials such as limestone, lead and coal. However, by 1861, this shop in The Square had become a kind of 'Selfridges of the Dales', but about 1920 the business ceased and the shop became the Café Royal which continued until more recent times.

Leave The Square proceeding up Main Street for a few yards to Ashfield Fold originally known as 'Summers Fold'. Note the new name plaque erected high up on Helen Midgley's building in 1997.

Ashfield House Hotel

On the right are some cottages dating from lead mining times and at the end is Ashfield House Hotel (12), dating from the late 17th or early 18th century. This attractive building has quite an extensive garden to the rear.

Continuing up Main Street on the left is Shenstone Gallery.

This little building (13), was a former smithy said to be owned by the notorious Tom Lee in the 1760s. He is thought to have been a blacksmith but with none too good a reputation! In 1766 Tom Lee murdered Dr Petty, the local doctor, when he was returning to Grassington on horseback through Grass Wood after both men had been drinking at the Anglers Arms at Kilnsey. At Lee's third trial his apprentice turned King's evidence and he was found guilty and later executed at York Castle. His body was then hung on a gibbet on the site of the murder, which is still known today as 'Gibbet Hill' at the northern end of Grass Wood.

A little higher up Main Street on the left is Number 47.

This property (14), and the adjoining cottage both date from the 17th century and have identical fireplaces. The Woggan, an ancient footpath, much older than the buildings fronting on to it disappears via a small archway at the side of the café.

The Dales Kitchen (15), a tall three storey building, was for many years in the late 19th century the chemist's shop run by John Crowther. At that time the entrance was on the corner of the building and Gemini Studios next door was his annexe where he bottled pop and perfume! This lean-to building was initially stables, then a lead miner's cottage and at one time a butcher's shop.

Opposite within Armstrong Terrace is located Clevedon house (16), a 17th century property which would originally be freestanding. It contains a fine inglenook fireplace and its main elevation is on the other side. The adjoining houses were built around it in the 18th and 19th centuries when there was a demand for additional housing for both the lead mining and textile industries.

Beyond and adjacent to the junction with Garrs End Lane is Number 53 Main Street.

This house (17), was originally known as 'Sunnyside' and at one time rents from this property were used to support the parish's poor fund. At another time it was divided into three cottages known as 'Town Fold', and was also an inn known as the 'Robin Hood' for a few years. As recently as 1970 this property comprised two separate cottages, a workshop and the library occupied the lean-to building as at present. In 1846 the present library was a blacksmith's shop. The fine fireplace and beehive oven probably date from the middle of the 17th century.

Beyond Garrs End Lane the cottage next to the Acorns to Oak showroom (18), dates from 1631 and contains a fine fireplace and beehive oven.

Behind the furniture showroom is Chamber End Fold, which was formerly known as 'King Street'.

Its present name is probably due to the tall house on the right-hand side (19), which may formerly have been used as a council chamber. It is dated 1675 and the barred window at ground level in the gable wall is said to have been a former town 'lock-up'. The buildings on the right of Chamber End Fold were originally connected with farming dating from the 17th century and later being subsequently converted into lead miners' cottages. The cobbles were repaired and additional new ones laid in 1988.

Turn left into Chapel Street. A few yards along on the left is Chapel Fold.

Chapel Fold (20), has had many names in the past. At one time it was known as St John's Fold which may have been on account of John Broughton, the Grassington poet. It has also been called Smith Fold and Ranters Fold. 'Ranters' was the nickname given to the early Primitive Methodists. The original Primitive Methodist Chapel, erected in 1837 and closed for worship in 1908, still remains and was partly converted into a guest house about 1990 and is now used as a dwelling house.

Proceeding along Chapel Street Rathmell Fold is soon seen on the left.

Rathmell Fold (21), comprises opposite the entrance, two cottages dating from about 1674 which were originally one house containing two fine fireplaces. The barn, which may be older, was converted into dwellings in 1986. The upper end gable window was formerly a door, which was left open to enable tramps to go in and sleep at night. This fold is named after Jacob Rathmell, a previous owner who died in 1849.

Opposite on the right is the Methodist Church.

The Methodist Church (22), was formerly a Wesleyan Chapel. The site, together with an old building, was acquired in 1809 and came into use as a chapel in 1811. In 1825 the present frontage, gallery and pews were added. In 1996 the roof was extensively repaired and the facilities have been greatly improved including the provision of disabled ramps, new toilets, a spacious new kitchen and a meeting room extension into an adjoining cottage named the 'Howgill Room' in memory of Howgill Chapel, which is now closed. These enhancements were designed and supervised by Stephen Calvert and Richard Appleyard of the Pearce Bottomley Partnership, architects. This building is often open for coffee mornings and other events and in the Church is a beautiful Lectern made by John Ely and based upon the design of a Celtic cross 'In Memory of Muriel Routh 1900-1990'. In the Chancel there are two fine chairs one of which is inscribed 'In Memory of John Helm Steward of this Church Entered into Higher Service June 14th 1957'. John Helm started a Sweets, Jewellery and Fancy Goods shop in The Square where Robinsons is now located and his son and daughter-in-law presently have the Dales Book Centre.

Continuing along Chapel Street, passing Intake Lane, the three new houses on the right will soon come into view.

These detached houses, known as 'Chapel Croft' (23), were built in the garden of the older building adjoining Endicot in 1988. The architects who designed these properties were Allison and MacRae.

Endicot

Endicot (24), dates at least from the 17th century and contains a fine inglenook fireplace with a beehive oven. A derelict barn adjoined the rear of this property and about 1990 Alan Dodd of the Dodd Frankland Stocks Partnership, architects, skilfully prepared the scheme to extend this cottage into the barn. Personally, I have a feeling that this property may go much further back in

time and could have started its life as a timber framed or cruck building.

Opposite is High Wisphill (25), and an adjoining cottage which were very attractively converted from old farm buildings in the early 1980s by local craftsmen.

A little further along Chapel Street on the right, behind Endicot, is a group of cottages dating mainly from the 18th and 19th centuries formerly occupied by lead miners.

In the middle of this row of properties is No 24 Chapel Street (26), which dates from the 17th century and was originally a free-standing building known as 'Banks Farm'.

Beyond Bank Lane we enter the part of Grassington known as 'Town Head'. Beyond the next group of cottages on the right we come to a long block of property at right angles to the road generally referred to locally as 'The Nook'.

This building (27), was originally known as 'Leyland's Farm' being named after the first freeholder. A datestone over a former entrance doorway inside the later projecting front wing is inscribed '1628 WS' probably referring to William Stockdale the second owner. The earliest part of this building located to the right of and behind the projecting front portion, today with fine ashlar stonework to the front elevation, probably dates from very early in the 17th century and is a good example of a small 'yeoman farmhouse'. This older portion contains two small fireplaces and plaster friezes having distinct Jacobean characteristics, but there are similar details in some West Yorkshire houses which date from about the middle of the 17th century which suggests that these details were probably added when the owners became more prosperous. In addition there is some fine timber panelling and a large fireplace with imitation joggled voussoirs again dating from later on in the 17th century. The projecting front portion of the building, which has an extremely badly built east elevation, together with the first extension towards the road would appear to date from the latter part of the 17th century. The extension nearest to the road was probably built in the 18th century as a barn and at the north-east end there are some much later extensions. The

Town Head Farmhouse

fine barn nearby, which was converted into a dwelling about 1990, was doubtless part of the original farm complex.

Behind is one of Grassington's finest old buildings.

Known as 'Town Head Farmhouse' (28), this property may date from the 15th century, since evidence from a number of reused timbers and other features suggest that this building may have started its life as a Medieval timber framed structure. The building we see today largely dates from the early part of the 17th century, possessing fine decorative features near the eaves. It was formerly known as 'Rathmell's Farm' and contains a somewhat unique inglenook fireplace, with adjacent timberwork in the Jacobean style. The left-hand section of the building was originally a barn. In 1997 a major restoration scheme was embarked upon and the ground floor mullioned window to the former barn was installed at this time. This farm complex, together with a large acreage of land extending up to and including Bastow Wood belongs to the Trustees of the Fountaine's Hospital in Linton.

Here we leave the Dales Way. Bear left down the hill.

On the right is Scaw Ghyll (29), which may be on the site of an early manorial corn mill and probably being the most northerly building in the old Saxon town. The present building, dating from about 1729, is thought to have originally comprised a separate cotton worsted spinning mill and three cottages, long since joined together to form one building. In 1857, the building was used

for a time as a butter factory and in more recent times as a guest house.

Continuing down the hill across the garden of Scaw Ghyll will be seen, in Cove Lane, a property known as 'Meadowcroft'.

This house (30), was built in 1991 in part of the original garden of Scaw Ghyll. It is of timber framed construction and was designed by Ralph Stocks of the Dodd Frankland Stocks Partnership.

Bear left at the seat under the tree into Garrs End Lane.

Garrs End Lathe (31), on the right is said to have marked the northern entrance to the old Saxon town.

A few yards further on is the property known as 'Garrsdale' (32), which has been beautifully extended in the early 1990s to the designs of Robert Groves of John Moore & Partners, architects. The stonework in this extension is so excellent that already it appears to have been built at the same time as the original building.

Some distance further on at the end of the meadows bear right for a few yards into Moody Sty Lane to view Rylstone View Cottage on the left.

This property (33), is probably amongst the more interesting of the newer buildings in the town sitting astride an ancient lynchet. It has a carefully designed terrace to the front elevation and the attractive two storey end elevation, with beautifully designed steps leading down to the lower lawn, very much resembles an old Dales cottage. It was built by Peter and Stuart Gill of Otley to a design prepared by Alan Dodd.

Between the gate to Rylstone View Cottage and Garrs End Lane is Mount Pleasant, a late 18th century cottage which was very carefully restored in the late 1980s. The reroofing, pointing of the stonework and the construction of the new porch were all carried out by David Easterby.

Continue along Garrs End Lane.

On the right over the wall and situated in a most attractive garden is Ellesmere (34), which probably dates from the 17th century. In the 19th century it comprised two cottages and the delightful three storey section was added early in the 20th century.

Ellesmere in the late 19th century when it was two cottages and The Woggan went past the front

On the left-hand side of Garrs End Lane is Summers Barn (35), which was converted into a house in 1987 and may have its origins in the latter part of the 16th century. The adjacent section of Garrs End Lane was once gated and known as 'Leyland's Fold'. Rokeby, the adjoining farmhouse, dates from the 17th century and although refronted in the 19th century still retains an old fireplace.

Turn left up Main Street and right in front of the Town Hall to continue along Garrs Lane. This part of the town was originally known as 'Well Head' on account of the ancient drinking troughs which can still be seen outside the Craven Cottage. At one time Main Street was known as 'Well Lane'.

The Town Hall and Devonshire Institute (36), was

Town Hall and Devonshire Institute

built by the Duke of Devonshire in 1855 as a Mechanics Institute, on the site of a pinfold, to help to educate the lead miners. The Duke added the right-hand bay in 1895 and, in 1896, he handed over the building to the newly formed Parish Council for a nominal sum. The chiming clock was also given by the Duke towards the end of the 19th century. In 1923 the original Mechanics Institute building was greatly extended by the addition of a large hall, entrance foyer, stage and dressing rooms. In 1997-98 a third major restoration and extension plan was carried out to the designs of Brian Foxley of Brian Foxley Associates, architects, the main contractor being William Birch of Harrogate. As a result of this work an attractive external feature is the new octagonal Studio Theatre seating approximately one hundred people with the provision for a playgroup below, both having an independent entrance. The old mean and unattractive main entrance has been replaced with a most attractive new entrance adjacent to the old Mechanics Institute building, together with a greatly enlarged entrance foyer and modern toilets, including disabled facilities together with a disabled ramp and access to the building. The Foundation Stone was laid by Councillor John Edgar Darwin the Chairman of Grassington Parish Council on 25th February 1998 and the completed building was officially reopened by the Marquess of Hartington on 24th August 1998.

Just beyond the Town Hall bear right down the rough and partly cobbled Water Street.

Ahead you will see the ancient Pletts Barn (37). Today better known as 'The Mountaineer', this building was formerly in the ownership of a Mr Pletts and is also known locally as 'Wesley's Barn' since John Wesley preached here on his first visit to Grassington in 1780 when he was 77 years old. There is a datestone which was still legible in the 1960s inscribed 'E' over 'R 1688 B' standing for Roger Blackburn and Elizabeth Frankland who were married in 1688. Since this building is described as 'New Barn' in Pierse's survey of 1603 I think that it dates from the latter part of the 16th century. For many years it was in a derelict and ruinous state and in the very early 1980s the entire roof collapsed. This was followed by a very careful and extensive restoration of this important building.

Continue along Water Street and turn right for a few yards down Garrs Lane to view Theatre Cottage and the Congregational Church.

Theatre Cottage (38), has been formed out of part of the barn in which Tom Airey's theatre operated for many years. Thomas Airey started the mail-coach business in Grassington and his son Tom, who was born in 1771 and educated at Threshfield School, was inspired to be an actor about 1807 when he visited a theatre held at the Hole-in-the-Wall Inn in Skipton. He was lucky enough to get a part with the company, acting alongside Edmund Keen who was then unknown, and Harriot Mellon who later became Duchess of St Albans. Airey later started his own theatre in Grassington in the upper room of an inn. It was soon moved to the large barn in Garrs Lane and a young local man, Richard Garrs, was appointed as stage manager. Many Shakespearian plays were given here and instead of posters to advertise these events a bellman used to go around the town proclaiming the performance in rhyme! Tom Airey died in 1842.

Across the road in a landscaped Churchyard is the Congregational Church (39), dating from 1811 with later extensions and being the earliest Nonconformist building in Grassington. This little building has a very friendly and welcoming atmosphere, but sadly many years ago the upper part of this Church was closed off at gallery level to conserve heat and make the running costs more economical. Now with the advent of mains gas here, which is gradually coming down in price, it would be nice once again if the gallery could be opened up and this delightful little building be restored to its former glory!

Leaving the Churchyard turn right and then right again into Scar Street.

The building at the road junction (40), was built and used as The Manse for the Congregational Church until the mid 1970s and since then it has been a private house.

Beyond the Congregational Church buildings set back on the right is Gills Top.

This sheltered housing scheme (41), was erected by the Anchor Housing Association in 1989 on land owned by the Congregational Church and used as allotments. It was designed by Howard Riley of the Bowman Riley Partnership, architects, and the scheme is linked on to a former barn which has been converted into the manager's flat at first floor level with garaging and storage below.

On the other side of Scar Street is Scar Field approached by a steep drive.

Scar Field (42), comprises three detached dwellings designed by John Wharton, architect. The first two houses namely 'High Ghyll' and 'Rowan House' were built in the early 1990s. The third property, known as 'Elder House' was faced in stone quarried on site in the former quarry in which these properties are located. This house bears a datestone inscribed 'JW 1996', which stands for John Wainwright, the present owner and local fireman.

Continuing along Scar Street, on the right beyond Gills Top is Yew Tree House.

This large house (43), which takes its name from an old yew tree in its garden, was built in the grounds of The Grange in the late 1980s by Jim Cotterill.

At the end of the next long block of property on the right of Scar Street is No 17 Hardy Grange.

This cottage (44), has been very carefully extended on a rather difficult and awkwardly shaped site, to the designs of Barrie Birch, architect, in 1994.

Ahead, where Scar Street bends round to the right is Hardy Barn.

This property (45), was converted into a house in 1988 and the adjacent garage is a completely new building which was erected shortly afterwards. The

Scar Lodge before alteration in the early 1990s

owners possess a considerable length of nearby hillside which they are gradually incorporating into the garden, together with the planting of a number of copses.

Opposite and adjacent to an old workshop building is a new property.

This house known as 'Gills Stones' (46), was built in 1997 to the designs of Jan van Pagh, a Danish architect, and the very carefully executed stonework was carried out by David Easterby and John Longstaff. This dwelling is so named since a little of the stone for its construction came from the former Gill House located high up on Grassington Moor.

At the end of the garden to Gills Stones turn right on to the tarmacadamed footpath.

On the right, in an elevated position is Beech Cottage (47), which has been so named on account of the large copper beech tree in its front garden. This house was designed by Malcolm Thornton, architect, and completed in 1997.

On the left through a narrow opening is Springfield Court (48), a delightful little scheme of three houses on an enclosed walled site built by the Century Housing Association to the designs of Robert Groves in 1997.

Continuing along the main footpath to the right in Hardy Grange are two properties namely The Grange and Scar Lodge.

The Grange (49), may even date back to the time when the monks of Fountains Abbey drove their animals through the land of Grassington Manor. Careful restoration work in 1988 revealed a fine beehive oven and the remains of a second beehive oven, indicating that the property once possessed two 17th century stone fireplaces, possibly dating from a time when it comprised two cottages.

These were doubtless destroyed at the time of an extensive restoration in the 1860s. A datestone inscribed 'HL 1653', formerly at the rear of the building, has been incorporated in a new porch at the front of the house.

The adjoining house (50), known as 'Scar Lodge', may originally have been part of The Grange possibly being used as a malthouse. In the 19th century it was probably increased in height with many Victorian features being added to the front elevation as shown in the drawing. However, the last owner in the early 1990s altered the front appearance of the building by inserting an additional floor to make it three storeys in height.

Returning to the footpath there is a large disused barn.

This building (51), probably dates from the 18th century or very early in the 19th century, and for a number of years was used by the St John Ambulance Service. It is to be hoped that this fine and interesting building will soon be sympathetically restored and converted to a suitable new use.

Continuing back towards The Square note the building with a flight of steps leading up to the first floor, alongside Hardy Cottage.

This property (52), now known as 'No 6 Manor House Mews', served as Grassington's First Youth Hostel from about 1935 until 1940 when it was replaced by Linton Youth Hostel. This building was then used by the Local Defence Volunteers followed by the Home Guard during the Second World War.

After walking another few yards we find ourselves back in The Square. Did you manage to stay the course and look at all the buildings? If so, congratulations and no doubt now you will need to visit the Grassington Pharmacy either to get your film developed or to purchase some of Dr Scholl's foot comforts after standing

for lengthy periods reading my epistle about each building. However Peter, with Susan and Sarah his two charming assistants if necessary will be pleased to help you. Also you will be able to see the lovely 17th century fireplace behind the counter!

The building (53), originally comprised two 17th century cottages. It was extensively altered, and a second storey added in the early years of the 20th century. For many years it housed the telephone exchange and in the 1960s the carefully detailed bow windows were added, which have now become an accepted feature in this part of Grassington!

No doubt now you will want some refreshment in one of our many cafés or perhaps in an ancient hostelry. If not perhaps you would like to sit on a seat to rest for a while.

The circular seat (54), constructed around the tree at the bottom of The Square was erected in 1987 by local residents and friends in memory of Shirley Spencer who helped to start the Dickensian weekends. It has been beautifully designed and made by Allan Thompson.

Perhaps this is a suitable place to sit for a few minutes and watch the world go by, or unfortunately rather to be sprayed with petrol and diesel fumes from the many vehicles that go past! You would really think that there is a town the size of Bradford where the lead mines are located, or perhaps all the cars are taking disabled relatives round who couldn't otherwise walk, or even maybe it's the Yorkshire folk due to their renowned careful ways who are first looking for the odd vacant parking space instead of paying to park at Colvend!

It is only a short walk back to Colvend and take heart because the walks around the other villages are all very much shorter, apart from the one around Kettlewell.

STARTING POINT: This walk starts at the National Park car park at Colvend.

DISTANCE: Approximately three miles.

TIME REQUIRED: Two hours, but extra time should be allowed if Linton Church and the buildings and other features, in both Linton and Threshfield villages are to be looked at in some detail.

TERRAIN: This is a very easy walk provided that you have suitable footwear. The first section is along a fairly steep, flagged and partly tarmacadamed, path leading to the falls and beyond the route can be wet after heavy rain until the road to Linton Church is joined. The path to Linton climbs gradually up to a minor road leading into the village. The route to Threshfield is relatively level and grassed for most of the way. The bridleway from Threshfield is mainly grassed rising slightly to the bridge over the dismantled railway, then dropping down to Threshfield School. After a short section of road the path back to Linton Falls, which is partly grassed, can be wet in places.

Attractive features of this walk are the many fine views, especially where the path crosses pleasant meadows. The first section of the track from Linton along Well Lane, in the little valley of Linton Beck, is especially beautiful.

First a look inside the National Park Information Centre is well worthwhile if it is open at the time of your visit.

This building which was opened in 1988, is a good example of present day craftsmanship and almost appears to have been a conversion from an existing building, but this is not so. The Centre, which is open daily during the summer months and at weekends and some weekdays during the winter period, is well worth inspection especially in order to see the excellent exhibition explaining much about this part of the Yorkshire Dales National Park.

From the Information Centre head across the car park in a southerly direction to a gate in the far corner.

The people of Grassington have welcomed ramblers and tourists for generations and, if this hadn't been so, we should not have the wonderful range of shops and other facilities that exist today, since otherwise our small population would perhaps just about support a post office and possibly one shop if we were lucky! The hikers and walkers who come here are, for the most part, great lovers of the countryside and it is extremely unusual to see any litter on the footpaths with the one exception of the Snake Walk going down to Linton Falls. A few years ago this was much worse than it is today, being badly littered with rubbish

and dog dirt much to the annoyance of the locals. However, we now have brightly coloured red dog litter boxes around Grassington and so there is no longer any excuse for this latter problem; this reminds me of the parents who came with their young son shortly after these boxes had been installed. Young John enquired of his father as to what the bright red boxes were for to which his father replied, 'they are doggies' toilets' to which the little boy quickly responded 'well they are a bit high up aren't they!'

Pass through the gate turning right on to the Snake Walk.

Opposite is an interesting house known as 'Lynchets' which has a datestone over the front door inscribed '19 CC 81', standing for Christine Chisholm the present owner. This property was designed by Jim Wales of Wales, Wales and Rawson.

Just below is a very fine property with outstanding views known as 'The Outpost' which was built in the early 1990s to the designs of Barrie Birch. This site had the benefit of outline planning permission for many years and I often wondered what the outcome would be like. The stonework is superb and the building makes a most fitting entrance to Grassington at the end of the steep walk up from Linton Falls.

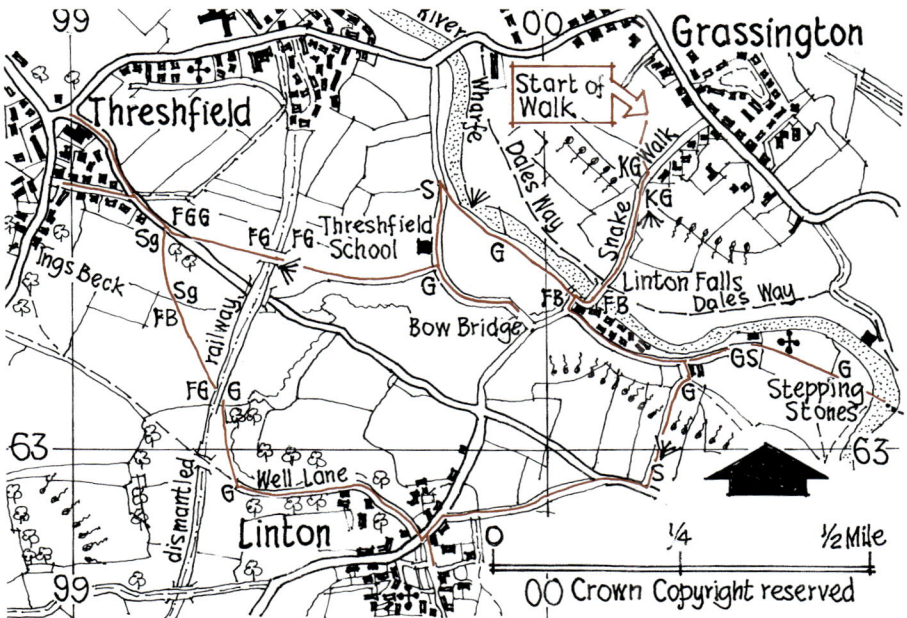

Pause at the old kissing gate with the new kissing gate to the left to admire the fine view.

The metal kissing gate is very old and dates from about 1814, the time when this footpath was constructed by the Birkbecks to give their workers who lived in Grassington easier access to Linton Mill.

Stop here for a few moments to admire the fine panorama dominated by Burnsall and Thorpe fells to the left and beyond Cracoe and Rylstone fells crowned by Cracoe Cairn 1,650 ft (500m) above sea level, which was erected by the residents of Cracoe, and paid for by Col Maude, in memory of their loved ones who lost their lives in the First World War and whose names are recorded thereon. In more recent times a bronze plaque has been added listing the names of those residents killed in the Second World War.

In front, from left to right, the green reef knolls, Kail Hill, Elbolton, Stebden Hill and Butter Haw are clearly visible. Below Kail Hill and Elbolton one of the finest examples of lynchets in Wharfedale will be seen. Beyond will be seen the excellent new housing at Linton Falls and to the left the old mill

houses, some of which are painted white, dating from the time the first textile mill was erected in 1790. To the right the roof of the former Threshfield Mill can just be seen, and much further to the right the long terraces of houses in Threshfield. These properties were built early this century for Bradford commuters, who came to live here after the railway opened in 1902.

Pass through a kissing gate and a further gate, descending the four steps to continue ahead.

The Snake Walk, no doubt, is so named because the old wall on the right bends round slightly over its whole length.

This wall dates from about 1780 and was here before the footpath was constructed. The wall on the left dates from the time the path was laid out. On the Ordnance Survey map this footpath is shown as 'Sedber Lane' being named after the ancient field out of which it has been carved. However, it has a third name 'The Flags' since initially the path was grassed, which soon became very muddy with constant use and so the Duke of Devonshire laid the flags which were covered with tarmacadam in more recent less enlightened times,

49

I am told so that it would be more easy to take children in push-chairs along this route. Thankfully, due to the tremendous use that this popular path gets, the dreaded tarmac is rapidly wearing off and perhaps before long the paving will be restored back to its former glory!

As you approach the barn pause to look at the attractive view to the left.

This beautiful view is dominated by Simon's Seat, which is 1,544 ft (485m) above sea level, in the background and below, from the left, Grassington Mill, Linton Church and Kirk Yett can be picked out.

Sedber Barn on the left has a datestone inscribed 'HW 1682'. The initials may stand for Henry Wrathall. The barn, of course, takes its name from the ancient field within which it is situated. During a survey a few years ago, the following pencil inscriptions were found on various joists of the main cattle house loft floor, namely 'F Sedgwick July 1914, H Nicholls, Mallinson and W.H.S. 1922'. The walls have all been increased in height at some stage and the building was reroofed after a fire in the late 1970s.

Adjacent to the River Wharfe the Dales Way crosses.

This delightful long-distance footpath goes all the way from Ilkley to Windermere, much of its route being through some of the beautiful valleys of the Yorkshire Dales.

Proceed on to the bridge to view the spectacular Linton Falls.

The falls are caused by the North Craven Fault which crosses the river at this point. The viewing area at the far end of the bridge was opened in 1988. Of course, many of the local people walk the numerous footpaths in the area and marvel as you do at the breathtaking views at almost every turn in the route being followed. If you are lucky enough to see the river in one of its many angry moods after heavy rain, you will no doubt be rubbing shoulders with many of us on the bridge, standing in awe as we watch the millions of gallons of water flow over these falls. At times like this it makes you wonder why we should ever be short of water but, I suppose, it is all a question of the water authorities being able to store enough water

to supply the population in dryer periods.

'Tin Bridge' was the name given to the first footbridge across these falls built by the Birkbecks for their employees in 1814. It was covered with sheets of tin from old oil drums to stop feet wearing away the timber and this caused a clatter, and thus its name. The second bridge which was also constructed in timber was erected in 1860 with a central stone support pillar and four pairs of iron stay rods, and remained until replaced by the third bridge, a metal structure, in 1904. The bolts which held the stays can still be seen on the rocks below. The third bridge became dangerous and was closed in 1988. The fourth bridge, erected by the Royal Engineers when the river was in flood and paid for by the Yorkshire Dales National Park, is wider and constructed in timber with an expected life of one hundred and fifty years. It was made by Hugon UK Ltd of Bramhall near Stockport and opened in 1989.

Looking upstream from the bridge there is a good view of Threshfield Mill, which was formerly a manorial corn mill. The mill, itself, was the left-hand of the three cottages and dates from the 17th century. It was powered by a small leet taken from Captain Beck and its route can still be traced through some nearby fields. The mill operated until the latter part of the 19th century and early this century it was for a time used as a creamery. It is interesting to note that there has been a mill on this site since the 14th century.

The downstream weir was constructed to power the Birkbeck's Linton Mill, which initially had a waterwheel. Beyond is a second higher weir which was constructed to power the Hydro-electric Station, this being opened in 1909 after a successful campaign by John Crowther to get electricity and sewerage to the town. The first generating house was a timber structure on a brick plinth which was enlarged and reconstructed entirely in brick in 1920. The remains of this building can be clearly seen at the left-hand end of the weir.

Linton Mill stood on the site occupied by the excellent new housing known as 'Linton Falls'. You will be able to see the original concrete retaining walls constructed to support the old mill buildings on top of which the new houses have been sited. It is recorded that there was a mill on this site as early as 1258, which would have been a manorial soke mill for grinding corn. J & W Birkbeck built the first textile mill here and about the same time they built a similar mill at Aysgarth which still survives today. Incidentally Birkbeck College was named after a brother, George, who was a sleeping partner and a scientist and whose portrait hangs in the College. This mill was larger than the one at Aysgarth and was interesting for the 'long-drop' toilets located on the four upper floors which were cantilevered out on the gable fronting on to the river. It was five storeys in height and was destroyed by fire in 1912. It was soon afterwards rebuilt as a largely single storey building with northlight roof trusses and demolished in 1983, apart from Falls Cottage and Falls House which front on to the footpath leaving the bridge.

Follow the footpath as it bears round to the left pausing to look at Little Emily's Bridge on the right.

IAN GOLDTHORPE

Linton Mill destroyed by fire in 1912 showing the 'long drop' toilets

This is a small packhorse bridge located on the original church path from Threshfield Village and it dates from the 14th century. It is thought to have been named after Emily Norton, daughter of Christopher Norton who was a patron of Linton Church, and was executed after the Rising of the North. Little Emily was fostered with the miller at Threshfield Mill after her father's death. Another theory for the bridge's name is that it was invented by Halliwell Sutcliffe, who mentioned it in his writings.

Across the bridge, on the right-hand side alongside Captain Beck there is usually a group of ducks waiting to be fed, dominated by a larger black duck with a red face which always seems to be fully in charge!

Return to the path proceeding up the seven steps ahead turning left on to the road.

A few yards along on the left is the entrance to Linton Falls, an excellent housing scheme commenced in 1986 and completed in 1988 to the designs of Jim Wales, who had working with him at the time a young man, Andrew Metcalfe, who was twenty years of age and lived with his parents in Linton Village. Sadly Andrew, who had just been offered a place at both Hull and Liverpool to study architecture was tragically killed, along with his cousin, in a road accident on the way to Skipton.

The lower section of the original mill wall has been retained as the garden walls to the properties fronting on to the road.

Beyond on the left are the two rows of former mill cottages.

The front block was built in 1912 and the whole group became known as 'Botany Cottages' after cheap wool started to be imported from Botany Bay in Australia, at the same time undercutting the wool produced by our local farmers.

Opposite in the car park is an old spring which keeps flowing even in times of drought, and originally supplied the nearby cottages before the mains supply was laid.

Continue ahead past the toilets and Holme House Cottage on the right.

Look over the wall into the small field on the right before the lane to view John McGuinn's collection of farm animals and birds. Just beyond Holme House Cottage note the beautiful dry stone wall with a little garden in front that he has recently constructed.

Beyond on the right is the Glebe Field.

The large stone in this field is said to mark a pagan religious site. On the left are Kirk Yett and Kirk Yett Cottage, which date from the 17th century and originally belonged to the church. This was originally one building and was for many years used as an inn. However, legend has it that the inn was closed by the Archdeacon when he found that drinking here was much more popular than going to church! In more recent times it was the home of Reginald Brundrit, the artist. He was obviously bothered by people thinking that it was either the Rectory or a tearoom for he painted a beautiful sign with the following words which was displayed outside: 'This is not the Rectory. We do not make teas. The way to Grassington is past the mill and over the bridge. The way to Burnsall is over the stepping stones.' This sign can now be seen in the Upper Wharfedale Museum.

Note the interesting steps and stile on the right of the gate leading into the Churchyard.

These steps and stile are a most interesting feature and obviously of great antiquity.

On entering the Churchyard of the ancient Church of St Michael and All Angels pause for a few moments to study the outside of the building.

This is a rather unusual but nevertheless delightful structure dating back to Romanesque and Medieval times. But it is only one of a great number of very old and well-loved churches in the Yorkshire Dales and it didn't escape the hands of the Victorian restorers. In 1861 a major restoration took place under the care and supervision of John Varley, architect, at a time when this church still had two rectors one of whom was Rev'd Alexander Nowell, whose great uncle built Netherside Hall about 1820. Incidentally, this church still has four churchwardens today.

Here it is perhaps worth mentioning, especially for those of you that are not particularly inspired by Victorian architecture, that during the 18th century morals were very lax and churchgoing was at a very low ebb and, consequently, very little money had been spent upon the maintenance of church buildings and it is even recorded that horses were being stabled in some churches! Of course, also until the 19th century church buildings were the main focus of each community, being extensively used for secular as well as religious activities, since there were no town or village halls.

As a result of the Industrial Revolution many of the new mill and factory owners became very rich and paid for some of the great Victorian churches in our industrial towns and cities, since there was also a great revival in religious worship. Famous Victorian architects often designed these new

buildings but it is debatable whether many were really built to the Glory of God, or more as a monument to the individual industrialists themselves.

I am not going to say a lot about the architecture of the Church building itself.

However, may I commend to you the excellent little guide book giving a history and description by John E Wright MBE, on sale inside the church at a modest price of £2. There is also a number of information boards, in different European languages, to carry around the building pointing out particular items of interest.

Note the new entrance door which was made by John Ely in the late 1980s. We are fortunate here that the 19th century restoration work was carried out, on the whole, very sensitively before Victorian architecture became too flamboyant and ornate in the 1870s and 80s. The ancient arcades have survived, more or less, intact as have many of the windows in the Nave. Also in the Nave, the clerestorey was extensively reconstructed with new windows and a most attractive timber roof replacing the 18th century plaster ceiling; in addition new aisle roofs were installed. A number of new windows were inserted in the Chancel and Lady Chapel, and the lovely Medieval timber roof in the Chancel, which had been plastered over, was uncovered and restored. Some of the tracery from the windows which were removed was reused to support the stone seats in the new porch.

As I worship in this church Sunday by Sunday, I very much regret that the original late 15th century East Window was not restored rather than being replaced by a pointed window of no special merit architecturally, which doesn't relate very satisfactorily to the relatively flat roof above. Nevertheless, the stained glass which was installed in this window, as a memorial to Queen Victoria's Jubilee in 1887, is very pleasing. But it is the two delightful altar frontals that give me the greatest pleasure, which were made about three years ago by Fiona Marsden, a member of the congregation. The kingfisher blue frontal, which is used other than on Feast Days is centred on the Holy Spirit, symbolised by the dove, spreading its light throughout the world. The design is a mixture of the traditional and the contemporary, as befits the

Church in the 20th century. The dove is worked in ivory silk and gold thread whilst the background has echoes of computer-generated designs of today, and reflects a period in which we have seen men on the moon. The frontal is made up of nearly 3,000 small squares and triangles, all hand-stitched, in colours which pick up all those present in the East Window of the Church, again emphasising the continuity of worship that has existed in this Church throughout the centuries. The predominant kingfisher blue is associated with both the colour in the Church and the flash of blue from this bird in the river outside.

This building is said to be haunted by a monk who is usually seen going through the most westerly window in the North Aisle, since until the 1861 restoration this window was a Devil's Door. He is thought to have belonged to either Fountains Abbey or Bolton Priory and may have taken services here in Medieval times. To the right of this window are the Royal Arms which came to light during a restoration that was carried out in 1994 under the supervision of Andrew Forman of Forman and Co, architects. These Arms had been used one hundred and thirty years ago to line a built-in cupboard in the Clergy Vestry. When removed a complete George III Royal Coat of Arms was found to be painted on the reverse side. There was little damage to the boards and perhaps the old churchwardens were apprehensive about the removal of the Arms and ensured that having rejected them they could readily be replaced. At the time of the 1994 restoration a new door was made to the West Vestry by Peter Merrell. Peter also made the door to the new Choir Vestry which stands on the site of the former pipe organ.

Mention should also be made of the beautiful Stall in the Chancel to the memory of Thomas Elwyn Wood 1913-1987 who was Honorary Assistant Curate here from 1977 until 1987. I remember Tom very well; he was a kindly man and delivered his excellent and amusing sermons in his fascinating Welsh accent. This Stall has been skilfully carved by John Ely. John has also made a number of memorial seats in the area, two outside the West End of the Church being in memory of Jos'e Gallaher 1952-1993 and Keith Lockyer 1929-1990. Keith was a well-known local dentist and Chairman of the Yorkshire Dales National Park Committee for a number of years. Another of John

Ely's seats is to be found near Yarnbury Lodge where Nick Nicholls lived. Nick was a keen radio ham, who was taken ill on a cruise and died suddenly, being buried at sea off the coast of Mexico. The symbol 'GØNOI' was his call number. Returning to the Church, the Lady Chapel was refurnished in 1973 with furniture made by Thompson of Kilburn, whose trademark is the mouse – each item of his furniture bears a carving of a mouse. The Altar Rail was made by Norman Clark of Burnsall and the ladies of the Church embroidered the hassocks with designs of local wild flowers. The Lectern, Altar Cross, Candlesticks, Prayer Desk and Chair – also by 'Mouse' Thompson – were installed in 1989. The Jacobean Communion Table in the Lady Chapel is thought to be the table that was used after the main stone altar had been removed in the 16th century.

Leaving the inside of the Church there are two memorials in the Churchyard that I find of particular interest. Walk along the south side of the building to the south-east corner. Nearby you will see a small memorial with the carving of a little boy on the top.

This is to the memory of Oliver Gordon Maufe, who was buried here on 1st February 1926 aged two years. Oliver was the son of Carl and Joyce Maufe who lived at Far Scar in Grassington. Oliver had taken part in a procession through Grassington, presumably at the time of the Grassington Feast, in the nude posing as Cupid with two wings attached to his body. Shortly afterwards he developed pneumonia and sadly died a few months later. This memorial was probably designed and carved by Eric Gill since the Roman lettering seems to me to be identical to another memorial that he carried out in Burnsall Churchyard.

Now return to the Church Porch and take the slightly worn grassy path between the tombstones across at a slight angle in order to join the footpath leading to the stepping stones.

The last memorial on the right is to the Grassington lead miners and is inscribed as follows: 'In memory of John and Henry Davis, lead miners, late of Grassington, formerly of Foolow, Derbyshire. John died July 8th 1835 aged 54 years.

Henry died March 17th 1845 aged 61 years. They are both interred in this churchyard. This stone is erected by a friend, to commemorate their great musical talent, John had one of the deepest, and most extensive, bass voices in this kingdom and Henry was alike celebrated, for his clear melodius tenor voice. Had they lived at this day, when musical talent is so much appreciated, they would have ranked as first, among the musical celebrities of the present time'.

Continue along the path passing through the gate and down the steps in order to view the stepping stones and Low Mill.

Low Mill, sometimes known as 'Grassington Mill' dates from the latter part of the 18th century and was also built upon the site of a former manorial corn mill. For many years it stood empty and derelict until it was restored for residential use in 1974. The covered sun lounge, designed by Brian Moxham a local architect, was added to the balcony in 1989. To the left of the stream are the remains of the old smelting mill built early in the 17th century by George Earl of Cumberland, when he became Lord of the Manor and started to develop the lead mining industry.

Before the Church was built in Hebden the route over the stepping stones was part of the church path to Linton Church from Hebden.

Now retrace your steps back as far as Holme House Cottage.

In the winter months as you approach Holme House Cottage you will get a fine view of the Linton Falls.

Holme House Cottage and Holme House were originally built in the 19th century by the owners of Linton Mill as one property known as 'Holme House'. At one time the property was split into three dwelling units.

Turn left just beyond the barn to Holme Cottage on to the unsurfaced lane. Just beyond Holme House, where the lane begins to climb turn right on to the footpath marked 'To Linton via B6160'. Pass through the little gate.

This path climbs fairly steeply at first and then gradually flattens out, being the original footpath linking Linton with Linton Church.

Pause at the summit of the hill and look back at the view with Grassington to the left and straight ahead, to the left of the electricity pole, Kirkfield and on the right Elbolton.

These two houses were built in 1921/22 by Theodore Taylor, a textile manufacturer from Batley, who lived to be over 100 years of age. He built Kirkfield, then known as 'Moraine', for himself and Elbolton for his daughter after she married a Dr Harrop. Theodore was at one time Member of Parliament for Radcliffe near Manchester. Both of these houses are typical of many houses built at the time by wealthy manufacturers, in beautiful countryside, well away from their factories.

Over to the right below some farm buildings you will see another excellent example of lynchets, or early field systems, and to the left Grass Wood comes into view.

Ahead Elbolton and to the right Stebden hills linked with a fine belt of mature trees will be seen. Cross the stile and turn right on to the road.

Beyond will be seen the remaining derelict buildings of the former Linton Residential School. Much of this site has now been returned to agriculture and it is to be hoped that the remainder of the site can be similarly cleared and restored.

In a hundred yards or so bear left at the 6'-6" restriction sign into the narrow lane.

Note the old milestone on the right at this junction inscribed to the left 'Linton Skipton' and to the right 'Kilnsey Threshfield'. This is a pretty little lane with several lengths of hedge in front of the stone wall on the left.

Soon some of the old buildings on the edge of Linton Village come into view ahead at a bend in the lane.

On the left as we drop down into the village across a field to the left with a high stone wall is the former Linton Rectory, now the Youth Hostel. There were two rectories until 1866, one for each Rector of the two Medieties. To the right the cupola to the Fountaine's Almshouses can be seen through the trees.

At the 'Give Way' sign bear left into the village.

IAN GOLDTHORPE

White Abbey

At the time I did this walk in early February the grounds of Linton House appeared as a carpet of white snowdrops, when seen from this point.

Cross the road bridge and turn left.

We come into a most perfect and idyllic Anglian village with a delightful green and a stream running through it, and a monument inscribed: 'A tribute to Linton-in-Craven on being adjudged first in the News Chronicle Loveliest Village in the North Contest 1949'. Incidentally this competition was judged by L du Garde Peach, who later became the Editor of the Ladybird series of books.

Could this peaceful place be Yorkshire's most beautiful village?

This is a most difficult question to answer, especially since for various reasons we all have favourites. Personally, I can think of well over a dozen, or so, other villages within the Yorkshire Dales National Park that could well merit this title. Again in the North Yorkshire Moors National Park there are as many of which Coxwold is my favourite with Egton Bridge with its recently rebuilt bridge and Robin Hood's Bay high on the list. The Yorkshire Wolds also have many little known villages of which Bishop Burton, Sledmere and Langton deserve a special mention, but Brantingham with its lovely little dale shouldn't be

forgotten. The Howardian Hills contain another fine group of which Hovingham must surely be the finest. Further outstanding villages are to be found around York, also to the north of Knaresborough and in the lower Wensleydale valley, together with some real gems such as for instance Hooton Pagnell, scattered throughout the four counties that make up the great expanse of the North of England known as 'Yorkshire'. So trying to decide upon which is Yorkshire's most beautiful village is no easy task, but aren't we fortunate that we have so many of these delightful and ancient settlements still surviving today, every one of which is a real joy to visit!

FOR INFORMATION ON THE BUILDINGS AND OTHER FEATURES TO BE SEEN HERE REFER TO THE CHAPTER DESCRIBING A WALK AROUND LINTON VILLAGE.

Leave Linton Village by taking the footpath marked 'To Threshfield' alongside Linton Beck known as 'Well Lane'.

Note the delightful 17th century barn on the left with the attractive ferns and other plants growing on its roof and gutters.

Just beyond are the stepping stones leading to the lovely house known as 'White Abbey' the front part of which probably dates from about 1630, having something of the character of the Cotswold buildings. It has nothing to do with monks and was never part of a monastery, but was given this name by Halliwell Sutcliffe, the author, when he lived here.

Across the beck will be seen the village pinfold and to the left a house that was converted from a barn in 1982.

The lane bends round to the right with the view of a barn ahead.

At this point the fine 18th century front elevation of Linton House can be glimpsed over the high wall on the left.

The nearby barn is in effect an example of a 'long house'. Note the former dwelling at the left-hand end. This building appears to date from the late 17th or early 18th century, but the front lean-to portion and the porch to the right are later additions.

A little further on a lane goes off to the left to a gate and a barn. To the right at this point, across the beck on the top of a small hill between the trees, you will see a small stone obelisk.

The exact purpose of this is unknown, but it has been suggested that it may have been used for a beacon to guide the monks and others connected with either Fountains Abbey or Bolton Priory when they passed along this route to their lands in Upper Wharfedale and beyond.

This section of the path is, I feel, very beautiful at all times of the year.

Pass through the gate and follow the grassy footpath marked 'To B6160 and Threshfield', going straight ahead parallel with the beck.

From here there are glimpses of Grassington between the trees.

Pass through the gate at the end of the copse of trees on the right, and then bear left under the railway bridge and through another gate.

Ahead there is a fine view of the old village of Threshfield, and at the right-hand end some newer buildings.

Cross the old stone slab bridge over Ings

Beck and then the gated stile, proceeding ahead to the left-hand corner of the copse of trees. Pass through the gated stile. This area is known locally as 'Monkholme'. Turn left and follow the road for two hundred yards, or so, if you wish to view the old part of Threshfield Village.

FOR INFORMATION ON THE BUILDINGS AND OTHER FEATURES TO BE SEEN HERE REFER TO THE CHAPTER DESCRIBING A WALK AROUND THRESHFIELD VILLAGE.

Returning back to this point of the walk, cross the road passing through the small gate to the right of a field gate on to the bridleway marked 'To Threshfield School'. This grassy path gradually climbs up to the railway bridge with fine views opening out ahead.

To the right, there is an excellent view of the old railway embankment carrying the former single track line that crosses this little valley. This branch line had a comparatively short life being opened in 1902 and closed to passenger trains, except for excursions, in 1930. It was closed down finally and the track removed in 1969. However, the first part of the line from Skipton still remains as far as the Swinden Quarry in Cracoe, being used to transport limestone. At the time this line was opened there were ambitious plans to extend it up Wharfedale and by tunnel either under Park Rash, or Kidstones Pass, to join the Wensleydale line. The route from Grassington Station would have gone roughly along the line of Wharfeside Avenue, crossing the Ghaistrill's Strid on a viaduct, then passing through Grass Wood and along the east side of Upper Wharfedale.

Pass through the gates, one at each end of the railway bridge, and continue ahead.

Soon the newly formed Captain Beck will be seen winding around in the bottom of the valley to the right. Grassington quickly comes into view to the left dominated by the red roofs of Bridge End and ahead Colvend, the National Park office, with an excellent example of lynchets in the field below.

The wall on the right of this track, winding round as it does, is quite old possibly dating from before the 18th century.

Pass through the gate.

Here, for those interested, it is worthwhile first to make a short detour of approximately two hundred yards along the road to the right to see the Victorian post box in the wall on the left just before Bow Bridge.

Turn left on to the road passing Threshfield Primary School.

IAN GOLDTHORPE

Threshfield Grammar School

This was originally known as 'Threshfield Free School' or 'Threshfield Grammar School' and still keeps up its tradition of the ghostly schoolmaster, 'Pam the Fiddler'. Though it is not a church school, it has links with the church since its founder was the Rev'd Matthew Hewitt, a rector of One Mediety of Linton who, in 1674, left an endowment to provide a free school at Threshfield. Matthew Hewitt was the uncle of Richard Fountaine who founded Linton Hospital. Matthew also endowed four Exhibitions at St John's College, Cambridge for pupils from Threshfield Grammar School, which remained a grammar school until 1865. This little school, which has an outstanding academic record, is shortly to be extended at the rear.

A few yards further on, the hillside on the right is often covered with cowslips during the spring. This road is very old, being part of the original highway from Grassington to Skipton.

A little distance ahead take the footpath on the right marked 'Linton Falls ¼ mile.'

The stile here is probably very old and may even date from the latter part of the 17th century.

The path soon runs alongside the river.

To the left across the river, is a fine view of the very long block of houses known as 'Bridge End' and further left the beautiful old Linton Bridge

now usually described as 'Grassington Bridge'. Bridge End belongs to the 'railway age' and was known as 'Boiled Egg Row' since the wives put on the eggs to boil when they heard the train enter the station. Note especially the red tiles to the front elevation. The roof at the rear is covered with slates, since at the time, although quite out of character with the area these tiles were fashionable but more expensive, and fortunately the developer couldn't afford red tiles for both sides of the roof. Gradually during the railway era some of these houses started to be let by their owners as holiday accommodation and as a result of this the Bridge End locality became known as 'Manningham on the Wharfe', since most of the people using this facility came here by train from Bradford.

This section of the path is rich in wild flowers during the summer months and nearby on the hillside to the right, some new tree planting was carried out in 1997.

We soon have a close view of the remains of the Hydro-electric Station generating house and weir.

This company known as the 'Grassington Electric Supply Company' was not entirely successful, since when the flow of water in the river was below a certain level it was impossible to generate any power, which was not exactly a very satisfactory state of affairs. However, about 1918, William Lowcock, who by this time was the owner of Linton Mill, bought out the company. The mill had changed over to steam power, and so when there was insufficient water in the river Lowcock generated the electricity at his factory. William was not a particularly popular member of the community and had now got a monopoly of the electricity business in Grassington, in addition charging batteries and selling electric light bulbs, etc. There was one notorious occasion when he put up the cost of the electricity and the Grassington Parish Council refused to pay the additional charge; he therefore cut off the street lighting for part of the winter to compensate for the electricity for which he was not being paid.

Pass through the gate and follow the grassy path over the meadow back to Little Emily's Bridge, turning left then back over the falls and up the Snake Walk to Colvend.

STARTING POINT: This walk starts at the National Park car park at Colvend.

DISTANCE: Approximately three and a half miles.

TIME REQUIRED: Two and a half hours, but extra time should be allowed if you are going to look at the buildings and other features in Grassington on the first part of the walk.

TERRAIN: This is a very easy walk, again provided that you have suitable footwear. It is a gradual climb up through Grassington to Town Head Farm, then undulating as far as Grass Wood. The path is fairly level along the edge of Grass Wood, dropping down through Lower Grass Wood to follow the river downstream to Linton Falls. The path back to Colvend along the 'Snake Walk' is uphill.

Attractive features of this walk are the many fine views, often backed by Cracoe and Rylstone fells. Very appealing wooded meadows border Grass Wood and the return path along the river, passing Ghaistrill's Strid is especially beautiful.

First a look inside the National Park Information Centre is well worthwhile if it is open at the time of your visit.

This building which was opened in 1988, is a good example of present day craftsmanship and almost appears to have been a conversion from an existing building, but this is not so. The Centre, which is open daily during the summer months and at weekends and some weekdays during the winter period, is well worth inspection especially in order to see the excellent exhibition explaining much about this part of the Yorkshire Dales National Park.

Turn left outside the entrance to the Information Centre, pass through one of the small gates and follow the sign marked 'To the Village' first crossing Hebden Road on to the footpath.

FOR INFORMATION ON THE BUILDINGS AND OTHER FEATURES TO BE SEEN ON THE FIRST PART OF THIS WALK REFER TO THE CHAPTER DESCRIBING A WALK AROUND GRASSINGTON.

At Barclays Bank bear right into Main Street.

Here we join the Dales way. This part of Grassington is known as 'Town End'.

The cobbled square is soon reached. Leave The Square proceeding up Main Street and at the Town Hall turn left into Chapel Street.

Beyond Bank Lane that goes off up a steep hill on the right we enter the part of Grassington known as 'Town Head'.

Where the road bends round to the left continue ahead alongside Town Head Farmhouse, through the farmyard as indicated by the green painted metal footpath sign marked 'Conistone'.

Just in front of the stable block on the right there is a further sign pointing the direction and marked 'Footpath to Conistone and Grass Wood', with the Dales Way logo attached. A few yards on the left, during the winter months, you will usually see a number of cows eating silage.

Leave the farmyard passing through a wide gateway into a rather muddy field where the paths divide, the upper one marked 'Dales Way footpath to Kettlewell'. Here we leave the Dales Way taking the lower path marked 'Footpath to Grass Wood', heading across to a narrow stile constructed with a vertical stone at each side. The path now continues ahead across a very grassy field through a little valley to the right of a little knoll with a tree in front of it.

The top of the roof of a barn can just be seen.

Pass through the stile.

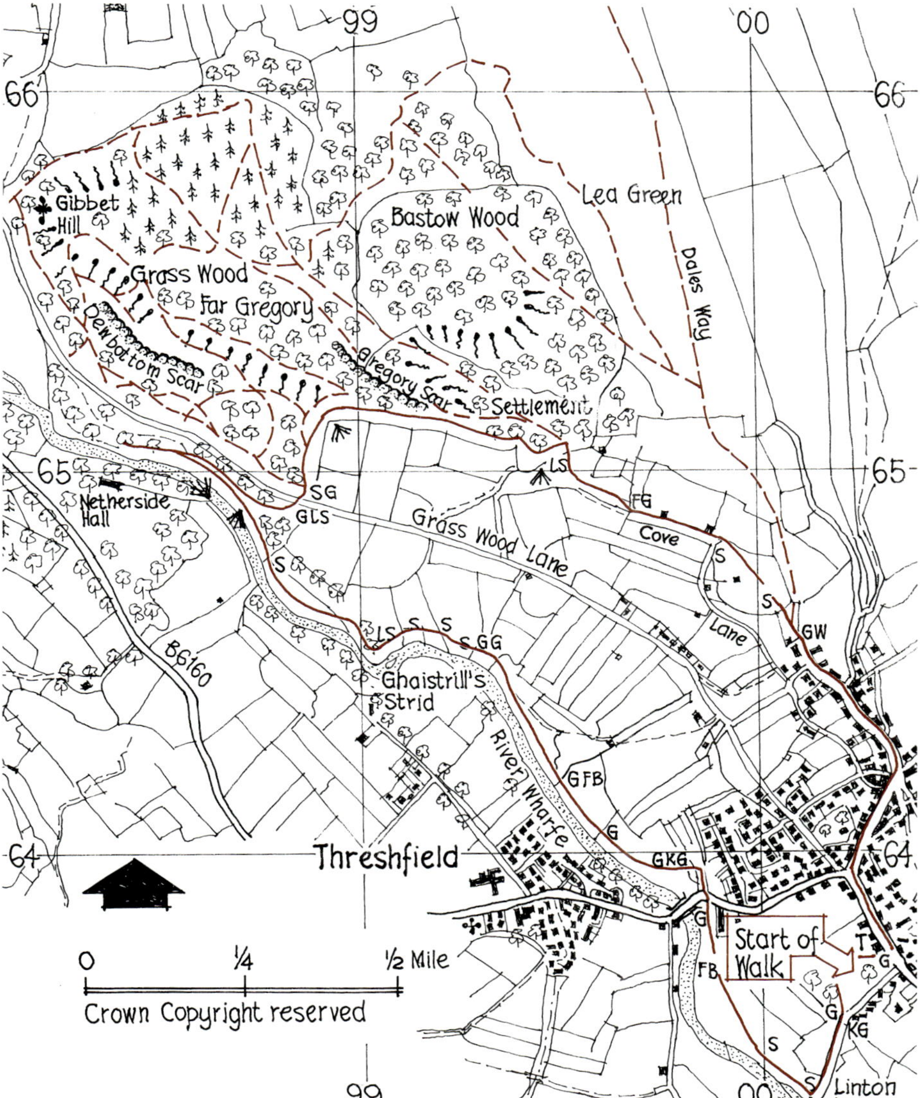

Gibbet
Hill

Bastow Wood

Lea Green

Grass Wood

Far Gregory

Dales Way

Pewbottom Scar

Gregory Scar

Settlement

Netherside
Hall

SG

GLS

Grass Wood Lane

LS

FG

Cove

S

Lane

GW

S

B6160

LS

S

S

S

GG

Ghaistrill's
Strid

River Wharfe

GFB

G

Threshfield

GKG

G

Start of
Walk

T

G

FB

G

G

KG

S

S

Linton
Falls

0   ¼   ½ Mile

Crown Copyright reserved

99

99

00

00

66

66

65

65

64

64

Note how the stile itself is made in gritstone, although the walls hereabouts are all limestone. This is quite a common feature in this part of Wharfedale.

Descend the nine steps and continue ahead along the walled lane past the barns.

Behind in the limestone escarpment may be glimpsed a cave.

The first barn on the right probably dates from the early 18th century. Note the large quoins at the corners and in the west gable, facing Grass Wood, the projecting stones in courses at intervals of approximately three feet, or one metre. These may have been used to support the scaffolding during construction.

The second barn probably also dates from the early 18th century, and is interesting with its front lean-to portion and fine entrance porch with old timber lintels over.

At the end of the narrow grassed road known as 'Cove Lane', pass through the right-hand metal gate continuing ahead through a long narrow field, passing through an opening.

Hereabouts there are many ancient walls dating back, I would think, at least to Medieval times. They can easily be picked out by their shape (very wide at the base with many large stones). The walls on each side of the opening through which you have just passed are good examples.

Proceed to the ladder stile at the edge of the wood

The barn on the right again probably dates from the 18th century.

Pause here and look back at the fine view with Grassington, behind the barn, straggling along the skyline. Between the trees ahead you will see the four arches of Grassington Bridge. Behind are Burnsall, Thorpe, Cracoe and Rylstone fells and below them the five reef knolls including Skelterton Hill to the far right, with a group of trees climbing up to its summit. To the right of the bridge much of the newer part of Threshfield can be seen and the cream gables of Threshfield Court are clearly visible above. Further to the right, between the rugby posts, can just be seen the

pointed top of the Roman Catholic Church of St Margaret Clitherow.

The ladder stile is known locally as 'Park Stile'.

Cross the stile and turn left on to the footpath running alongside the wall.

Grass Wood, originally in the ownership of the Duke of Devonshire, is a classic example of an ash wood on limestone with a hazel understorey, having an extremely rich and varied ground flora and has been designated as a Site of Special Scientific Interest. It is now owned and managed by the Yorkshire Wildlife Trust whose long-term objective is to restore later areas planted with alien species, mainly conifers, back to broadleaf woodland. Management of this Reserve relies almost entirely upon volunteers and anyone interested in helping with this work, which takes place mainly during the winter, should telephone The Yorkshire Wildlife Trust office at 10 Toft Green, York (01904 659570) for further information.

The flora includes such characteristic plants as lily-of-the-valley, bloody crane's-bill, rockrose, melancholy thistle, burnet rose, mountain melick and blue moor grass. Some plants found here – wood sorrel, yellow pimpernel and lily-of-the-valley – are amongst those believed to be indicators of ancient woodland. During most years there is a wealth of fungi. Uncommon species occur in the leaf litter, on dead and living wood and in association with the remaining conifers.

Birds also flourish and these include nuthatch, treecreeper, dunnock, woodcock, green and great-spotted woodpeckers, great, blue, coal and marsh tits, and various warblers.

Mammals include roe deer which have increased in number since they first appeared in the 1980s and the rabbit population has also increased.

Features of the wood include Fort Gregory, the Brigantian hill fort at Far Gregory, an Iron Age settlement near Park Stile and some remains of mining.

There is a number of concessionary paths through Grass Wood and for completeness they are shown on the map for this ramble. Beyond is Bastow Wood, which has also been included, an ancient wood containing silver birch, which belongs to the

Trustees of the Fountaine's Hospital in Linton. This wood, being more open than Grass Wood, has a rather different flora. Especially noteworthy are the yellow mountain pansy and the bird's eye primrose.

The path soon bears round to the right, leaving the wall and cutting across the corner of the wood rising uphill slightly. At the small green post don't take the path which rises, but bear left on the path marked 'gate'. The path soon runs alongside the wall again, being narrow and quickly passing over some limestone outcrops, with a limestone escarpment at the top of a steep slope to the right. The path then becomes wider and less rocky.

Note the countryside on the left which is delightful, being pleasantly wooded and treed with a medley of stone walls and limestone outcrops and two stone barns with monopitch roofs. Some of the stone walls hereabouts are falling into a state of 'graceful decay'! Pigs were reared locally in this area for many years.

The path bears round to the left.

Here, especially in the winter months, there is a good view of the Wharfedale RUFC ground and in front of it three houses built early this century when the railway came. The house with the red roof, which has a superb view of the river looking up the dale, was for many years a guest house; the block to the left is actually two houses.

Ignore the path coming in from the right and continue ahead gradually going downhill towards Grass Wood Lane. Cross the stile to the left of a gate. Cross the road and then the ladder stile to the right of a gate leading into Lower Grass Wood.

This wood also belonged to the Duke of Devonshire and in the late 1980s he sold it to the Woodland Trust.

Follow the path straight ahead and in about fifty yards take the path off to the right in order to get a view of Netherside Hall.

Soon there is a fine view of the River Wharfe far below. For a short distance the path becomes naturally paved with limestone.

A little distance further on the path drops

down towards the main path alongside the river. Continue ahead until you are abreast of Netherside Hall.

Netherside Hall was built about 1820 by Alexander Nowell. As mentioned earlier in this book his great-nephew Alexander Dawson Nowell was Rector of Linton from 1855 until 1866 and was partly instrumental in arranging the major restoration of the church in 1861, six years before his death. This former residence is a fine building in a most impressive location, being almost reminiscent of a Scottish castle! Internally there is a fine hall going the full height of the building with a rooflight and lovely cast iron balconies at each floor level. On the back of one of the ground floor doors are marked, in pencil, the heights of three Nowell children in the late 1870s namely, Roger, Walter and ME Nowell. For many years now it has been used as a school first by the former West Riding of Yorkshire County Council and now by North Yorkshire County Council.

Continue a few yards further along the path and above the river on the opposite side will be seen a square base.

This base supported one of the pylons for the suspension bridge which crossed the river at this point. The route of the original path leading down to the bridge from the hall can just be picked out. This bridge was constructed by William Bell, the Hebden blacksmith, probably in the late 1870s but before he constructed the Hebden Suspension Bridge.

Now retrace your steps back keeping to the lower path alongside the river.

This part of the river, which doesn't appear to flow very quickly, is known as 'Lang Dub'. It is nevertheless very deep and dangerous.

Initially the path gradually climbs before dropping steeply down to the grassy path alongside the river.

From here there are fine views of Cracoe and Rylstone fells. Take care as you descend the steep, rocky and well worn path leading down to the riverside. As you go down the path note the very fine view looking upstream with the limestone fells behind. The river soon becomes more interesting as it starts to flow over a number of minor rapids.

Cross the stile in the fence ahead.

This marks the boundary of Lower Grass Wood. The houses above Ghaistrill's Strid come into view. Ghaistrill's Strid, itself, is located behind the rocky and wooded knoll.

Here there are various paths, possibly through the stone gateposts, or for the botanist over the rocky edge by the river itself.

Many different plants grow here including crow garlic and greater knapweed.

Overlooking Ghaistrill's Strid is a seat suitable for a short rest, or a picnic.

This seat has been placed here in memory of John Michael Howard who was tragically drowned whilst negotiating his canoe from Ghaistrill's on 23rd December 1991. He was only 28 years of age. Ghaistrill's Strid, like the Strid in Bolton Woods, is extremely dangerous and very deep having a whirlpool underneath. Of course, it is wider than the Strid in Bolton Woods and is ,therefore, less likely to attract people to try to jump over it. Sometimes known as 'The Grassington Strid', it disappears completely when the river is in flood.

Continue alongside the river crossing the ladder stile.

The next section of the river is very beautiful.

After crossing two more stiles the path runs over the edge of the river's bed and passes through a stile on the left and then through two gates.

Note the old stile to the right of the first gate. The second gate gives access to grazing land alongside the river. Ramblers are requested to walk in single file and avoid spreading out over the grass. The arches of Grassington Bridge and the red roofed properties known as 'Bridge End' soon come into view.

The path soon passes through a gate and over a footbridge.

This little stream, which can be a raging torrent after heavy rain, is known as 'Braith Kill' and only rises a short distance away at the end of the field and before the barn. 'Braith' means impetuous, violent or wrathful; 'kill' means spring. It starts as a small still pool and the flow of water rapidly gathers momentum over the first few yards. As a result of dyeing the water in the streams which suddenly disappear in the area, some years ago, the source of this particular one was found to be in Mossdale not far from Great Whernside. However, Braith Kill has a rich flora. Many plants will be found growing from stones, or wood, on the stream bed especially the yellow mimulus. From this point as far as Grassington Bridge the botanist should take the path closest to the river. A diligent search among the rocks will reveal horse-shoe vetch, a comparatively rare member of the pea family resembling bird's foot trefoil.

After passing through another gate the path soon veers off to the left rising up to the left-hand end of Grassington Bridge, first passing through a kissing gate to the right of a field gate. Pause here for a short time and sit on one of the nearby seats to admire the view.

As mentioned earlier in this book the bridge was originally known as 'Linton Bridge'. Note the cantilevered pedestrian footpath that was added on this upstream side in 1984. The actual footpath is supported on reinforced concrete which can just be picked out under the original parapet wall, that was carefully taken down and rebuilt in the new position. The concrete has now weathered so well that today it matches, almost perfectly, the stone of the bridge.

Grassington Bridge

Station Road, going up the hill behind us and ahead across the bridge into Threshfield, is a comparatively new route. The old approach to the bridge was along the little road to the left at the far side and at this side the road would pass well below where we are sitting joining Wood Lane near the barn just beyond Bull Ing Lane. The way into Grassington in those days would be by turning right at the junction with Wood Lane.

Before the earliest section of the present bridge was built in 1603 there was a timber bridge, which we are told was in a very bad state of repair. This bridge may have been similar in design to the old Toll Bridge at Selby, but would have been no wider than the first part of the present stone bridge. It would only be long enough to span the actual width of the river and the carriageway would only be high enough above the river to avoid the worst of the floods. In even earlier times there was a ford here and still today you can clearly see in the woodland opposite where the graded carriageway ran down from the level of the present bridge carriageway to the edge of the river, between two and three hundred yards upstream. This is where the actual ford across the river was located and it would be nice to think that this dates back to Roman times, but my friends in the Archaeology Section of the Upper Wharfedale Field Society assure me that this is most unlikely, for in any case the Romans would not have tolerated a right-angled bend in their highway at each side of the ford. However, it is thought that the Roman road along this section of Wharfedale would run on the west, or Threshfield, side crossing the river just above Mill Scar Lash waterfall near Kilnsey. This route would enable the road to be constructed without any severe bends which was usual with Roman highway engineering.

Cross the road and after going slightly uphill pass through the gate and down the steps on to the footpath signposted 'To Hebden and Burnsall'.

We are now back on to a section of the Dales Way.

Pause a few yards along the path to look back at the bridge.

From here you can clearly see on this downstream side, under the arches, the narrow width of the original bridge which has a number of masons' marks. You can also see from the changes in the

stonework how it ran downhill on the Grassington side and would then have turned sharp left passing well below where the seats are presently

Lady Well Cottage

located. In 1661 this initial narrow and humpbacked packhorse bridge was repaired and then, in 1780, it was widened to its present width by the addition of the upstream section. In 1825 the carriageway was raised on the Grassington side to remove the former hump, which was probably about the same time as the road going straight up the hill and today known as 'Station Road' was constructed.

At the end of the bridge across the river is Lady Well Cottage which probably started its life as a 'cruck' building, with a thatched roof and walls constructed of wattle and daub. The original building would be encased in stone in the early part of the 17th century, which is the building we see today having been beautifully restored in the early 1990s. Beyond is Bridge End Farm which dates from the 17th century and has been skilfully extended at its northern end by its present owner so well, in fact, that it is impossible to distinguish the old work from the new.

On the left towering above the path is the long terrace known as 'Bridge End'. This property belongs to the 'railway age' and was known as 'Boiled Egg Row' since the wives put on the eggs to boil when they heard the train enter the station, being cooked to perfection by the time their husbands arrived home! Note especially the red tiles to the front elevation. The roof at the rear is covered with slates, since at the time, although quite out of character with the area these tiles were fashionable but more expensive, and fortunately the developer couldn't afford red tiles for both sides of the roof. Gradually during the railway era some of these houses started to be let by their owners as holiday accommodation and as a result of this the Bridge End locality became known as 'Manningham on the Wharfe', since most people using this facility came here by train from Bradford.

Pause at the end of Bridge End, near where the path becomes grassy, to look back at the famous view.

This view of the bridge backed by Grass Wood and the dale beyond is probably one of the most photographed in this part of Upper Wharfedale. Ahead note the embankment along the edge of the river that was constructed to contain the additional water at the time the Hydro-electric Station was built.

Across the river is the property known as 'Gams Bank' which has a datestone '1631 SM', although it has been much altered in recent times.

We soon cross a stream on a wooden plank bridge, made of old railway sleepers.

This is the stream that originally supplied water for Grassington at Well Head and The Pump in The Square. To the left you can see the pipe carrying the sewage, which appears on the hillside a little further on and terminates at the Sewage Works beyond the stepping stones below Low Mill.

The Hydro-electric Station weir and generating house soon come into view and, to the left, the old Threshfield Mill and cottages.

This company known as the 'Grassington Electricity Supply Company' was not entirely successful, since when the flow of water in the river was below a certain level it was impossible to generate any power, which was not exactly a very satisfactory state of affairs. However, about 1918, William Lowcock, who by this time was the owner of Linton Mill, bought out the company. The mill had changed over to steam power, and so when there was insufficient water in the river Lowcock generated the electricity at his factory. William was not a particularly popular member of the

community and had now got a monopoly of the electricity business in Grassington, in addition to charging batteries and selling electric light bulbs, etc. There was one notorious occasion when he put up the cost of the electricity and the Grassington Parish Council refused to pay the additional charge; he therefore cut off the street lighting for part of the winter to compensate for the electricity for which he was not being paid.

Either cross the next stile or walk round the end of the wall alongside the river.

Soon there is a good view of Threshfield Mill across the river, which was formerly a manorial corn mill. The mill, itself, was the far three storey property and the whole group dates from the 17th century. It was powered by a small leet taken from Captain Beck and its route can still be traced through some nearby fields. The mill operated until the latter part of the 19th century and early this century it was for a time used as a creamery. It is interesting to note that there has been a mill on this site since the 14th century.

We now approach the weir in the river.

This was constructed in order to power Linton Mill which stood on the site of the excellent new housing, known as 'Linton Falls', behind the attractive footbridge. This footbridge is the fourth on the site and was made by Hugon UK Ltd of Bramhall near Stockport and erected by the Royal Engineers when the river was in flood. It was paid for by the Yorkshire Dales National Park and opened in 1989. In order to get access to the site to dismantle the third bridge and erect the new one the Royal Engineers had first to take down a section of wall, across the field in front of Threshfield Mill and adjacent to Bow Bridge, in order to lay down one of their temporary metal track roads across the meadow to the edge of the river. They were then able to drive their crane into the river over the rocks to a point at the top of the falls just above the central stone support pillar. 'Tin Bridge' was the name given to the first footbridge across the Linton Falls built by the Birkbecks for their employees in 1814. It was covered with sheets of tin from old oil drums to stop feet wearing away the timber and this caused a clatter, and thus its name. The second bridge which was also constructed in timber was erected in 1860 with a central stone support pillar and four pairs of iron stay rods, and remained until replaced by the third bridge, a metal structure, in 1904. The bolts which held the stays can still be seen on the rocks below. The third bridge became dangerous and was closed in 1988.

It is recorded that there was a mill on the site of the new housing as early as 1258, which would have been a manorial soke mill for grinding corn. J & W Birkbeck built the first textile mill in 1790 on this site and about the same time they built a similar mill at Aysgarth which still survives today. Incidentally Birkbeck College was named after a brother, George, who was a sleeping partner and a scientist and whose portrait hangs in the college. This mill was larger than the one at Aysgarth and was interesting for the 'long-drop' toilets located on the four upper floors, which were cantilevered out on the gable fronting on to the river. It was five storeys in height and was destroyed by fire in 1912. It was soon rebuilt as a largely single storey building with northlight roof trusses and demolished in 1983, apart from Falls Cottage and Falls House which front on to the footpath leaving the bridge.

Pass over the stile and turn right on to the bridge in order to view the Linton Falls, both from the bridge and also the viewing area adjacent to the new housing.

Here we leave the Dales Way. The falls are caused by the North Craven Fault which crosses the river at this point. The viewing area was opened in 1988, at the same time as the housing scheme designed by Jim Wales was completed.

Now retrace your steps back over the bridge and continue ahead uphill along the Snake Walk, noting the barn on the right a few yards beyond the end of the bridge.

This is Sedber Barn which has a datestone inscribed 'HW 1682'. The initials may stand for Henry Wrathall. The barn, of course, takes its name from the ancient field within which it is situated. During a survey a few years ago, the following pencil inscriptions were found on various joists of the main cattle house loft floor, namely 'F Sedgwick July 1914, H Nicholls, Mallinson and W.H.S. 1922'. The walls have all been increased in height at some stage and the building was reroofed after a fire in the late 1970s.

Pause just beyond the barn to look at the attractive view to the right.

This beautiful view is dominated by Simon's Seat, 1,544 ft (485m) in the background and below, from the left, Grassington Mill, Linton Church and Kirk Yett can be picked out.

The Snake Walk, no doubt, is so named because the old wall on the left bends round slightly over its whole length. This wall dates from about 1780 and was here before the footpath was constructed. The wall on the right dates from the time the path was laid out. On the Ordnance Survey map this footpath is shown as 'Sedber Lane' being named after the ancient field out of which it has been carved. However, it has a third name 'The Flags' since initially the path was grassed, which soon became muddy with constant use and so the Duke of Devonshire laid the flags which were covered with tarmacadam in more recent less enlightened times, I am told, so that it would be more easy to take children in push-chairs along this route. Thankfully, due to the tremendous use that this popular path gets, the dreaded tarmac is rapidly wearing off and perhaps before long the paving will be restored back to its former glory!

Ascend the steps and pass through the gate.

Here there is a convenient seat where, if you so desire, you can sit for a few moments and look back at the fine view. Ahead the fine property known as 'The Outpost' which was built in the early 1990s to the designs of Barrie Birch makes a fitting entrance to Grassington.

Pass through one of the kissing gates.

The kissing gate on the left was put here at the same time as this path was laid out by the Birkbecks. Beyond on the right is an interesting house known as 'Lynchets' which has a datestone over the front door inscribed '19 CC 81', standing for Christine Chisholm the present owner. This property was designed by Jim Wales.

Pass through the gate on the left opposite to Lynchets and you are back at the National Park car park.

Ramble No 3

From Grassington along High Lane to Hebden
and the Suspension Bridge
returning along a section of the Dales Way

STARTING POINT: This walk starts at the National Park car park at Colvend.

DISTANCE: Approximately four miles.

TIME REQUIRED: Two and three quarter hours, but extra time should be allowed if you are going to look at the buildings and other features in Grassington on the first part of the walk, and similarly the buildings and other features in Hebden Village.

TERRAIN: For this walk it is essential to have suitable footwear since the first part of the route to Hebden is through gritstone country. After a gradual climb up through Grassington to the Town Hall the path climbs steeply out of the built-up area then very gradually to a more or less level route. From the end of the former Grassington Hospital site the path gradually drops down into Hebden Village and then down into the valley of Hebden Beck returning alongside the River Wharfe which is relatively level.

Attractive features of this walk are the fine and extensive views of Upper Wharfedale and the valley leading to Skipton, then the rocky valley of the Hebden Beck and in contrast the beautiful river scenery on the return route.

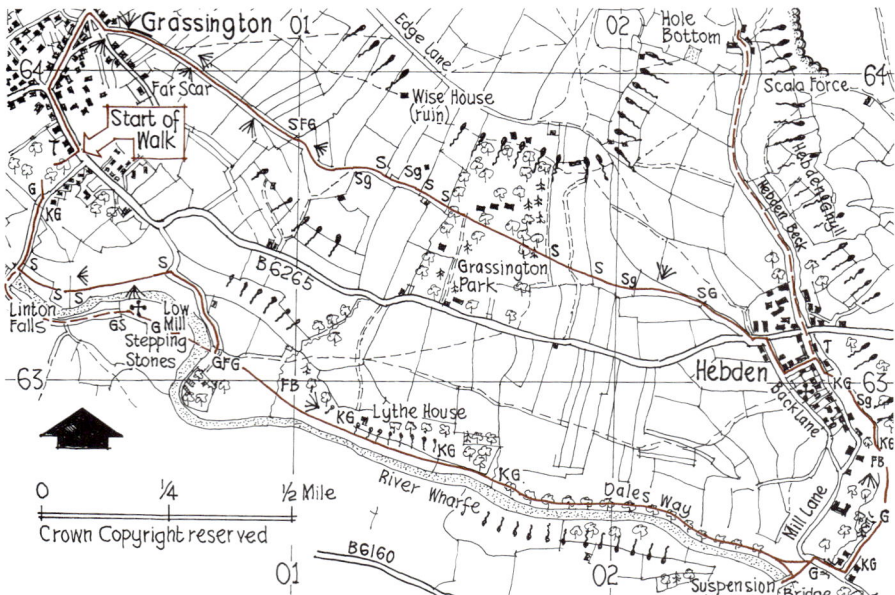

First a look inside the National Park Information Centre is well worthwhile if it is open at the time of your visit.

This building which was opened in 1988, is a good example of present day craftsmanship and almost appears to have been a conversion from an existing building, but this is not so. The Centre, which is open daily during the summer months and at weekends and some weekdays during the winter period, is well worth inspection especially in order to see the excellent exhibition explaining much about this part of the Yorkshire Dales National Park.

Turn left outside the entrance of the Information Centre, pass through one of the small gates and follow the sign marked 'To the Village' first crossing Hebden Road on to the footpath.

FOR INFORMATION ON THE BUILDINGS AND OTHER FEATURES TO BE SEEN ON THE FIRST PART OF THIS WALK REFER TO THE CHAPTER DESCRIBING A WALK AROUND GRASSINGTON.

At Barclays Bank bear right into Main Street.

Here we join the Dales Way. This part of Grassington is known as 'Town End'.

The cobbled square is soon reached. Leave The Square proceeding up Main Street and at the Town Hall turn right.

IAN GOLDTHORPE

Town Hall and Devonshire Institute

Here we leave the Dales Way.

In a few yards take the left-hand road that climbs steeply marked 'Low Lane'. Again a few yards further on pause to look over the wall on the right just before the property known as 'Hazelwood'.

You will see a delightful view looking over the roofs of Grassington with Threshfield Moor in the background.

Just beyond Hazelwood we take High Lane on the left marked 'Public footpath Hebden'. However, first go a few yards further along Low Lane and look over the wall on the right adjacent to the single storey white painted property known as 'Rock Cottage'.

The view of the little courtyard far below gives some idea of how valuable space was in Grassington during the lead mining times, and this view is almost reminiscent of scenes in the older parts of Whitby or Robin Hood's Bay.

Now retrace your steps back turning right into High Lane. Grassington is soon left behind and views open out all around.

Note the brown dome to the left which is the reservoir which supplies Grassington with water. Above and to the left of the reservoir, near the skyline, are the buildings of the Royal Oak Furniture Company. To the right fine views of Burnsall, Thorpe, Cracoe and Rylstone fells soon appear. It was roughly on the line of this little lane that about 1190 Nigel de Plumpton gave the Abbot and the community of Fountains Abbey right of passage through his land for their beasts, carts, horses and men, which continued until 1539. (However, perhaps it should be noted that as a result of research work currently being carried out by local historians in connection with the Hebden area, it is now thought that the route granted by Nigel de Plumpton to Fountains Abbey between Hebden and Grassington is more likely to have been on the line of the present Edge Lane which runs along the skyline when seen from this point on the walk and marked the boundary of the arable land at the time).

Soon the dale ahead opens out towards Bolton Abbey and the conifer plantations on the fells near Barden can be clearly seen. Just at this point where there are two metal field gates, opposite to each other, pause and look over the gate on the right.

From here you will get a very good view of the fine house known as 'Far Scar' designed by Sir Edward Maufe in 1920 for his brother Carl and Carl's wife

Joyce. Each end of the building was to have been symmetrical and sadly the right-hand end was never completed due to inflation at the time. Sir Edward Maufe is probably best known for designing Guildford Cathedral, but nearer here, in Bradford, he designed much of the later extensions to the Cathedral which was formerly a Medieval parish church being raised to Cathedral status in 1919. Note the fine barn on the hillside to the right of the house.

Soon the lane levels out and where it bends slightly to the left with a metal gate facing pause and look over the wall to the right.

From here you will have a fine view of the extensive expanse of lynchets across the valley above a new barn.

At the end of the walled section of the lane cross the stile to the left of the field gate and continue along the track.

Ahead there is a fine view of the trees at the edge of the former Grassington Hospital site dominated by Simon's Seat beyond. To the left on the hillside are the ruins of Wise House and beyond on the skyline the radio and television booster station which enables people living in these deep valleys to get better reception.

Where the track bends sharply round the end of the wall to the right there is a footpath sign. Head straight across the grass to the corner of a stone wall, which can just be seen, with a yellow marker nearby, well to the left of a large barn.

The section of the path where it runs alongside a wall, crossing a bridge made of old railway sleepers and then some stone slabs over a stream, can be rather wet at times.

We soon join the track again passing through a wide opening with a gated stile on the right and some steps. Ten yards before the metal gate ahead turn left alongside the wall.

Here there is a sign marked 'Stile 20 yards'.

Cross the stile and then a gated stile at the other side of the track.

Note the nice barn to the left with a lean-to porch which probably dates from the early part of the 18th century.

Cross two more stiles and enter the grounds of the former Grassington Hospital.

This site is now known as 'Grassington Park' and ramblers are requested as follows: 'Please keep to public footpath and keep dogs on a lead. Part of this Park is designated as a Site of Special Scientific Interest. Please help us to ensure that it is kept this way'.

Descend the steps crossing the road, then going up the steps at the other side.

In the springtime there are many daffodils hereabouts.

The path now crosses open grass land and below to the right will be seen a pair of former hospital houses, the right-hand one having been considerably extended.

The former hospital was opened by Bradford in 1919 as a TB sanatorium. In 1966 the hospital became a Psycho-Geriatric hospital and finally closed late in 1984, most of the buildings being demolished in 1997. To the left are three large houses built on the site of some of the former hospital buildings designed by Ken Robinson of Dales Designs.

Ignore the tarmacadamed footpath and instead continue ahead on the grassy path clearly marked with the footpath sign. Pass through the conifer woodland and where the footpaths cross, pass over the stile ahead. Continue ahead, crossing the track leading up to Garnshaw House on the left, to the stile at the far side of the field, then through another field to a gated stile.

To the left there is a fine view of the valley of Hebden Beck and the disused quarries on Hebden Scar.

Here we enter a long field that gradually narrows.

The walls on each side of this field are very old probably dating from Medieval times, and constructed to safeguard Hebden crops and stock from encroachment from those passing through. The wall on the right-hand side was originally part of the boundary that surrounded the West (arable) field consisting of old hawthorns and a broken-down wall. The wall on the left-hand side bends round to run in a northerly direction partly surrounding another large enclosure to the north-west of the village opening on to Edge Lane and Tinkers Lane, which was formerly a major drove route.

Towards the end of this funnel-shaped field, to the left up the valley of Hebden Beck on the distant moor, the Grassington Lead Mines Chimney can be clearly seen.

Cross the stile to the left of the gate and continue ahead along the walled lane soon emerging on the B6265 Grassington Pateley Bridge road.

FOR INFORMATION ON THE BUILDINGS AND OTHER FEATURES TO BE SEEN HERE REFER TO THE CHAPTER DESCRIBING A WALK AROUND HEBDEN VILLAGE.

This road marks the line of an ancient east-west route, which probably existed in prehistoric times. This particular section of the road was also part of the route used by the drovers of flocks and herds moving between Fountains Abbey and its grazing grounds around Kilnsey, Malham and beyond. It later served the markets at Ripon, Knaresborough and York. In the late 1750s the line of the present road from Grassington to Pateley Bridge was turnpiked, probably in anticipation of a boom in lead production from the mines at Grassington, Hebden and Greenhow.

A few yards to the left is Hargreaves Bus Garage and behind Longthorne's Haulage Depot. Hargreaves provide the transport for many organisations in Grassington, the most frequent user being the Upper Wharfedale Concert Club. Longthornes transport much of the limestone from the quarries in Upper Wharfedale.

Turn left for a few yards and then first right into Back Lane, which has a Clarendon Hotel sign to the left of it. In a short distance turn left down Chapel Lane and then right on to Main Street. A few yards beyond the former school on the left, pass through the kissing gate signposted 'Hebden Suspension Bridge 1 Hartlington Raikes 1½'.

The first part of the path, which is setted, drops steeply down to run alongside Hebden Beck. No doubt the kissing gate and this footpath were made by the owners of the former Hebden Mill, further down the valley, as a short cut for their workers who lived in this part of the village.

Just beyond the footbridge, leading to the house across the beck, cross over the gated stile and continue ahead.

The old workings across the valley are the remains of a trial level dating back to the lead mining days in the latter part of the 19th century. Although it was driven almost one and a half miles underground, it never yielded any lead.

Former lead mine waterwheel

On the left, before passing through the next kissing gate, you will see the old lodge, or reservoir, which was built to provide water power for the old Hebden Mill lower down this little valley.

Pass through the kissing gate and over the footbridge.

The nearby fish farm known as 'Yorkshire Salmon', which is a salmon hatchery, was established in 1982.

Looking down from the footbridge the valley of Hebden Beck is very beautiful dominated by Burnsall and Thorpe fells behind.

The path goes between two old trees and across a small stone slab bridge, then across the track leading to the downstream part of the fish farm, and up towards the footpath signpost. Take the path signposted 'Hebden Suspension Bridge'. In a few yards pass through a gate and the path quickly drops down to run alongside a conifer wood.

On the left you will see an old retaining wall comprising a part of the original goit carrying the water from the lodge to power Hebden Mill.

After passing through a kissing gate the path drops further to pass between two fairly new properties emerging on to Mill Lane.

To the left at this point, high up above some terracing, is a house which has been built upon the site of the former textile mill which was five storeys in height being initially operated by an undershot waterwheel. This mill was erected in 1791 and closed after the First World War and was finally demolished in the mid 1960s. Beyond the site of the former textile mill the former mill cottages still remain. The building nearest to the road, now a house called 'The Grange' was previously a corn mill.

Note the delightful bridge which was originally a packhorse bridge, which was extensively reconstructed with the addition of parapets in the 18th century.

Turn right on to Mill Lane and after a few yards pass through the gate on the left on to the footpath. First have a look at the Suspension Bridge before taking the

footpath upstream marked 'Grassington Bridge 2 miles'.

There are some stepping stones below the Suspension Bridge referred to in 17th century documents as 'Hebdin Hippins'. The age of the stepping stones is not known, although in the Middle Ages there was a ford nearby. After the partial destruction of Burnsall Bridge in the great flood of 1883, there was a need for a link between Hebden and Burnsall and so a temporary bridge was erected. However, there was soon a demand for something more substantial and a few years earlier William Bell, Hebden's local blacksmith, had built a suspension bridge at Netherside Hall. After inspection of this bridge by some of the local people, Bell was commissioned to build a similar bridge which he did for the sum of £87. This was built by subscription with additional help from the Duke of Devonshire. William used scrap metal obtained from the Hebden Moor Lead Mines, with hollow cast iron columns at each end nine feet in height and nine inches external diameter, supported upon masonry blocks. However, the cast iron columns did not come from the lead mines but the wire rope did. In 1936 this bridge was badly damaged in another great flood, that probably surpassed that of 1883, and the County then rebuilt it at a slightly higher level. Prior to 1936, this bridge had a central support, the remains of which can still be seen in the river, and it wobbled about quite a lot and thus became known amongst local people as the 'Swing Bridge'.

Here we join the Dales Way again.

Now follow along the footpath upstream on the Hebden side of the river.

Note the fine line of horsechestnut trees which are thought to have been planted in 1897 to commemorate Queen Victoria's Diamond Jubilee. Here we are back again into the limestone country. The views ahead soon become very attractive as the river gradually bends round slightly to the left and Threshfield Moor comes into view behind.

After a fairly long level stretch the view ahead becomes more wooded and eventually we pass through a kissing gate.

Please note the sign which reads 'In the interests of stock dogs must be kept under close control preferably on a lead'.

Pass through a further kissing gate.

In the winter months Lythe House comes into view in its wonderful location on the hilltop to the right. As the view opens out towards another kissing gate you will see in the distance Linton Church, and to the left Kirk Yett, backed by Kilnsey Moor.

The steep bank to the right has many characteristic limestone plants such as wild thyme, bird's foot trefoil and milkwort.

Note the ram pump at the side of a stream, just as we approach the kissing gate, which is used to pump water up to Lythe House. The wet area near the little stream is known as 'Lythe House Bog' and contains a number of water loving plants. These include the more common water mint and watercress, together with the rarer grass of Parnassus and bog-bean.

The gate has a sign painted on it which reads 'Bull in Field'. I have seen the bull here on a number of occasions, but it is usually with a herd of cows and I have never heard of it attacking anyone.

Now pass through the kissing gate and then cross a footbridge where the river veers off to the left.

On the hill to the right can be seen two large houses, Kirkfield on the left and Elbolton to the right. These were built in 1921/22 by Theodore Taylor, a textile manufacturer who lived to be over 100 years of age. He built Kirkfield, then known as 'Moraine', for himself and Elbolton for his daughter after she married a Dr Harrop.

Theodore was at one time Member of Parliament for Radcliffe near Manchester. Both of these houses are typical of many houses built at the time by wealthy manufacturers, in beautiful countryside, well away from their factories.

Ahead, in the trees, is the Grassington Sewage Works.

The path makes towards a tree to the right of the church where there is a gate. But first go to the edge of the river to view the stepping stones and Low Mill.

If the water level is low an alternative route may be taken here if desired, crossing the stepping stones then following the path through the churchyard across the bridge over the Linton Falls and up the Snake Walk to Colvend.

Low Mill, which is sometimes known as 'Grassington Mill' dates from the latter part of the 18th century, being built upon the site of a former manorial corn mill. For many years it stood empty and derelict until it was restored for residential use in 1974. The covered sun lounge, designed by Brian Moxham a local architect, was added to the balcony in 1989. Beyond the stream on the north-west side of the mill are the remains of the old smelting mill built early in the 17th century by George, Earl of Cumberland, when he became Lord of the Manor and started to develop the lead mining industry.

Now retrace your steps and pass through the small gate to the left of the field gate and continue ahead on the unsurfaced road.

From here there is an extremely fine view of Linton Church across the river. The new property on the right known as 'Mayfield' was built in the early 1990s and replaces a former timber holiday cottage.

To the right at a bend in the road, by a large tree, emerges the fairly large stream which flows into the river alongside the mill. Today this stream is used extensively to supply the nearby fish farm and like Braith Kill, above Grassington Bridge, has its source in Mossdale not far from Great Whernside.

The road has now become surfaced and where it starts to climb and bend round to the right take the stile on the left, with steps down on the other side, signposted 'Grassington and Linton Falls'. Soon there is a fine view across the river of Linton Church.

This is a rather unusual but nevertheless delightful building dating back to Romanesque and Medieval times, with an attractive little belfry. However, it didn't escape the hands of the Victorian restorers for in 1861 a major restoration took place under the care and supervision of John Varley, architect. All the pointed windows to the Chancel were inserted at this time and the Nave clerestorey was substantially rebuilt and new windows were put in, together with a new pointed Victorian window being the most westerly in the north aisle, which replaced a former doorway. This building is said to be haunted by a monk who is usually seen going through this window. He is thought to have belonged to either Fountains Abbey or Bolton Priory and may have taken services here in Medieval times.

Beyond there is a fine view of the rear of Kirk Yett with two windows dating from the latter part of the 17th century or early in the 18th century.

From the top of the next stile look back at the fine view of Low Mill, Linton Church and Kirk Yett.

This field has some fine examples of lynchets on the slope to the right.

Pass through the narrow stone stile.

From this field there are fine views of the Linton Falls and the new housing across the river also known as 'Linton Falls'. The falls are caused by the North Craven Fault which crosses the river at this point.

The excellent Linton Falls housing scheme was designed by Jim Wales and together with the viewing area completed in 1988. From here you can see how the new housing has been built upon the original concrete retaining walls constructed to support the old buildings of Linton Mill. It is recorded that there was a mill on this site as early as 1258, which would have been a manorial soke mill. J & W Birkbeck built the first textile mill on this site and about the same time they built a similar mill at Aysgarth which still survives today. Incidentally Birkbeck College was named after a brother George, who was a sleeping partner and scientist and whose portrait hangs in the college. This mill was larger than the one at Aysgarth and was interesting for the 'long-drop' toilets located on the four upper floors which were cantilevered out on the gable fronting on to the river. It was five storeys in height and was destroyed by fire in 1912. It was soon afterwards rebuilt as a largely single storey building with northlight roof trusses and demolished in 1983, apart from Falls Cottage and Falls House which front on to the footpath leaving the bridge.

Pass through the stile, first turning left on to the bridge in order to get a better view of the falls.

Here we leave the Dales Way.

'Tin Bridge' was the name given to the first footbridge across these falls built by the Birkbecks for their employees in 1814. It was covered with sheets of tin from old oil drums to stop feet wearing away the timber and this caused a clatter, and thus its name. The second bridge which was also constructed in timber was erected in 1860 with a central stone support pillar and four pairs of iron stay rods, and remained until replaced by the third bridge, a metal structure, in 1904. The bolts which held the stays can still be seen on the rocks below. The third bridge became dangerous and was closed in 1988. The fourth bridge, erected by the Royal Engineers when the river was in flood and paid for by the Yorkshire Dales National Park, is wider and constructed in timber with an expected life of one hundred and fifty years. It was made by Hugon UK Ltd of Bramhall near Stockport.

Looking upstream from the bridge there is a good view of Threshfield Mill, which was also formerly a manorial corn mill. The mill itself was the left-hand of the three cottages and dates from the 17th century. It was powered by a small leet taken from Captain Beck and its route can still be traced through some nearby fields. The mill operated until the latter part of the 19th century and early this century it was for a time used as a creamery. It is interesting to note that there has been a mill on this site since the 14th century.

The downstream weir was constructed to power the Birkbeck's Linton Mill, which initially had a waterwheel. Beyond is a second higher weir which was constructed to power the Hydro-electric Station, this being opened in 1909 after a successful campaign by John Crowther to get electricity and sewerage to the town. The first generating house was a timber structure on a brick plinth which was enlarged and reconstructed in brick in 1920. The remains of this building can be clearly seen at the left-hand end of the weir.

Now retrace your steps back over the bridge following the Snake Walk up the hill to Grassington.

Sedber Barn, immediately on the right, has a datestone inscribed 'HW 1682'. The initials may stand for Henry Wrathall. The barn, of course, takes its name from the ancient field within which it is situated. During a survey a few years ago, the following pencil inscriptions were found on various joists of the main cattle house loft floor, namely 'F Sedgwick July 1914, H Nicholls, Mallinson and W.H.S. 1922'. The walls have been increased in height at some stage and the building was reroofed after a fire in the late 1970s.

The Snake Walk, no doubt, is so named because the old wall on the left bends round slightly over its whole length. This wall dates from about 1780 and was here before the footpath was constructed. The wall on the right dates from the time the path was laid out. On the Ordnance Survey map this footpath is shown as 'Sebder Lane' being named after the ancient field out of which it has been carved. However, it has a third name 'The Flags' since initially the path was grassed, which soon became very muddy with constant use and so the Duke of Devonshire laid the flags which were covered with tarmacadam in more recent less enlightened times, I am told so that it would be more easy to take children in push-chairs along this route. Thankfully, due to the tremendous use that this popular path gets, the dreaded tarmac is rapidly wearing off and perhaps before long the paving will be restored back to its former glory!

Ascend the steps and pass through the gate.

Here there is a convenient seat where, if you so desire, you can sit for a few moments and look back at the fine view dominated by Burnsall and Thorpe fells to the left and beyond Cracoe and Rylstone fells.

Ahead the fine property known as 'The Outpost' which was built in the early 1990s to the designs of Barrie Birch makes a fitting entrance to Grassington.

Pass through one of the kissing gates.

The kissing gate on the left was put here at the same time as this path was laid out by the Birkbecks. Beyond on the right is an interesting house known as 'Lynchets' which has a datestone over the front door inscribed '19 CC 81', standing for Christine Chisholm the present owner. This property was designed by Jim Wales.

Pass through the gate on the left opposite to Lynchets and you are back at the National Park car park.

The Outpost

A Walk Around Linton Village

Linton means the village by the hlynn, or lake, and the flat area to the south-west of the village was known as 'Linton Tarn', later becoming marshland and finally being drained late in 1850. It was ideal for growing flax which was still being produced in 1812 and two 'retting' troughs still survive in the village. This village is a good example of an Anglian settlement with the buildings being grouped around a green. The Green, which is cut into two unequal areas by Linton

Beck, was formerly 'Waste of the Manor of Linton', belonging to the Lord of the Manor of Linton, who for many years has been the Duke of Devonshire. About 1930 Linton Parish Council bought the Green and at the same time made a series of bye-laws regulating its use. No animals are allowed to graze on the Green and similarly fires and camping are not allowed. In 1935 the posts and chains were erected around the perimeter, the present maypole being fairly new.

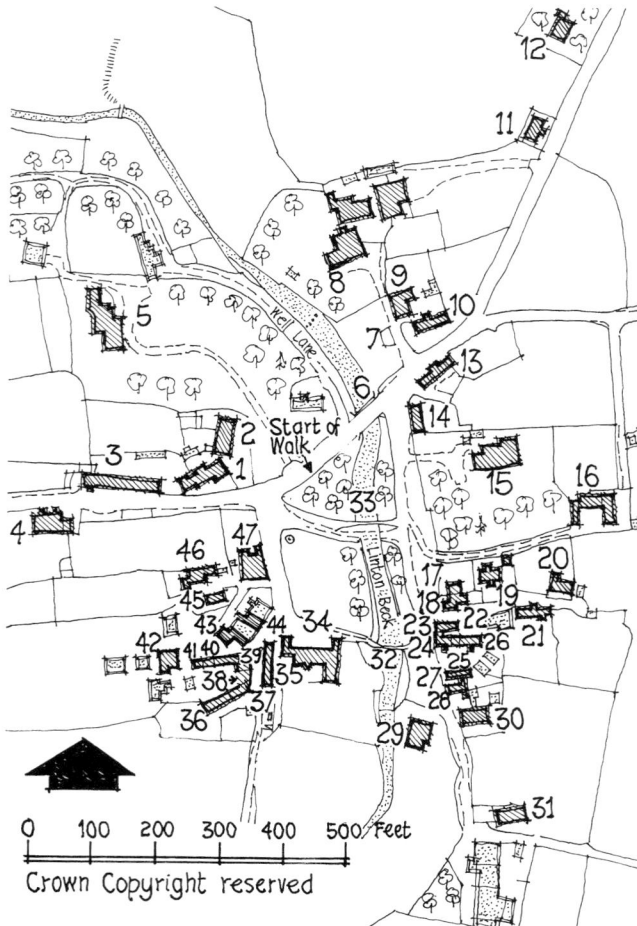

0   100   200   300   400   500 feet

Crown Copyright reserved

Linton Old Hall

IAN GOLDTHORPE

This walk starts at the bus stop on Skipton Road.

Outside the village, to the south, this road is known as Lauradale Lane.

To the north of the road is a delightful property known as 'Linton Old Hall'.

There has been a hall in Linton since the 13th century with the present building replacing an earlier timber framed structure. The present building (1), which dates from 1664 shows much of its history in its structure the left-hand section with its mullioned windows dating from the 17th century, some of the mullions having been removed over the years to allow larger windows to be inserted. Richard Fountaine left a considerable sum of money to his niece, Lydia Atkinson, who was the daughter of the owner of Linton Old Hall. It has been suggested that Lydia built the later 18th century three storey right-hand section after a visit to Holland, where in Amsterdam at the time the tall buildings with large windows were being built alongside the canals. She lined the new extension up with the original projecting porch, altering and refacing it to match the new part of the building, complete with what might be described as a 'Yorkshire Dales Dutch Gable'.

The barn (2), behind the Georgian extension to Linton Old Hall probably also dates from the 18th century.

Beyond Linton Old Hall is a fine range of farm buildings (3), dating from the middle of the 17th century with later modifications. There are many ventilating openings and a projecting porch at the western end. The mullioned window midway along the first floor level was for the wool chamber and this building was at one time used to store flax.

A few yards further on across the road is Tarn Laithe (4), a fine barn with a rear lean-to portion which was converted into a dwelling in 1977. The garage was built in the mid 1990s.

Now retrace your steps back beyond Linton Old Hall as far as the setted driveway on the left which leads off through wooded grounds. From here you can get a glimpse of Linton House.

Please note that the approach to Linton House is private and the residents do not like tourists walking up their drive.

This building (5), which was originally a 17th century house having one surviving mullioned window, was later owned by the Atkinson family and Lydia probably built the new frontage in the 18th century. This front extension had small Georgian panes to the windows up to the beginning of this century, when the owner at the time removed the glazing bars and put in the present plate-glass single panes.

Proceed along Skipton Road in a north-easterly direction as far as Linton Beck.

The Bridge (6), was built in 1892 and replaces

75

the old ford across the beck to the south. Prior to this the Clapper Bridge, the oldest of the three bridges, was sited here. It was subsequently moved and re-erected to cross the beck close to Fountaine's Hospital, replacing some stepping stones.

On the little green, to the north of the bridge, is the old Sheepfold or Pinfold (7), which probably predates many of the drystone walls in the area. Here stray animals were kept until a fine was paid by their owners in order to reclaim them.

Beyond is White Abbey (8), which was originally known as 'Troutbeck' and was then a farmhouse. It was given its new name by Halliwell Sutcliffe, the Yorkshire novelist, whose books dealt almost exclusively with the Craven district but there was never an abbey here. He lived here for over twenty years until he died in 1932. The front part of this building probably dates from about 1630 with mullioned windows of various types and a large 19th century extension at the rear. In the garden near to Linton Beck is an old stone building that was formerly a privy, which it is said originally had a seat with three holes of varying sizes, to suit all age groups. It was 'flushed' by a narrow channel of water diverted from the beck, since filled in. The farm buildings to the rear largely appear to date from the 18th century.

Adjacent to the Sheepfold is a former barn (9), now known as 'Linbeck' with a datestone inscribed 'PCP 1982 KNP', the initials standing for Preston C Pickles and Kathleen N Pedley. This building has a fine barn entrance on its rear elevation.

Next to the approach to White Abbey is the Manor Farm (10), known locally as 'The Old Post Office'. The west end of the building is the original dwelling and probably dates from the early to mid 17th century. The extension to the property was probably added in the late 17th or early 18th century. Linton Manor goes back to Norman times and the name suggests that this was the farm of the Manor and may, therefore, have a very early origin, but there is no evidence of a timber framed building. There is a stone fireplace yet to be discovered and a blocked up fire window.

Continue along the road uphill in a northerly direction.

The Anderton Memorial Institute and Men's Reading Room (11), is soon reached on the left. It was built in 1911 in memory of Arthur Anderton who formerly lived at Linton House. The new toilet block at the southern end was designed by Andrew Metcalfe and completed in 1986. Note how well the new stonework matches the old.

Beyond is Llyn Bank (12), another property which was built after the railway was opened.

Now retrace your steps back down into the village.

Between Llyn Bank and the Anderton Institute there is a beautiful view across the fields to the limestone hills and Threshfield Moor to the right.

Note the interesting weather vane on one of the outbuildings to White Abbey.

On the left as we re-enter the village is the Manor House and ajoining it Ivy Cottage (13). Like the Old Hall there was a Manor House before the present one of stone was built. This building dates from the early 17th century and on the roadside elevation are some mullioned windows. However, in line with fashion the southerly rear elevation has had new larger windows inserted in the 18th and 19th centuries. On the north-easterly gable at the rear are two stone quoins, one with a Roman letter 'H' carved upon it and below one with a Roman letter 'S' carved.

Turn left before the road bridge.

The property on the left known as 'Stoneycroft' (14), was converted from a barn about 1970.

Beyond is the former Linton Rectory (15), which is now the Youth Hostel. Until this building was extended in recent times there was a mullioned window to the rear elevation indicating that it dates back to the 17th century and it ceased to be the rectory about 1930. Formerly in the right-hand corner of the garden were a few scattered stones indicating the site of the former rectory of the Second Mediety at the time when the parish had two rectors. After the two medieties were united, the second rectory was used as a farmhouse for the glebe land, but was allowed to fall into decay and was finally pulled down in the late 19th century. The south elevation shows in its windows the various changes since the building was first erected. In the 18th century the building was extended at the east end and sash windows replaced the mullioned windows, especially on the south side. In the 1890s the glazing bars to the small panes in the windows were removed, apart from one window at the west end at first floor level and the Victorian bay window was added at this time. The south entrance doorway and door date from Regency times. The garden has a fine show of snowdrops and daffodils in the spring.

At the entrance to the Youth Hostel is a metal sign which reads as follows: 'A request from the holiday fellowship. Friend when you stray or stand your ease. On moor or fell or under spreading trees. Pray, leave no traces of your wayside meal. No paper bag, no scattered orange peel. Nor daily journal littered on the grass. Others may view these with distaste and pass. Let no one say, and say it to your shame. That all was beauty here until you came. These words printed on a card can be obtained from the Holiday Fellowship Ltd, Fellowship House, Great North Way, Hendon NW4'.

The rough lane at the end of the Youth Hostel grounds along which there is no public right of way is known locally as 'Corpse Lane'. This was the route used from the village to Linton Church since this lane runs into the minor road running eastwards linking with the B6160 road for a few yards then taking the ancient church path off to the left.

At the end of this lane are the buildings of Glebe Farm (16), which probably. in the main, date from the late 17th or early 18th centuries and were originally connected with the Second Mediety rectory.

On the right of this track is Sunny Bank (17), and adjoining it West Cottage (18) which both date from the 17th century, their west elevations having been much altered in the 18th century.

Now walk up the little lane on the south side of West Cottage.

This property has a fine mullioned window at ground floor level which was originally of five lights and a three light one above. Also on the south elevation is a fine 17th century doorway, which is no longer in use, and some other interesting little windows. This doorway has a lintel which bears a crossed 'I' followed by the

letters 'T' and 'A'. The 'T' stands for Topham and the crossed 'I' is really a 'J' and stands for John, the 'A' being for Alice.

Beyond in this lane, on the left, is 'Benersyde' (19), which is located behind the site of an old barn which was pulled down, the stone being reused in the present building.

At the end of the lane is Grange Cottage (20), which was converted from a barn about 1952 retaining the original walls, roof and roof timbers, with the main rooms all being located on the south side.

Opposite to the garden of Grange Cottage is Holme Croft (21), which was also converted from an old barn possibly dating from the 17th century. It also retains its original walls, roof and roof timbers and bears the inscription 'R' over 'AE 1940

Beckside and adjoining cottages

B' over 'HR' over the doorway since this building was converted into a dwelling by Dr Arthur Raistrick and his wife Elizabeth who both wrote many books about the Yorkshire Dales. Arthur Raistrick lived here until he died at a great age in the late 1980s. Here again the design has provided for all the main rooms to face south.

Beyond on the left as we return to the Village Green are two small cottages.

Primrose Cottage (22), and Glebe Cottage (23), were both built in 1851 to house the increasing number of textile workers coming to live in the village and working at Linton Mill. These properties well illustrate the poor quality of dwellings that were erected before there were any building regulations. They were squeezed on to an odd piece of land almost touching the house next to them, also facing north having a minimum of sunlight and the smallest amount of accommodation.

Turn left proceeding in a southerly direction.

The three cottages immediately on the left (24, 25 and 26), are of special interest, nos 25 and 26 originally being one property and a very good example of a yeoman's house. The cottage nearest the road (24), is a later addition and the stonework is rather crude in comparison. The far two doorways have simple headstones, one with the initials 'AP 1642' indicating that the house was built by Anthony Proctor, a member of one of the old families. The far property is known as 'Beckside'. A number of fine mullioned windows remain complete with a string course.

Across this little courtyard is Dove Cottage (27), which has been nicely restored and probably dates from the 18th century.

Miles Cottage (28), in my opinion dates from the late 17th century, but has been significantly altered and rather spoilt over the years.

A few yards further on, on the right is a fine barn (29), which probably dates from the early part of the 18th century.

Proceeding southwards along the lane, the next property on the left is traditionally known as the birthplace of Richard Fountaine.

This house known as 'Brows View' (30), also built in the 17th century, has had some very nice mullioned windows installed to its south elevation in more recent times.

Beyond is a property now known as 'The Grange' (31), which for many years was known as 'Sheepshanks' after a family who occupied it in the 18th and early 19th centuries. Much of this house, which may have its origins in the 17th century, probably dates from about 1730, has two staircases, one leading to a room that was once a wool store and there is also evidence of a former beehive oven. The north elevation has a fine Venetian window and the front elevation, which has late Georgian windows, has probably been refaced in the late 19th century. The east elevation indicates that the roof has been raised, possibly at the time of the refronting.

Now retrace your steps back as far as the Packhorse Bridge.

Abreast of the Fountaine's Hospital you will see the ancient Clapper Bridge (32), with three openings, which formerly stood at the other end of the village beyond the road bridge. The asphalt covering the flags and the railings are fairly recent additions to make the crossing safer, since the flags especially were rather uneven. In my opinion the asphalt greatly detracts from the attractiveness of this bridge and how nice it would be if the Linton Parish Council could remove this unsightly addition and repave with large smooth York stone paving slabs and a more sensitively designed handrail, perhaps to mark the Millennium in their beautiful village. The stone steps leading down to this bridge are fairly new and replaced the former steps made from old railway sleepers.

The Packhorse Bridge (33), dates from the 14th century. It was repaired in the late 17th century by Dame Elizabeth Redmayne, who added the parapet. Immediately on the south side of this bridge is the old ford which formed part of the original highway from Skipton to Grassington until the nearby new road bridge was built.

Now cross the Packhorse Bridge, passing in front of the Fountaine Inn to the Fountaine's Hospital.

JAN GOLDTHORPE

Fountaine's Hospital

This fine building (34), founded in 1721, is thought to have been designed by Sir John Vanburgh, the architect of Blenheim, Castle Howard and Seaton Delaval assisted by Nicholas Hawksmoor. It was paid for with money left by Richard Fountaine, who was born in 1639, his mother being a sister of Matthew Hewitt who endowed the Free Grammar School in Threshfield. Richard was part of a large family who were related by marriage to many of the other local yeomen families of the 17th century such as the Proctors and the Atkinsons. Young Richard went to London where he became a timber merchant and it is said he first made money providing timber for coffins in the 1665 Plague and consolidated his fortune during the rebuilding after the 1666 Fire. He became a member of the Merchant's Guild and lived at Enfield where he may have been an Alderman. He traded with many parts of Europe and invested in many overseas enterprises including the Hudson Bay Company, the East India Company and the South Seas Company. He died a very wealthy man, in fact a millionaire in terms of today's money. The executors bought farms in Grassington, Hebden and Threshfield in order to endow the Fountaine's Hospital. Initially the Hospital had four dwelling units and a Chapel to accommodate poor people from the parish, and in the 19th century two more units were added to the rear of the east wing. A fund was also provided to pay the Rector of Linton for saying prayers in the Chapel twice a week. Many of the architectural details are similar to those of Castle Howard and, in 1992, following an architect's inspection, the Trustees of Fountaine's Hospital Charity decided to reroof the Hospital and restore the Chapel back to its original Georgian style. A Restoration Fund was established with donations, grants from many local charities and English Heritage, the Yorkshire Dales National Park and Craven District Council. The Restoration was controlled by English Heritage and carried out by local firms, the architect being Barry Rawson and the contractor Bob Middleton of Buckden.

From the Fountaine's Hospital go down the lane to the right known locally as 'Garris' or 'Garrows Lane'.

Fern Cottage (35), on the left, which has farm buildings to the rear, probably dates from the 18th century.

The property at the end, on the right and now divided, is a typical yeoman's house. The far portion known as 'Fell View' (36), is characteristic of the 17th century having a four light window with a hood mould at ground floor level, with a three light window above. The far end of this block is a later extension.

Yew Tree Cottage (37), is probably part of the original yeoman's house, but it has been extensively altered. New House (38), now rendered on the outside, is also 17th century with a fine fireplace, although much altered externally. Nook Farm House (39), similarly dates from the 17th century with a kitchen wing which may be later. This building, which has a circular stone staircase, was originally single storey. There is thought to be a 17th century fireplace which is not exposed at the present time. Eldon House (40), The Cottage (41), and Nook Barn (42), all date from the 17th century. Nook Barn was converted into a house in 1990.

Croft Cottage (43), was greatly enlarged by adding to the existing building in the mid 1960s. The block of four cottages with Oakwood House in the middle (44), may date from the late 17th century, but the two storey units were probably refronted in the 18th century and the three storey ones later in the 19th century.

Turn left up the lane just before the Fountaine Inn.

The Minns (45), probably dates from the late 18th century, but has been much altered in more recent times. Fountaine Cottage (46), on the right, is probably late 17th century, and the adjoining barn with a nice archway is rather later.

The Fountaine Inn (46), though much altered at the front in the 18th century probably dates from the latter part of the 17th century. In the late 1960s the inn was extended at the rear by converting some old buildings and roofing over the rear yard.

So now we are almost back at our starting point and it is worthwhile reading the wording on the nearby monument on the Green since this is, indeed, a most delightful village with a great wealth of fascinating buildings. Note the hornbeam tree in the little woodland behind the bus stop.

79

A Walk Around Threshfield Village

Threshfield means threshing field and originally the Manor of Threshfield belonged to the Norton family, but it was confiscated by the Crown after Richard Norton and some of his sons supported the Rising of the North in 1569. The Manor remained with the Crown until 1606, when Earl Francis Clifford purchased it from James I. At this time the mineral rights passed to the Earl of Burlington and then to the Duke of Devonshire. In more recent times the Manor of Threshfield passed to Sir Matthew Wilson of Eshton Hall, who sold the whole village in 1923 the majority of the properties being purchased by his tenants.

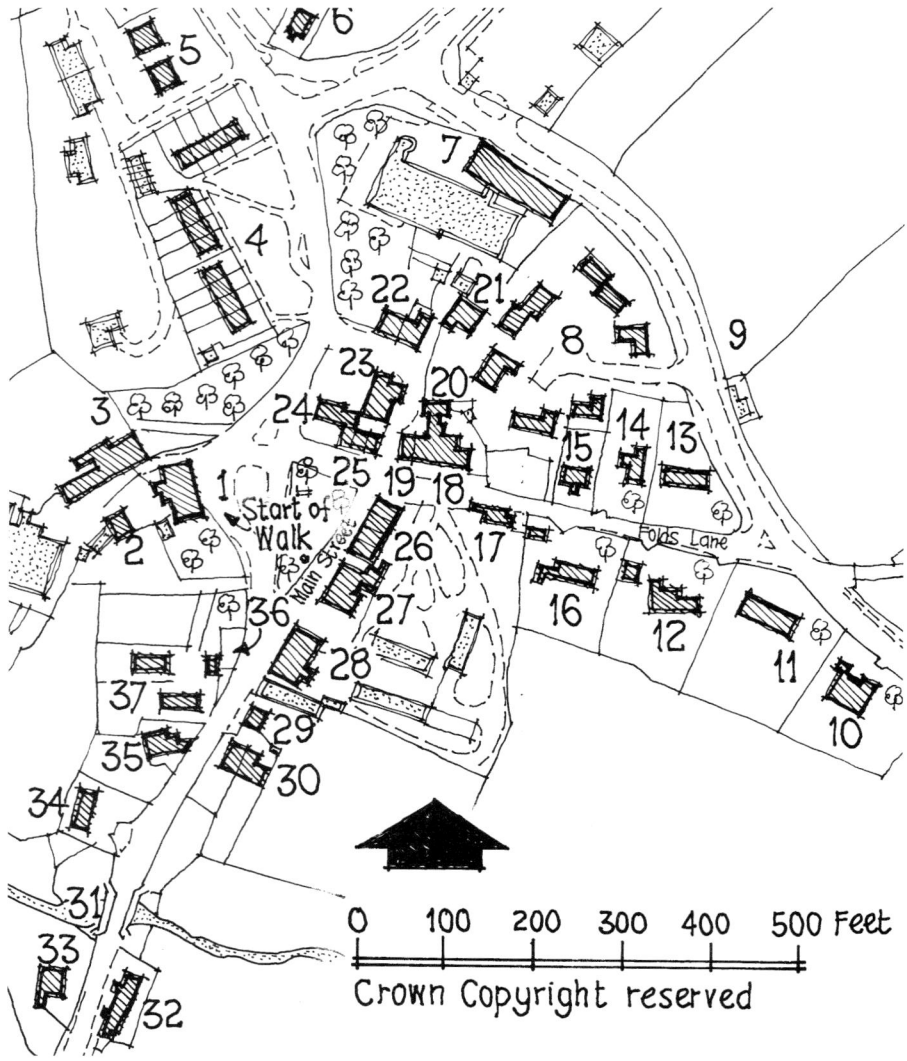

Start of Walk

Main Street

Olds Lane

0   100   200   300   400   500 Feet

Crown Copyright reserved

This walk starts outside the Old Hall Inn.

The centre part of the Old Hall Inn (1), dates from the late 18th century and was originally known as the 'New Inn', 19th century windows replacing the original small paned windows at the front. This building was extended on the north side in the early 1980s and on the south side in the early 1990s.

If you go down the driveway along the north side of the inn you will see to the rear all that remains of the original Threshfield Old Hall.

Threshfield Old Hall

This small single storey building (2), now converted into a holiday cottage, has a seven light mullioned window on the east elevation each having a semi-circular head and carved spandrels; to the left of this window is an old doorway. On the north side is a similar four light window and it is interesting to note that these windows are identical to those remaining in the gatehouse portion of the original monastic grange at Kilnsey. This Old Hall could date back to the early part of the 14th century in which case it would be almost as old as the original section of Grassington Old Hall.

The block of buildings to the right of this driveway (3), were all formerly farm buildings in the main dating from the early part of the 18th century. The first two sections have been converted into residential units, in more recent times the initial one having been nicely restored as a holiday cottage.

Now retrace your steps back to the main

road turning left for a few yards, taking care to avoid the traffic which moves fairly fast, to follow along the footpath around the front of Caxton Garth.

Caxton Garth (4), which comprises twelve dwellings, was built in 1966 by Skipton Rural District Council and is quite a good example of local authority housing built about this time since some attempt was made to fit in with the character of the local buildings, the attractive projecting stone porches and stone surrounds to the windows being worthy of mention.

Continue a few yards beyond Caxton Garth to view the two new detached houses.

These two dwellings (5), the first of which was completed in 1997 and the second in 1998, fit in very well with the local buildings and were designed by Raymond Cryer.

Now cross the road to the Methodist Chapel.

This little building (6), has carved over its doorway '1878 Primitive Methodist Chapel' and is typical of Victorian buildings of the time.

Standing with your back to the Church bear round to the left into Station Road for a few yards, then cross the road into the B6160 road signposted 'Burnsall 3'.

This section of the road is known locally as 'Back o' th' Town'. The farm buildings on the right (7), probably date from the late 17th century. Beyond, on the right, is an attractive little housing scheme known as 'Home Croft' (8), which was designed by Brian Kaupe and erected in the late 1980s.

Note the fine wall on the left (9), which continues down the hill as far as the railway bridge. This was built, together with a shorter stretch on the right which was lowered in front of Home Croft, when the road formerly a very narrow little lane was widened in 1938 by the West Riding County Council. These beautifully constructed walls were erected by Fred and Walter Walker using stone from demolished mills in Bradford. Walter still lives in Appletreewick.

Continue ahead along the footpath on the left of this road, past the road going back into the village on the right, as far as the last property on the right.

This house known as 'Monkholme' (10), which is the name given by the local people to the area near and beyond this road junction, was built in 1902 at the time the railway was opened.

Now retrace your steps back bearing left down the little roadway known as 'Folds Lane'.

The property on the left at the junction with Folds Lane, known as 'Meadow Croft' (11), was built in the mid 1980s. It was erected on land, formerly part of the grounds of Farcroft Hall (12), which was built in 1926.

Opposite is Rosewood (13), which was built in the late 1980s and extended in 1998. The adjoining property known as 'Throstle Nook' (14), was built about 1926. The next property (15), was built in 1997 and opposite is Nethercroft (16), built in 1924.

Beyond on the left is Threshfield Village Institute (17), which was originally Sir Matthew Wilson's estate shop used for maintenance work and was converted into the Village Institute in 1945. The upper floor has external steps at the east end.

A few yards beyond on the right is a fine yeoman house now known as 'Park Grange' (18), its modern name, being one of the finest buildings in the village with mullioned windows and fine ashlar stonework to its front elevation. It contains two fine stone fireplaces with moulded stone surrounds and an interesting cast iron fireplace. On its doorhead is carved 'F 1640 H' indicating that it was built by Francis Hewitt, a member of a large local family. It has been said that this property was once an inn known as 'The Bay Horse'.

Two cottages known as 'Park View Cottage' and 'South View' (19), were added on to Park Grange, probably in the late 17th or early 18th century and, during recent restoration work in South View, an old blocked up mullioned window was uncovered in the party wall, formerly the exposed west gable wall of Park Grange.

Turn right into the little lane which doesn't have a name.

On the right is a slightly later rear extension to Park Grange and adjoining it Pemba Cottage (20), both probably dating from the latter part of the 17th century with more recent windows to the front elevation. This block was originally a separate building, the ground floor of which was for many years used for making a famous local Wensleydale Cheese. The Pemba Cottage section was used for storing cheeses and the right-hand section was used for the manufacture of the cheese. The making of cheese ceased in the 1960s. The top rooms of this building were used to accommodate the 'haytime men' who came here each year from Ireland to help with haymaking.

Ahead is Toft House (21), which probably dates from the early part of the 17th century, having moulded kneelers and a projecting two storey front porch. There is a large 17th century fireplace with stones inscribed to imitate joggled voussoirs. The front windows have been altered and enlarged, probably in the 18th century, but two original 17th century mullioned windows remain at the east end of the north elevation, one at ground floor level and the other immediately above.

To the left is a large house (22), with a datestone inscribed 'MWW 1905', which was built incorporating part of an existing building by Sir Matthew W Wilson. This building is now divided into two dwellings known as 'Netherby Cottage' and 'Greta Cottage'.

Now retrace your steps back along this little lane.

On the right is Park Grange Barn (23), probably dating from the 18th century, which was beautifully converted into a dwelling in 1997 to the designs of Barrie Birch.

Between this barn and the cottages fronting on to Park View the gable end of Rose Cottage (24), is clearly visible with the remains of an old fireplace at first floor level. Rose Cottage obviously originally comprised either a larger property, or at least two properties dating from the 17th century.

The Manor

Cross Park View into Main Street.

Looking back you will see that there were formerly three cottages (25), adjoining Rose Cottage, dating from the late 18th century. The right-hand cottage has the name 'Miriam's Cottage' inscribed over its front door. The doorway to the centre cottage has been converted into a window and the doorway to the left-hand cottage is now obscured by an attractive projecting porch.

Opposite to Miriam's Cottage, against the low wall, is an interesting stone which appears to have carved upon it the date 1769 and a metal sheep's head above. This low wall surrounds the ancient Village Green which is known locally as 'The Park', hence Park View which overlooks it. To me the word 'park' suggests a fairly extensive landscaped open area such as, for instance, the Royal Parks in London, Central Park in New York or even the delightful settings of most of our great country houses. Surely this must be the smallest park in Yorkshire, if not in the whole country or even the world! Perhaps it might qualify for the Guiness Book of Records! If you enter The Park through the gate midway along Main Street you will see the ancient stocks and, adjacent to the southern end of the wall fronting on to Main Street, an old trough again with a similar sheep's head with the following inscription 'This trough was moved from its original site to commemorate the coronation of Queen Elizabeth II 1953'. It was formerly located in the vicinity of the Methodist Church.

Returning to Main Street the block of four cottages at the northern end are particularly interesting.

These cottages (26), probably all date from the 17th century, the southern ones with fine quoins at each end, namely No 2 and West View, being the older. The top two cottages known as 'Stocks House' and 'The Goblins' were originally one property, the Stocks house section comprising a stable with living accommodation over. The Goblins has inscribed over its fine doorway 'W 1651 H', doubtless referring to a member of the Hewitt family. The front windows of this block have been replaced in the early 18th century with larger ones having simple square stone mullions. Over the stable arch are two sliding sash windows dating from the 18th and 19th centuries. However, within living memory there was an identical

archway to the rear elevation but it was blocked up. In the north elevation there is evidence of two 17th century windows that have been blocked up. Stocks House takes its name from the nearby stocks in The Park. This property for many years comprised the Post Office with a warehouse at the back until the late 1950s. For a few more years the village still had a post office which moved its location from time to time.

Immediately to the south is the property known as 'The Manor' (27), which has a surprising south elevation together with beautiful cast iron railings and a gate which survived the Second World War, when many fine railings were removed in case the metal would be required to help with the war effort. Note the name of the founder 'T Ashworth Burnley' on the left-hand gatepost. The delightful projecting three storey porch with a tall mullioned window at first floor level and a rose window above suggests that this building may date back to Elizabethan times, sadly having been much altered in the 18th and 19th centuries. There is a fine projecting plinth to the south and west sides of the building and evidence in these elevations of earlier mullioned windows which have been walled up. Originally this building would have been three storeys in height with its gable fronting on to Main Street. This property was originally known as 'Old Hall Farm' and the new name attractively carved in stone was put over the doorway in the 1920s. Incidentally the lean-to building adjoining the northern end of this house was for many years a butcher's shop but this use ceased about the beginning of the Second World War.

Beyond, adjacent to the junction with the main road, is a fine shippon (28). At first floor level at the left-hand end a two light mullioned window and old doorway remain complete with the original steps and railings. The loft part was originally living accommodation and in more recent times a workshop and below was a stable. At the southern end there are three fine old doorways, the first having the initials 'MH' carved in the lintel again doubtless referring to a member of the Hewitt family. Over the third doorway is the date '1661' and there is a further 17th century doorway in a lean-to section at the rear.

Continuing southwards the next but one building (29), was originally a stable, with living accommodation above and a flight of steps on the south side. This property was converted into a dwelling, with a lean-to extension at the rear, in the late 1980s. The small building to the rear was formerly a hen house with a pigsty below.

Bridge House (30), dates from the 17th century since, when alterations were carried out some years ago, a mullioned window came to light. The eastern section was originally a barn and the forking hole, on the north side, was converted into a window when the whole building was converted into two dwellings in 1975. The house adjoining the road was given the name 'Hewitt Gate' since the croft behind has always been known as 'Hewitt Croft'.

Proceed southwards crossing the bridge, with great care, since there is no footpath and the traffic often exceeds the thirty mile speed limit.

The Bridge (31), with its horizontal ribbed stonework is similar to a number of other bridges to be found within the Yorkshire Dales National Park; it was built in 1816 by Alexander Nowell and the stone may have come from the old quarries on Thorpe Fell. It is most attractive in the summertime when the bright yellow stonecrop is in flower on its parapets. There was once a ford immediately to the east of this bridge. In earlier times the road went along the north side of the Old Hall Inn, then in a southerly direction joining the line of the present road to Skipton near the junction with Moor Lane halfway up the hill.

On the left is a property originally known as 'Ling Hall' (32).

This was largely rebuilt many years ago after a disastrous fire and few old features remain except for the numerous shoes – horse shoes, pony shoes and cow shoes fixed on the barn door in the correct position so that the good luck they bring will not run out! This property was for a long time occupied by the Ibbotson family. The best known member was 'Besom Jamie', who made besoms, or brooms, from heather twigs or birch twigs. The 'engine' that he used to grip and tighten the bundles of twigs is now in the Craven Museum in Skipton. This building again probably dates from the late 17th or early 18th century and the residential part of the property is now two cottages, which have had nicely designed

projecting stone porches added in more recent times.

Across the road is Raikes Cottage (33), at one time known as 'Raikes Foot', which probably dates from the late 17th or early 18th century. On the north side was an old lean-to wash-house which was pulled down in 1964 and a larger lean-to kitchen and bathroom built in its place.

Now carefully retrace your steps back across the bridge.

On the left is Bridge Barn (34), which was beautifully converted into a house to the designs of Malcolm Thornton and completed in 1998.

Beyond, going uphill is Sunnybank (35), which dates from the 17th century. There are some mullioned windows to the rear and an old 17th century doorway fronting on to the road which has been converted into a window. The front of this house was altered in Georgian times and the later porch hides the old doorhead inscribed 'CD 1771'.

Nearing the top of the incline, where the road bends slightly round to the left, is the old Pinfold, or Pound (36), with its gate leading on to this busy road where stray animals were kept until claimed by their owners. This would be here before many of the stone walls in the locality were built. The line of this road at the time would probably have been only a minor track giving access to farmyards.

Behind the Pinfold are two properties known as 'Pinfold Garth' and 'The Sycamores' (37), which were designed by Leslie Ingham and completed in the mid 1990s.

So after walking a few yards further we arrive back at the Old Hall Inn, which in recent years has built up a good reputation for its fine cuisine as instanced by its sign, which is displayed outside in the car park during opening hours and includes the wording 'The Best Food in the Dale'. If you arrive back at the right time you may like to sample it! In conclusion the old part of the Village of Threshfield has a great wealth of interesting buildings dating mainly from the 17th and 18th centuries, together with a sprinkling of much later buildings, in the vicinity of Monkholme, many of which were built during the railway era.

JAN GOLDTHORPE

Roman Catholic Church of St Margaret Clitherow

If you are thinking of going on to Grassington, or would like a further walk on a good footpath along Station Road, there are three more buildings and schemes that are worthy of note. The first, on the south side of Station Road, is a small housing development known as 'Piece Croft', designed by Jim Wales and completed in 1987. This attractive scheme, with many of the properties linked together like so many of the older buildings in the Dales towns and villages, was refused planning permission by the Yorkshire Dales National Park Authority and subsequently won on appeal.

Adjoining Piece Croft is the Roman Catholic Church of St Margaret Clitherow which was designed by Peter Langtry-Langton of J H Langtry-Langton Partners, architects, and dedicated in 1973. The architect's inspiration for the design came from sketches of a simple church built by a priest in Africa. It is a most interesting building using local materials, and in my opinion has some similarities with the great Metropolitan Cathedral of Christ the King in Liverpool designed by Sir Frederick Gibberd and consecrated in 1967. Internally, the Threshfield Church has a large bas-relief depicting the Risen Christ, the work of John Ashworth and John Loker. There are also some fine modern windows designed by Jane Duff. This was the first church to be dedicated to St Margaret Clitherow after her

canonisation in 1970. Margaret was born in 1556, in York. After marrying she lived in The Shambles, was martyred at an early age and today there is a plaque there to her memory.

The third scheme is a little further on just beyond Doctor Laithe, being the Threshfield Court Care Centre. The original three storey building was formerly the Wilson Arms Hotel, which was built early this century to serve the passengers arriving on the new railway. Over the years the building, which never really matched the design and character of the traditional buildings of the Dales, was altered and extended. About 1990 the hotel became a nursing home and in the early part of 1995 it was acquired by the Yorkshire Care Group, who shortly afterwards embarked upon a major rebuilding and refurbishment programme and the completed project was officially opened by Freddie Trueman OBE on the 1st April 1988. A large extension to the original hotel building was demolished and a new purpose built wing was erected together with ten self-contained dwelling units grouped around a courtyard known as 'The Stables'. This very creditable scheme, now fitting in very well with the local Dales buildings, was designed by Simon Western of the George Trew Dunn Partnership, architects, and the main contractor was Roberts of Leeds.

The township of Hebden gets its name from the Old English hebban, meaning 'rose hip' or 'bramble' and dene meaning a 'small valley'. In the Domesday Book it is written as 'Hebedene' but its history goes much further back than the Anglo-Saxons. Like nearby Grassington it was almost certainly occupied during the Bronze Age. At the time of the Norman Conquest, the Saxon thegn was Dringel who continued as King's thegn although the manor was conveyed to the de Arches family. From the time of the Crusades, (c1160), the manor was held by the de Hebden family. It passed to the Tempests of Bracewell on the marriage of Grace de Hebden in about 1399 to Piers Tempest, who was knighted on the eve of the Battle of Agincourt. The Manor of Hebden remained with the Tempests until 1589 when it was sold to the freeholders of Hebden of whom the trustees were Messrs Topham, Bland and Eshton.

Crown Copyright reserved

This walk starts in Main Street opposite the Post Office. Proceed in a southerly direction along Main Street noting the old stone trough set in a recess in the wall on the left, which is filled with brightly coloured flowering plants in the summertime. A few yards further on the left are the Old School Tea Rooms (1).

This building is the former Hebden Primary School which was built in 1874 replacing an earlier school that was in use before 1851. It ceased to operate as a Primary School in the late 1980s and then was used for a few years as a privately run children's playschool. This use ceased in the mid 1990s and, after careful restoration and conversion into a house and a tea room, it opened for business in 1997. Here visitors will get a very warm welcome, but unfortunately it is not open every day.

Continue in a southerly direction noting another old stone trough set in a recess in the wall, and from here the delightful views across Hebden Ghyll with Hebden Beck flowing in the bottom.

Over to the left in the bottom of the valley is a property known as 'Thors Ghyll' (2), with a slate roof which probably dates from the 1920s. The next house on the left is Thruskill Cottage (3), which probably dates from the late 18th century or early in the 19th century.

Beyond, where the road bends round to the right, are the three houses Hebden Hall, Manor House and Manor Hill (4), in the main dating from the latter part of the 17th century and originally one property. It is likely that there was a Medieval manor house on this site in earlier times. On the north elevation of Manor House, which has had an extension added at the east end in the early 1970s, there is a tall two light 17th century mullioned window at ground floor level with a transom. However, this block of property has been much altered in the 18th and 19th centuries.

The last property of interest within the village itself is known as 'Braemoor' (5), being a little further along on the left. It probably dates from the 1920s and has an interesting classical styled porch on the south elevation, no doubt having been built by a Bradford commuter!

Now retrace your steps back along Main Street in order to view the properties on the left-hand side of the road.

The barn attached to Crag View (6), appears to have been at one time a freestanding very late 17th century structure. It has a 17th century doorway remaining on the front elevation and an interesting buttress on each side of the original barn entrance, obviously having been put there at a later date to stop the wall, which has been well tied together, moving further. The adjoining house may date from the late 18th century being refronted with rather nice coursed stonework and quoins in the 19th century style. It has a very Victorian entrance and porch with a Georgian styled door. Almost adjoining is the group of buildings known as 'Hebden Hall Farm' (7), which appear to date from the 18th, 19th and early 20th centuries.

Continuing along the road we soon come to Belmont (8), an imposing house having a fine Victorian south elevation with a classical styled porch together with a semi-circular headed staircase window on the north elevation, dating from the mid 19th century.

Chestnut House (9), dates from the latter part of the 17th century. There is evidence of mullioned windows to the south elevation and one to the north elevation, together with a doorway which could date from the 17th century.

Now walk up the little lane behind Chestnut House as far as the farm gate.

To the left is Saxelby Barn (10), which appears to date from the latter part of the 18th century having an interesting circular forking hole high up in the north-east gable constructed in brickwork and similarly an arch on the north-west elevation also made of bricks, these details obviously being of a much later date. On the right beyond the gate is Saxelby Farm (11), which dates from the mid to late 18th century, although much altered in later times.

Now retrace your steps back down towards Main Street turning left.

On the left is a large square property known as 'Saxelby House' (12), which dates from the early part of the 19th century, having many Regency features including a very tall semi-circular headed staircase window on its northerly elevation.

The first building on the left in Main Street is the Hebden Methodist Chapel (13), which dates from

Saxelby House

the 1850s. Note the rather fine iron railings and gates. Almost adjoining the church is Chapel Garth (14), which appears to date from either the very late 17th century or the early part of the 18th century and may have been built initially as either a lead miner's cottage, or a cottage for an agricultural worker. Note how the south-east gable wall has been rebuilt, possibly at the time Hebden Methodist Chapel was built.

Here turn left into Croft House Lane.

On the right are the properties known as 'Croft House' and 'Croft Cottage' (15), dating from the 19th century although Croft House has been much altered and refaced during the 20th century, possibly in the 1920s.

Continue along the lane passing through the double gates to turn right on to Back Lane.

On the left at the end of Croft House Lane are Lady Croft Cottage and Lady Croft Barn (16), which have been converted from a late 17th century barn admirably carried out to the designs of Andrew Durham, a local architect, in 1997.

In a few yards turn right into Church Lane.

On the right is the Church of St Peter (17). By the early part of the 19th century prosperity in Hebden had reached its peak, largely due to the flourishing lead mining industry, and the population had grown considerably. Fed up with walking the long distance to St Michael's, Linton,

especially when the river was in spate making it impassable via the stepping stones, the church members here decided to build their own church and an appeal was launched in 1838. The building which was designed by the Curate, the Rev'd John Feron, was completed in 1841. The Rev'd Henry Bailey gave the land on which the Church is built and donated the stained glass in the East Window. It is a simple, but pleasing, building in the Gothic Revival style which was attractively redecorated internally in the mid 1990s. This year beautiful new kneelers have been installed, all being different in design and made locally by members of the congregation and their friends.

On the left is a group of farm buildings known as 'Green Farm' (18), which may date from the late 17th century or very early in the 18th century. On the right is a new house known as 'Court Croft' (19), which was built in the mid 1990s to the designs of Richard Pearson of James Hartley & Son, architects. Beyond on the right are two further properties, namely Green Cottage and Green House (20). Note the interesting semi-circular projecting chimney stack on the south-west elevation of Green Cottage and the two light mullioned window. Over the entrance to Green House on the south-east elevation is a plaque inscribed 'R' then a Yorkshire rose followed by 'A', followed by another Yorkshire rose and 'R' over '16' then a symbol like two crossed anchors followed by '74'. On the next line below is the word 'DEVSET' and below this the word 'MEWS'. These two dwellings, which were originally one house, have been much restored very nicely, with many new mullioned windows installed, possibly in the 1920s.

Church of St Peter

Turn left into Main Street.

School House and the former barn behind (21), appear to date from the end of the 17th century or early in the 18th century. School House has two nice 17th century styled chimney stacks and there is the remains of a blocked up 17th century doorway on the south elevation, but the building has been much altered in the 18th and 19th centuries and later. Note the nicely designed garage to School House probably built in the late 1980s. In the barn behind, fronting on to the road, the original barn entrance can be picked out with a 17th century doorway inserted which may have come from another building.

The two cottages known as 'Bank View' (22), appear to date from the first half of the 19th century.

Now turn left and walk to the top of Chapel Lane, noting especially the gardens to the houses located on the left-hand side so similar to those in Chamber End Fold, in Grassington.

The top block of property comprising 'Swallows Nest', 'Dene Croft', 'Glebe Cottage' and 'Fell View' (23), dates from the early 19th century with some later alterations. Walking back down the hill the next pair of houses, being slightly set back and known as 'No 5' and 'No 6' this latter property also having the name 'The Ives' (24), appear to date from the 1840s No 6 having a distinctive Victorian doorway. The next pair of semi-detached houses, namely No 7 known as 'Avondale' and No 8 (25), probably date from the 1930s and have been built on the site of the former Primitive Methodist Chapel. The Wesleyan Methodists arrived in Hebden about 1812 and the Primitive Methodists around 1840.

Next is a long block of buildings extending to the bottom of Chapel Lane and northwards along Main Street (26). The section fronting on to Chapel Lane comprises some older buildings and some 19th century buildings, all having been refronted in Victorian times. Roseanne Cottage and Maryan Cottage are originally thought to have been a local inn much frequented by the lead miners and mill workers. From an internal inspection it would appear that these two buildings with their very thick walls and comparatively low ceilings may well date back to the 17th century. At first floor level between these two cottages is a metal plaque

inscribed 'TF.MA' over 'H' over '1877'. The 'H' is said to stand for a member of the Hammond family. It is also said that the last landlord of the inn was very good at betting and with the proceeds was able to buy the adjoining land on which he built the neighbouring properties, refacing the existing ones and building Angle House at the corner, for himself. The Green Terrace section, fronting on to Main Street probably dates from the second half of the 19th century.

The next block of cottages set back at an angle to Main Street is known as 'Moor View' (27), and complete with kneelers and copings to each gable probably dates from about the middle of the 19th century.

Now turn left up the little lane to view the properties known as 'Rose Bank' and the farm buildings beyond (28).

This block of houses is largely 19th century, but the top house and the adjoining barn may date from the 18th century.

Retracing your steps back down the lane and turning left you will see the Ibbotson Institute (29).

Opposite are the toilets which date from the 1960s and beyond is a bus shelter with a datestone inscribed 'ER 1953'. The Ibbotson Institute is Hebden's Village Hall having two foundation stones one of which was laid by Mr & Mrs T F Hammond of Hebden on February 24th 1903.

Now cross the B6265 Grassington to Pateley Bridge road.

Immediately opposite is the Bridge House block of buildings (30), which probably date in the main from the 18th century, although the south section and parts of the eastern side date from the 19th century. Part of this group of buildings was used by a corn chandler at one time. Behind down a little lane are the houses known as 'East View' (31), the first two of which originally appear to have been a barn dating from the late 18th century, the houses beyond having been added on later, probably during the first half of the 19th century. Flatts Farm and the adjoining Clarendon Hotel (32), date from the 19th century.

Now retrace your steps back eastwards in order to view Hebden Bridge.

This large structure (33), which spans Hebden Beck far below, has embossed on the coping stone to one of the buttresses to the south parapet the date 1827. It was built by Bernard Hartley Senior to replace the delightful earlier bridge, just to the north, at the same time as this section of road was straightened and improved, the route formerly going along Orchard Lane. A few yards to the north the Old Bridge (34), has many similarities in its detailing to both Conistone and Arncliffe bridges and is said to date from the middle of the 19th century although in my opinion it may be a little earlier.

Now cross the bridge in order to look at the old cottages in Brook Street.

Facing is the block known as 'Nos 1, 2 & 3 Brook Street' (35), which dates from the late 17th century. There is what has originally been a four light mullioned window at ground floor level in the middle of this block, which has now lost two of its mullions, and also some 18th century two light mullioned windows, although these cottages have been much altered, certainly at the rear, in much later times.

Continue northwards along Brook Street.

Note the nice pair of beautifully designed garages on the left (36), built in the late 1990s. The next group of buildings, partly set back behind a small paved courtyard, including Scala Glen Cottage (37), probably date from the late 17th or early 18th century but have been much altered in later times. Pinfold Cottage also forms part of this group. This is a very new name for this property. The Pinfold may have been on High Green at the end of Brook Street, but a site within the village has also been suggested. The remainder of the cottages in Brook Street (38), are interesting. Property No 8 known as 'Beck Cottage' together with Nos 9 and 10 are older than the rest of the block, probably dating from the latter part of the 17th century since there is the remains of one two light mullioned window at ground floor level in cottage No 9. Cottage No 7, although probably externally appearing a little later in date, possesses a fine 17th century fireplace and some plasterwork with Jacobean characteristics which in all probability date from the second half of the 17th century. The two at the north end with rather nice ashlar stonework date from the 19th century.

No retrace your steps back along Brook Street and across the bridge over Hebden Beck, turning right along the little road leading up Hebden Ghyll, then after a short distance turning left in order to view the block of houses known as 'Mount Pleasant' (39).

These properties with an attached barn at the western end date from the late 17th and early 18th centuries, but they have been much altered in later times possibly in the 18th and 19th centuries.

Now retrace your steps back on to the lane turning left and left again in a few yards in order to view the properties on Town Hill.

On the right at the head of this little lane are two cottages known as 'Rosemary Cottage' and 'Town Hill Cottage' together with an attached barn beyond (40). The two cottages appear to have their origins in the 17th century since Rosemary Cottage has what appears to be a doorway from this period, although the barn is probably 18th century. The two cottages have been much altered in the late 18th century, or later, and the barn has an attractive south elevation with a nice forking hole and entrance doorway.

Retrace your steps back looking at the other properties on the north side as you proceed.

The first is Phoenix Cottage (41), which has a datestone over the main entrance inscribed 'HI 1677'. The building has obviously been extended later at the west end by the addition of a barn, the property now having been beautifully restored and extended into the barn portion. The drive has been paved with York stone setts, with the initials 'JPJ 1988' picked out in granite setts, standing for Jonathan Paul Jowett who restored the property at this time to the designs of Howard Riley. Beyond are the two houses known as 'Town Hill' (42), which could have their origins in the late 17th century, although they have been much altered in the early 19th century.

Continuing northwards the last property in the village is Town Head (43), which dates from the second half of the 17th century. There is a fine

Hole Bottom

four light mullioned window from this period in a lean-to section on the north elevation, and at first floor level the remains of a two-light mullioned window. There are two 17th century doorways on the south elevation and two 17th century two light windows which have had 18th century mullions inserted. In the west elevation is another nice 17th century doorway and at first floor level a two light window from this period that has lost its centre mullion. This window may originally have been a three light window since there is evidence that it has been altered very carefully and above is a superb chimney stack from this period. Internally the original stone staircase remains behind the four light mullioned window, together with a number of doors which may be original. The conservatory was added in 1995 and this property with its extensive and beautifully kept garden, complete with a large pond, located behind a high wall fronting on to the lane is probably the most delightful old house in the whole of Hebden Village. Behind Town Head up the track through the farm gate, which is private, are two barns. The one on the left (44), probably dates from the early part of the 18th century, but the one on the right (45), is a superb example of a 17th century barn with two doorways from this period, complete with spandrels, and a very lovely barn arch with beautiful stonework and in the lean-to section on this elevation are two ventilating slits. There is a similar barn arch on the north elevation together with copings and kneelers to the west gable.

Now either walk southwards back to the starting point or, alternatively if you are not too tired, it is well worthwhile continuing northwards along the little lane leading up Hebden Ghyll for half a mile, or so, in order to see Scala Force, a pretty little waterfall in a wooded glen, located a hundred yards before the hamlet of Hole Bottom is reached.

At Hole Bottom the house on the left facing the little car park, which has been carefully restored in more recent times, has a datestone over a doorway on the south elevation inscribed 'WR 1743'. This building has two nice chimney stacks that may date back to the 17th century and some 18th century window openings.

The two stone cottages on the right known as 'Jerry and Ben's Holiday Cottages' are both interesting. Their present name is derived from the novel 'Jerry and Ben' by W H Riley, a local regional novelist whose works were very popular when first published in the 1920s and are still in occasional demand. The first, which is older, dates from the 17th century having the remains of what has been an entrance doorway from this period, now with an 18th century sliding sash window inserted and above what has obviously been a three light mullioned window, now having lost its mullions, with a Yorkshire sliding sash window inserted. The adjoining cottage, which may date from the 18th century, has some very strange three light mullioned windows with pitched mouldings over made of stone slates, which have obviously been inserted in much more recent times.

Ramble No 4

From Threshfield along Moor Lane and over Threshfield
Moor to Higher Heights Holes, returning via Wood Nook
and Skirethorns Village

STARTING POINT: This walk starts outside the Old Hall Inn.

DISTANCE: Approximately five and a half miles.

TIME REQUIRED: Four hours, but extra time should be allowed if you are going to look at the buildings and other features in Threshfield Village on the first part of the walk.

TERRAIN: For this walk it is most essential to have suitable footwear since a number of sections of the footpath can generally be wet at most times of the year. After leaving the village and crossing Threshfield Beck the path climbs steadily up on to Threshfield Moor and then more steeply beyond the old coal workings. Our route is then fairly level for about one and a half miles until it drops steeply down from Higher Heights Holes into the valley of the Rowley Beck. The descent to Wood Nook is steep in places and from there on to the old village of Skirethorns is fairly gradual. The route from Skirethorns back to Threshfield Village is relatively level for the most part traversing pleasant grassy pastures.

Attractive features of this walk are the fine and extensive views back of Upper Wharfedale as the path climbs and once the summit of Threshfield Moor is reached there is a fine panorama embracing the Haworth Moors, Pendle Hill, the Ribble Valley and the Bowland Fells. On the return route the valley of the Rowley Beck is fascinating since the watercourse marks a very clear divide between the limestone on the north side and the gritstone of the south side. Once Height House is left behind the valley is delightful with fine views of Upper Wharfedale and Grassington in its attractive setting located on rising ground on the east side of the dale far below. The old part of Skirethorns Village is a lovely surprise before the last part of our route takes us through lush green meadows back into Threshfield Village. Overall this is a delightful ramble, though perhaps a little more strenuous than many described in this book, and surprisingly little explored by many of the ramblers who frequently come to Grassington and Upper Wharfedale.

Cross the road and proceed in a southerly direction along the narrow footpath along the B6265 road.

FOR INFORMATION ON THE BUILDINGS AND OTHER FEATURES TO BE SEEN HERE REFER TO THE CHAPTER DESCRIBING A WALK AROUND THRESHFIELD VILLAGE.

When crossing Threshfield Bridge take great care since there is no proper footpath and I find it best to walk on the right facing the oncoming traffic which often exceeds the thirty mile speed limit.

The road climbs steeply and is known locally as 'The Raikes'. Again there is no proper footpath and I find it best to walk on the grass verge on the right.

At the head of this first steep section turn right on to the attractive narrow walled road known as 'Moor Lane'.

The next section of the B6265 road along the summit of this little hill is known as 'Tarns Lane' probably on account of the fields here tending to flood alongside the road after heavy and prolonged rain.

Pause opposite the house on the left, which is soon reached and known as 'High Pasture', and look over the wall on the right.

This land, comprising the nearby large field and the three smaller fields beyond, was originally the site of the nine hole Grassington Golf Course. From here there is a pleasing view of the old village of Threshfield. Ahead there is a fine view of Upper Wharfedale and to the left the edge of the old village of Skirethorns can just be seen.

High Pasture and High Pasture Cottage were built in 1908, the latter originally being the Coach House for the main residence.

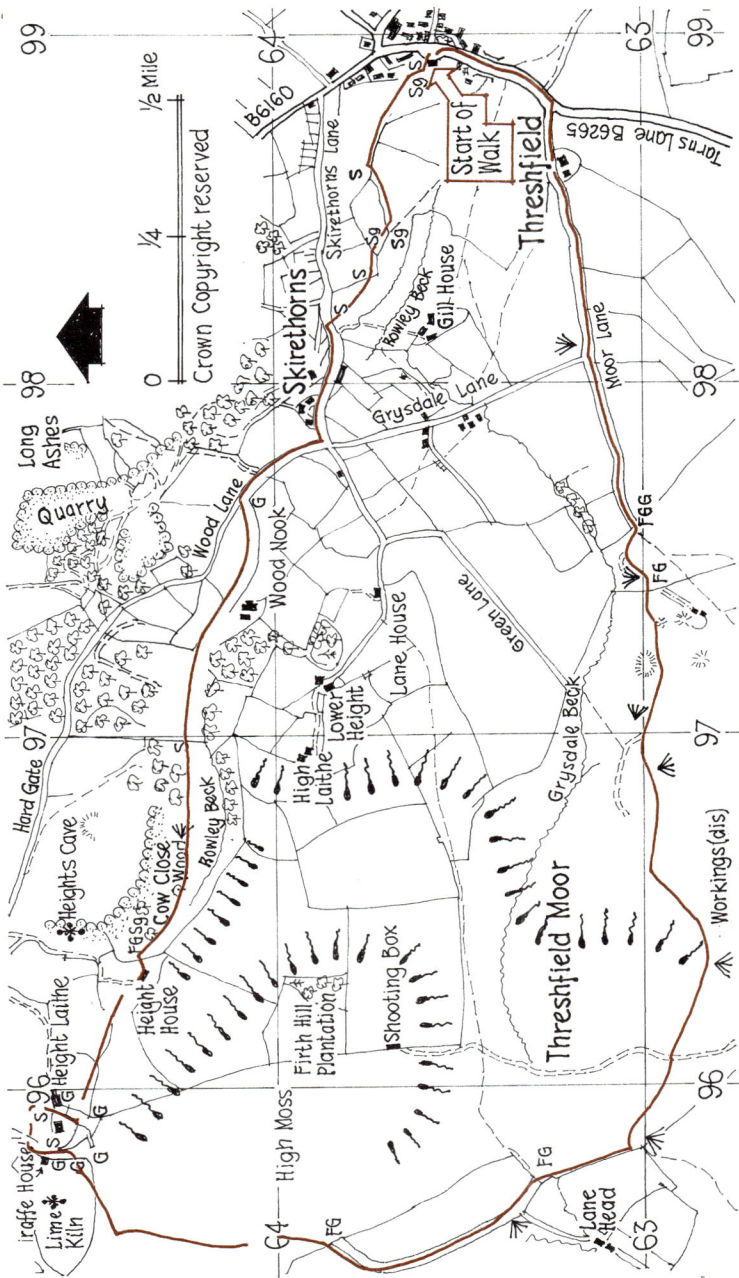

Continue ahead along Moor Lane.

A short distance further on note that the wall on the left has a substantial amount of gritstone used in its construction, whilst the wall on the right is built entirely of limestone which suggests that this part of the lane probably runs along the boundary between the gritstone and the limestone.

Pause at the road junction, where Moor Lane becomes unsurfaced and Grysdale Lane goes off down the hill to the right.

Here you will see in the bottom straight ahead the old village of Skirethorns and behind, and slightly to the left, the Skirethorns Quarry which was started about 1890 by John Delany. In 1939 the Ribblesdale Lime Company merged with John Delaney to form Settle Limes and in 1961 the company was taken over by ICI. In 1980 this quarry was bought by Tarmac and has been greatly expanded in recent years, much of the stone being used for road construction. Beyond is the large expanse of Grass Wood and Bastow Wood backed by Great Whernside and further right Grassington and in front of it Threshfield Village can again be seen.

Continue ahead along the unsurfaced track which gradually climbs.

Often there are cowslips hereabouts in the verges in springtime.

At the end of the walled lane pass through the pedestrian gate, to the right of the field gate, and continue ahead on the track marked 'Bridleway'.

Note the fine barn to be seen a field or two away over the wall to the right with a lean-to front portion, which probably dates from the late 17th or early 18th century.

Two hundred yards, or so, further on look to the right into the little valley where you will see the remains of two stone abutments.

These carried the light railway line on a single span bridge across Grysdale Beck which linked the colliery on Threshfield Moor with the quarry. This colliery, which started in the 1890s, was closed and then abandoned in 1905. Looking ahead from this point you will see a number of flat topped mounds which are the spoil heaps from the former colliery.

To the left of the left-hand heap can be seen the remains of the old buildings, comprising the washing floor and winding house connected with this colliery. It is interesting to note that there has been coal mining on Threshfield, Linton and Boss moors, together with Backstone Edge, since the 1600s. The Threshfield and Bordley coalfields were both being worked by Lancelot Johnson as early as 1607.

Pause before passing through a field gate in a post and wire fence.

The remains of the old railway track on the left are evident which, of course, originally crossed our path. This is a grouse shooting moor and so beware, from the 12th August, when grouse shooting may be taking place.

When you get abreast of the slag heap on the right pause for a moment.

Look back at the fine view of Grassington and the surrounding country.

Where the tracks fork, near a slag heap that has been excavated in recent years, take the more distinctive left-hand path rather than the more grassy track which forks right.

Over to the left, across the moorland, you will see a line of six grouse butts constructed in timber and externally clad with peat sods cut from the nearby moor and, over to the left of them, the green mass of Elbolton, probably the largest and most prominent of the reef knolls and further right Thorpe and Cracoe fells will be seen.

We now quickly reach the heather clad area which covers much of the higher part of Threshfield Moor.

It is clear to see that in certain areas the heather has been burnt usually during the winter months to encourage young shoots to grow which the sheep will eat.

At the next junction fork left onto the more stony track which soon starts to climb more steeply.

Soon there are fine views to the left of the long range of high moors extending to Rylstone Fell on the right dominated by a stone cross. There are two opinions regarding the origin of the first cross on this site. Some local people are of the opinion that the first one was put up to commemorate the Battle of Waterloo in 1815, others think that it was erected in memory of the Napoleonic Wars about 1820. However, some years ago the Yorkshire Dales National Park Authority put up a timber cross to replace the original stone one which had fallen down. In 1997 the timber cross fell down and the Generating Board shortly afterwards gave a new and slightly narrower stone cross, which was erected with the help of the National Park. Further to the left is Cracoe Fell, 1,650 ft (500m) above sea level, on which there is a cairn. This was given by Col Maude of Rylstone and erected in 1921 by the local men of the parish which consists of Rylstone, Hetton, Cracoe and Bordley. It is in memory of the men of the parish who fell in the First World War. The individual initials were each carved upon a stone on the site and then built into the north, east and south sides of the cairn. In recent years a bronze plaque has been added, secured to the west side of the cairn, listing those who were killed in the Second World War.

Pause where the track flattens out and bends sharply to the right.

Looking to the left there is a glimpse of the southern end of Swinden Quarry and to the right, in the bottom of the valley, Cracoe Village will be seen. Beyond are the prominent little mountains near Skipton, namely Rough Haw 1,050 ft (339m) and Sharp Haw, 1,171 ft (357m) above sea level.

The path now climbs only gradually up to a signpost.

The more traditional stone shooting butts on the moorland to the left are noteworthy, this time only having peat sods lining the top of each one.

Pause at the footpath sign to admire the superb panorama to the south dominated by Pendle Hill in Lancashire, 1,831 ft (557m) above sea level.

Behind Rough Haw and Sharp Haw the distant moors are near Haworth. In front of and to the right of Pendle Hill is a glimpse of the beautiful Ribble Valley and beyond the Bowland Fells can be seen.

At the signpost bear left on to the grassy and less distinct track marked 'Bridleway'. What appears to be the more obvious track ahead is in fact private and has a 'no access' sign.

The next section of our path can be very boggy in places. Take account of the track that soon crosses our route, partly paved with old railway sleepers making it safer for vehicles.

Head towards the footpath sign located in front of the wall ahead, to the right of a gate. As you approach the wall look over to the right.

You will see the Shooting Box on the top of the hill and the track paved with old railway sleepers, which we recently crossed, is the vehicular route up to the Shooting Box.

At the gate take the path to the right alongside the wall, signposted to Malham Moor Lane.

Note the heaps of stone to the right being a former wall, and judging by the distance from the wall to the left this must at one time have been an important route, possibly an old drove road.

The path becomes more clearly defined as it drops down to cross a stream and then rises up to a gate.

The footpath sign here is marked to the right 'FP to Skirethorns Lane' and ahead, the way we go, 'BW Malham Moor Lane'.

After passing through the gate the path soon becomes a grassy track with superb gritstone walls on each side of the fairly level lane. In a short distance a narrow walled lane goes off to the left to Lane Head.

Pause here and look over to the left where you will see Weets Top, 1,357 ft (414m) above sea level. A little further to the left there are fine views of the green pastures in the valley of the Bordley Beck.

The walled lane bears round to the right and terminates at a gate leading on to open moorland. After passing through the gate bear leftwards across the moor signposted 'Bridleway', the route being indicated with marker posts.

The path at this point heads towards the right-hand end of a distant rocky limestone hill. This section of the path can be very wet in places.

After passing through a gate in a post and wire fence our route, picked out with marker posts, crosses a little valley making for a green track back in the limestone

country, and a further post on a little hill.

This side of the valley can be very wet and boggy at times and it may be necessary to make a slight detour over to the left in order to traverse somewhat drier ground! The bottom of this little valley is important from a geology point of view since it marks the line of the North Craven Fault, the rock on this side being gritstone and on the other side limestone.

Note the limestone outcrop to the right where the two separate entrances to a cave are clearly visible.

Once you reach the limestone country and the green track you will see ahead a fine barn with two rather tall openings with segmental arches.

'Giraffe House'

This barn is known locally as the 'Giraffe House' on account of its lofty entrances, and probably dates from the early part of the 18th century. To the left of this barn, on the rocky escarpment, you will see the remains of a lime kiln.

Our path becomes very pleasant and grassy as it follows round by a fine limestone wall on the left. Pass through two consecutive gates, where there is a

Lime Kiln

sign marked 'Bridleway' pointing in each direction. We now enter what has obviously been a walled lane with a fine wall on the left and on the right a wall that has long since fallen down. The wall beyond on the right on the hillside, with the post and wire protection was built anew on the site of an old wall, in the early 1990s. At the footpath sign near the Giraffe House we take the footpath to the right marked 'Wood Nook', crossing a stile in the new wall. The path now descends steeply through large boulders, past a marker, to run alongside a wall on the right.

The fine new barn to the right with its timber cladding and artificial stone facing below, nicely designed to fit in with the standards set by the Yorkshire Dales National Park is noteworthy.

At the corner of the field we cross what is obviously a very old stile and continue along the lane up the hill to the right.

On the left is Height Laithe, which was originally a shippon at its western end and a farmhouse at its eastern end, probably dating from the middle of the 17th century.

Before continuing ahead up the walled grassy slope note the walled area to the left, with the drinking troughs for the animals, suitably paved to prevent it becoming muddy due to continual use. This was also the water supply for the nearby farmhouse whilst it was occupied.

Pass through the nearby gate where there is a footpath sign. Towards the top of this little hill pass through the gate on the left, where there is another footpath sign, keeping alongside the wall on the left.

Observe in the escarpment ahead the now much better view of Heights Cave. This is sometimes known as the 'Fairy Holes', or 'Calf Hole Cave' and often 'Anderson's Cave' since some people called Anderson once lived at the nearby Height House.

The path now veers away from the wall on the left, being clearly indicated by a series of markers, soon running alongside a wall on the right to another marker.

This wall is largely a mixture of gritstone and limestone indicating that we are again walking along the boundary between these two different rocks.

The Chapel, Scargill.

Peter Walbank (left) and John Wolfenden (right) at one of the Dickensian Saturdays.

Bridge End House – Ramble No 10 and Arncliffe Walk.

Wharfedale from Scaw Ghyll – Grassington Walk.

Barns on Cove Lane – Ramble No 2.

View of Kettlewell from near 'The Slit' – Ramble No 10.

Kettlewell and Great Whernside – Ramble No 10.

The River Wharfe above Grassington – Ramble No 2.

A pastoral scene near Kettlewell.

Arncliffe from Old Cote Little Moor – Ramble No 10.

Looking up Wharfedale showing the fine glacial valley – Ramble No 10.

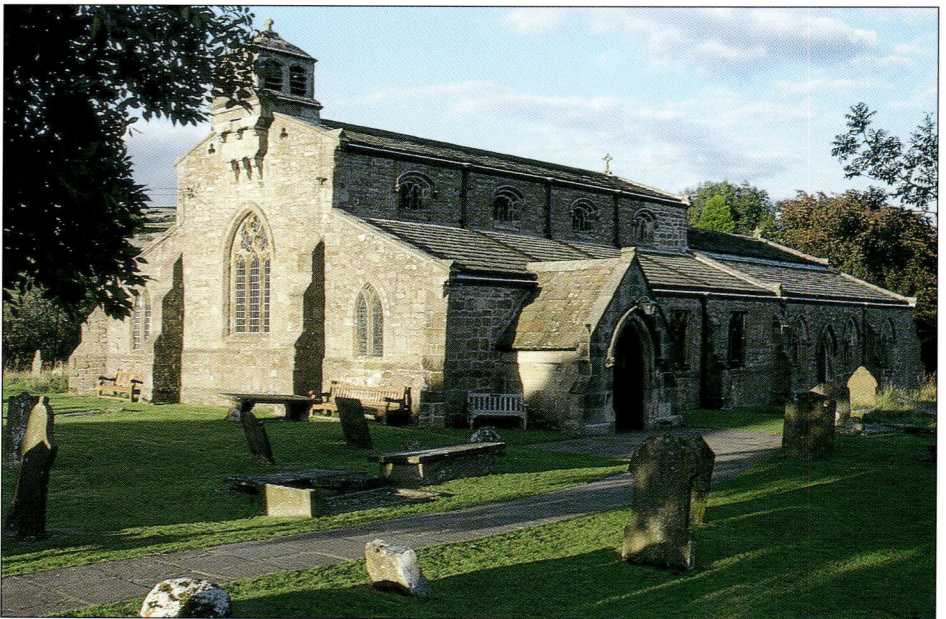

Church of St Michael and All Angels, Linton – Ramble No 1.

'Lang Dub' and Lower Grass Wood – Ramble No 2.

Burnsall and the lower slopes of Burnsall Fell – Ramble No 6.

Alongside the River Skirfare near Arncliffe – Ramble No 10.

Scala Force – Hebden Walk.

Linton Village – Ramble Nos 1 & 5 and Linton Walk.

Conistone Village.

The River Wharfe above the Ghaistrill's Strid – Ramble No 2.

Near Kilnsey.

On the Dales Way – Ramble No 3.

Littondale from near Hawkswick – Ramble No 10.

Above Bastow Wood – Ramble No 2.

Arncliffe Bridge – Ramble No 10 and Arncliffe Walk.

Loup Scar – Ramble Nos 6 & 7.

The roofs of Grassington – Ramble No 3.

Low Mill from the Dales Way – Ramble No 3.

Loup Scar – Ramble Nos 6 & 7.

Chamber End Fold – Ramble Nos 2 & 3 and Grassington Walk.

The beautiful River Skirfare – Ramble No 10.

Ancient barn in Thorpe Village – Ramble Nos 5 & 7 and Thorpe Walk.

The River Wharfe near Ghaistrill's Strid – Ramble No 2.

Arncliffe and Littondale with the long ridge of Fountains Fell behind – Ramble No 10.

Linton Village – Ramble Nos 1 & 5 and Linton Walk.

A quaint corner of Arncliffe – Ramble No 10 and Arncliffe Walk.

Grassington from above Wood Nook – Ramble No 4.

Looking down towards Thorpe Village – Ramble No 5.

Netherside Hall – Ramble No 2.

Linton Falls – Ramble Nos 1, 2 & 3.

Near Ings House – Ramble No 5.

We now go past the front of Height House.

This property is now used as a barn and was last occupied as a house in the early 1950s. There are the remains of a two light mullioned window on the north side which suggests that this building may date from the late 17th or very early 18th century. The little freestanding toilet block to the east of the building is interesting, complete with the original seat and the little door below, outside at the back, for emptying and cleaning out.

Leave Height House via a gated stile, to the right of a metal gate, in the wall to the east and continue ahead on a grassy path keeping a limestone wall immediately to the right. The path soon veers away from the wall to pass through an interesting area with hawthorn trees and beyond, ash trees on a limestone escarpment to the left.

This area has been designated as a Site of Special Scientific Interest. Of particular interest is the little tarn, which soon appears in the valley to the right.

As the limestone escarpment to the left becomes more pronounced a superb view of Upper Wharfedale opens up dominated by Grassington and in front of it the cream painted buildings of Threshfield Court can easily be picked out. Far below you will soon get a glimpse of the caravans at Wood Nook.

The path now drops down steeply to pass through an opening in a stone wall and then drops further into a pleasant wooded valley to run alongside the Rowley Beck. We soon pass through another opening in a stone wall and the boundary of the Wood Nook Caravan Site is soon reached.

At the entrance to the caravan site there is a notice marking the boundary of the Site of Special Scientific Interest.

Cross the stile into the caravan site.

The dog stile to the left, which lifts up is of special interest. Once inside the caravan site the wooded hillside on the right is usually a carpet of primroses in the springtime.

We soon reach the former coach house and house known as 'Wood Nook'.

Wood Nook was built in 1888 by James Lambert who was a mill owner in Leeds, but he sadly died quite young. The coach house has in the keystone the initials 'JFL' and below the date '1893'. The house has over the side door the initials 'J & FL' with an ogee arch over. The main front entrance on the south side also has an interesting ogee arch over the doorway.

Follow eastwards along the driveway leading from Wood Nook.

Note the farmhouse across the fields to the right known as 'Lane House', which was derelict for many years and was beautifully restored and extended in 1997. The restoration and extension was designed by Andrew Durham. There are some very fine dry stone walls hereabouts. Especially interesting is the wall running alongside the south side of the drive to Wood Nook which has been very carefully constructed, generally in courses of stone graded so that they are smaller towards the top.

From here there is a fine view down Wharfedale dominated by Simon's Seat in the distance. Note the interesting iron gate and fine stone gateposts at the entrance to Wood Nook.

Bear right on to the macadamed Wood Lane which gradually descends. At the little crossroads turn left into Skirethorns Lane.

Note the old Yorkshire West Riding signpost, our route being signposted 'Threshfield ¾ Grassington 1½! Croft House immediately on the left with its original iron gate leading to a rather fine barn is worth noting. There is a much more recent metal gate giving access to the house, this property probably dating from the latter part of the 17th century. The first floor windows were obviously originally two light mullioned windows.

In a few yards we reach the attractive little village of Skirethorns with its buildings grouped around a little green and a small stream running through.

The barn on the left probably dates from the late 17th or early 18th century. The house covered with ivy and known as 'Bell Bank' has two 17th century four light mullioned windows at first floor level and later 18th century mullioned windows to the ground floor and also to a third window at first floor level. Spiredale Beck Cottage was originally

Skirethorns Village

known as 'Meadowcroft' and was extended into an adjoining barn in the early 1990s and the garage to the right is a completely new building.

Continuing along Skirethorns Lane we soon pass the long building on the right known as 'Cobble Close' and 'Lowclose'.

Cobble Close originally comprised a barn and a small blacksmith's shop. Lowclose was originally known as 'Low House'. Don't miss the post box set in the wall here dating from the reign of Queen Victoria. I wonder how many letters were posted here bearing the first postage stamp in the world, the famous Penny Black? This stamp was invented by Sir Rowland Hill in 1840, quickly followed in the same year by the Twopenny Blue, both bearing a portrait of the head of Queen Victoria. Until 1854 stamps were printed in large sheets without any perforations and cut out in post offices with scissors. A Penny Black today with a nice postmark and good margins can be worth up to £150, a Twopenny Blue in a similar condition being worth up to £325.

The narrow lane soon becomes a wide road near the entrance to Skirethorns Quarry. Abreast of the far side of the

quarry entrance take the stile in the wall opposite signposted 'Threshfield'.

The final part of this ramble is through pleasant and grassy meadows.

The path goes diagonally across this field crossing a further stile at the far end of the left-hand wall. The path then follows alongside the wall on the right in the next field to a further gated stile on the right, then proceeding alongside a wall on the right in the third field. After crossing the next stile ignore the path that goes straight ahead, instead taking the path alongside the wall to the left to cross a further stile.

The land through which we are walking is on the edge of the land which formed the former Grassington Golf Course.

We are now in a very large field. After following fairly closely to the wall on the right, where it turns to the right, our path strikes out across the field up a small hill to a gated stile in front of the buildings ahead. After crossing a further stile and turning left into a little lane the Old Hall Inn is only a few yards away.

Ramble No 5

From Linton to Far Langerton passing between Elbolton and Stebden hills to Thorpe, returning along Thorpe Lane and the site of Waddy Lathe

STARTING POINT: This walk starts at the bus stop on Skipton Road.

DISTANCE: Approximately four miles.

TIME REQUIRED: Two and three quarter hours, but extra time should be allowed if you are going to look at the buildings and other features in Linton Village on the first part of the walk, and similarly the buildings and other features in Thorpe Village.

TERRAIN: For this walk it is essential to have suitable footwear since the first part of the path across the fields between Stebden and Elbolton hills can be very wet at times. The initial part of the route is relatively level until the track leading from Ings House is joined. From here it is a reasonably steep climb all the way up to Far Langerton. From Far Langerton to the shoulder of Elbolton Hill the gradient is much more gradual followed by a steep descent into Thorpe Village. From the centre of the village there is a fairly steep, but short, climb on to and up the first part of Thorpe Lane. From Waddy Lathe the path descends, steeply in places, all the way back to Linton Village.

Attractive features of this walk are the extensive views of Upper Wharfedale and the Bowland Fells including Great Whernside, Buckden Pike, Old Cote Moor, Simon's Seat and Parlick.

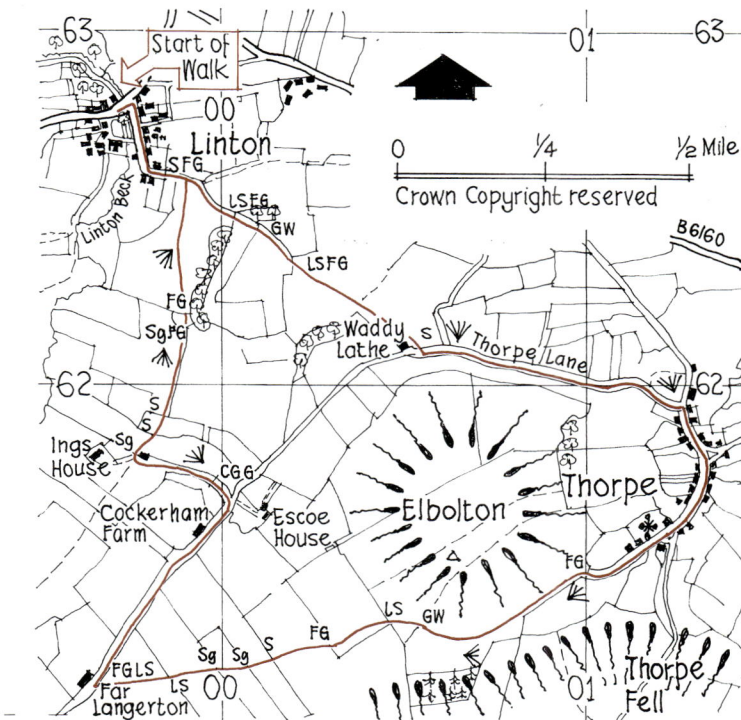

Proceed in a north-easterly direction across the bridge over Linton Beck, turning right on to the little lane running parallel with the beck, passing the Youth Hostel on the left, and continuing straight ahead.

FOR INFORMATION ON THE BUILDINGS AND OTHER FEATURES TO BE SEEN HERE REFER TO THE CHAPTER DESCRIBING A WALK AROUND LINTON VILLAGE.

Note the Fountaine's Hospital across the green which is said to have been designed by Sir John Vanbrugh.

At the end of the village pass over the stile to the left of a gate at the entrance to Grange Farm.

The surfaced road terminates here and the gate is usually open.

The Grange

In a few yards turn sharp left at the footpath sign marked 'Cracoe and Thorpe'. At the end of the farm buildings pass through a narrow stile to the left of a gate.

This section of the track can be very muddy at times and so it is advisable to walk along the causey stones, or move to the point the concrete blocks, alongside the wall on the left.

Look back here at the delightful view of the old buildings of Linton Village dominated in the middle by the campanile of Fountaine's Hospital. To the left there is a fine view of Cracoe and Rylstone fells dominated by Cracoe Cairn, 1,650 ft

(500m) above sea level, which was given by Col Maude and erected by the residents of Cracoe, in memory of their loved ones who lost their lives in the First World War and whose names are recorded thereon. In more recent times a bronze plaque has been added listing the names of those residents killed in the Second World War. Three of the reef knolls are visible and at the end of the valley Pendle Hill can just be seen. To the right Swinden Quarry comes into view and on the extreme right Grassington can be seen dominated by Great Whernside and Grass Wood to the left.

Proceed ahead for a few yards and take the track on the right leading straight towards Cracoe Cairn.

Note the lynchets to the left of this track, in fact our path actually passes along the bottom terrace. Pause halfway along this section of the path and look to the right and you will see how successfully the waste from Swinden Quarry has been reclaimed. You will see to the right of the quarry workings a farmhouse and barn and further to the right on the hillside a group of trees; the large green hill behind with some new tree planting is where the land has been reclaimed looking like another reef knoll, which of course is what the quarry area was originally! Just before passing through the gate ahead you will see a little woodland on the right that has recently been planted.

After passing through this gate take the right-hand track dropping down to a further gate with a gated stile to the left. The path now continues ahead alongside the wall.

There are now fine views of Stebden Hill ahead and Butter Haw to the right backed by the rugged gritstone ridge behind. Beyond, and slightly to the right, Ings House in its attractive landscaped setting comes into view. Two thirds of the way along this field note the fine 'creep hole,' or 'cripple hole,' to allow the sheep to pass from one side of the wall to the other. The two large stones at the base of this opening probably indicate that this is quite an old section of wall.

Cross the stile ahead noting how nicely it has been constructed in gritstone and inserted within the limestone wall. Proceed ahead first crossing a little

stream. The path now heads to the right of a small barn to a gated stile.

Ings House, which is now clearly visible to the right, has kneelers and copings to its gables and doubtless dates from the 17th century.

Turn left on to the track.

The nearby small barn probably dates from the early part of the 18th century. To the left of this track you will see some ancient lynchets on a south facing hillside to the right of a woodland.

Looking back from here there is a fine panoramic view to the right of the barn with Old Cote Moor and Buckden Pike just visible beyond a large tree and further right Grass Wood, Great Whernside and Grassington.

The track soon climbs fairly steeply and where it leads into a walled lane pass through the gate to the right of a cattle grid.

Ahead is Escoe House which has kneelers and copings with a barn to the left with a slightly steeper roof pitch, and it is most likely that these buildings date from the 17th century.

Turn right on to Thorpe Lane soon reaching Cockerham Farm on the right.

This building is probably early 18th century, but the adjoing barn to the south may date from the latter part of the 17th century having kneelers and a coping to its gable.

From here there are fine views down the valley to the south with the Bowland Fells in the distance. On the right-hand distant ridge at the left-hand end is Parlick, near Chipping in Lancashire.

Far Langerton is soon reached backed by Butter Haw Hill. Take the ladder stile to the right of a gate, opposite the building, signposted to Thorpe.

Far Langerton is probably early 18th century having a large barn at the southern end.

The path now crosses a series of fields heading towards the right-hand end of Elbolton Hill.

To the left of Elbolton the rocky valley of Hebden Beck can just be seen, and on the moors above a large clump of trees the Grassington Lead Mines

chimney can be picked out. To the left of the valley of Hebden Beck the wooded grounds of the former Grassington Hospital are visible.

First we cross a ladder stile, then two gated stone stiles, followed by an ungated stile and then another gated stile.

This part of the path can be very wet and, in parts, boggy at times. From here there are superb views of Upper Wharfedale to the left. This is also a good place from which to hear the curlew at the right times of the year.

The path drops down to pass through a gate in a fence, crossing a small stream then climbing up to cross a ladder stile at the foot of Elbolton. Bear right on to the grassy track soon passing through a stone gateway into, in effect, a small mountain pass, dominated on the right by Thorpe Fell with some young pine trees in a woodland below.

Soon Simon's Seat appears.

At this point you can take either the grassy path that climbs up to the left, or continue straight ahead on the narrow worn path. The footway gradually drops down to run alongside a fine limestone wall on the right.

Soon Thorpe Village comes into view far below and beyond it, stretched out across the bottom of the valley, the village of Hebden dominated in the middle by its small Victorian church and beyond Grassington Moor famous for lead mining in earlier times. High up in a small valley to the right can be seen the green swath of the dam of Grimwith Reservoir, the largest stretch of inland water in Yorkshire. Further to the right, over the trees, the Pateley Bridge road climbing up over the moors to Greenhow is visible.

You will see as you approach the village how hidden it is from all sides.

At the bottom of the hill, where the path flattens out, pass through a gate on to a walled lane which quickly leads into the village.

Crispin Hall

FOR INFORMATION ON THE BUILDINGS AND OTHER FEATURES TO BE SEEN HERE REFER TO THE CHAPTER DESCRIBING A WALK AROUND THORPE VILLAGE.

Bear left at 'The Triangle' or Village Green climbing up the steep short hill then bearing left on to Thorpe Lane marked 'unsuitable for motors'.

From this junction, looking slightly to the left, there is a fine view of Great Whernside and straight ahead the remaining buildings of the former Grassington Hospital with their red roofs.

This lane climbs up a little and then gradually levels out to give excellent views of Grassington and Upper Wharfedale beyond.

There is grass in the middle of this walled lane in many places and, for the most part, it is very narrow. Soon there is a superb view far below of Linton Church, Low Mill and the River Wharfe bending round.

Ignore the narrow walled bridleway on the right signposted to 'B6160', but a few yards further on take the footpath that heads towards the right-hand end of a belt of trees, next to the remains of Waddy Lathe, crossing a stone stile with a sign marked 'FP Linton'.

Ahead, below Grass Wood, can be seen the village of Threshfield and in the middle the pointed roof of the Roman Catholic Church of St Margaret Clitherow.

The path now rapidly drops down across this very large field to a ladder stile at the left of a metal gate, and then follows a clearly defined track ahead. The track passes through a gateway and drops steeply down to pass over a ladder stile to the left of a gate. The route now quickly leads to a stile to the right of a gate and then through Grange Farmyard and back to the starting point in Linton Village.

A Walk Around Thorpe Village

On old maps and legal documents Thorpe is often described as 'Thorpe-sub-Montem' or 'Thorpe-in-the-Hollow'; being an outlying farm or hamlet of a larger parent village, usually of Anglian origin, and in this case of Burnsall. After the Conquest Thorpe passed into the ownership of the de Romillies and by 1417 the Tempests owned some of the land here. By the end of the 15th century the Tempest family had acquired much more land in the area including Elbolton, where they were working the veins of lead and mining continued here until the end of the 18th century. Also in the 18th century the Fawkes family of Farnley Hall, near Otley, acquired parts of the Manor of Thorpe. The enclosure award is dated 1793 and shortly afterwards many dry stone walls were built within the township. At the beginning of the 19th century many of the properties in the village passed into the ownership of the Proctor family and, in 1918, Mr Wesley Newton Rhodes of Bradford acquired the whole of the estate. Today three of the farms are still owned and worked by his descendants.

Much mystery surrounds the many stories about the cobblers of Thorpe and it is not known whether it is fact, or fiction, for it is reported that at one time there were about forty people in the village employed in this trade. Many of the unusual buildings to be found here, mostly barns today, may have been their former cottages or where, in fact, they made shoes. The shoemakers are said to have been employed by the monks of both Fountains Abbey and Bolton Priory, and every so often they made the journey to these two monasteries with a sackful of new and mended shoes on their backs and returned with more shoes to be mended. It is said to have been a cobbler from Thorpe who met the Devil by the River Dibb, on the way to Pateley Bridge, and for the asking gained a bridge over the river. However, it is recorded that in 1822 there were, in fact, two shoemakers and one bootmaker in the village. The last of these craftsmen, Kit Inman, who lived in Burnsall, died in the mid 1930s. Kit sang in the church choir at Burnsall for over sixty years and was also a keen church bellringer; it was not unusual for him to walk over the moors in the summer to Middlesmoor, to ring the bells there on a Sunday morning. (My dear wife, Mary, and myself are both campanologists. In a rather romantic way we both met for the first time in the Ringing Chamber of Manchester Cathedral, where we were both bellringers for many years and Mary was a member of a number of Cathedral committees, including the Fabric Committee. Although Mary was always a much more competent ringer than I shall ever be, for four years I was the President of the Manchester University Guild of Change Ringers, known in ringing circles as 'The MUGs' – I think that the students must have asked me to do this job because they liked the look of me! Mary and I were to have been married by our old friend Hetley Price, the Bishop of Ripon, but sadly he died a month before our wedding). In 1804 the cobblers

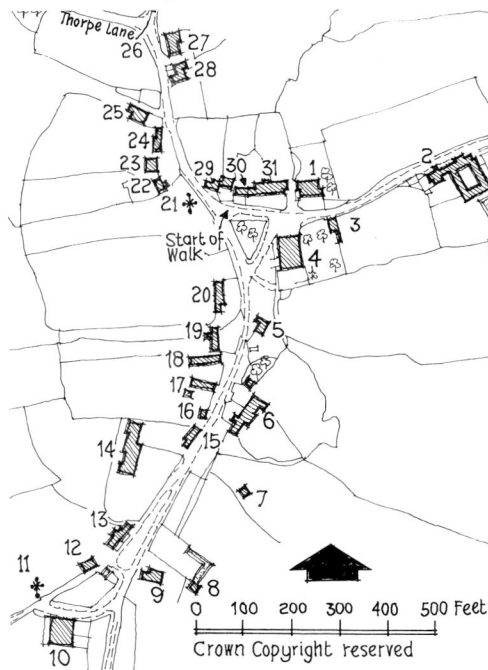

fetched the maypole from Burnsall in the middle of the night, and put it up in Thorpe; it was quite a time before the Burnsall residents discovered where it had gone! However, it is interesting to note that the present-day residents of Thorpe repeated this prank again in 1991.

This walk starts at the walled and treed area in the centre of the village which is known locally as 'The Triangle'. Before trees were planted here in 1860 this was an unenclosed grassed area usually referred to as 'The Green'. The original trees were felled about twenty years ago and the area replanted, the new trees now becoming very attractive.

Walk along the road eastwards to view the Manor House.

This building (1), originally known as 'Manor House Farm' dates from the 17th century initially comprising a much narrower property which was extended southwards, in effect doubling its width, in the 18th century. This fact is confirmed by the very thick wall which runs through the centre of the house. The rear elevation has changed little since it was originally built. At first floor level there are three identical two light mullioned windows with transoms and a very tall two light staircase window, also with a transom. At ground floor level are two three light mullioned windows, each with a stone slate drip head. Also at ground floor level is a wider mullioned window which again may have had a transom at some stage, into which 18th century sliding sash windows have been inserted.

Manor House

The 17th century west elevation was completely refaced at the time of the 18th century extensions and a nice two light 18th century mullioned

window was inserted into the new widened gable, complete with a moulded surround. The Georgian front elevation is extremely elegant possessing fine stone quoins at each end and a stringcourse, together with cills and moulded surrounds to the windows and a refined entrance doorway, all being picked out in limestone. The infilling stonework is a contrasting gritstone with very fine joints, but it is very likely that this was originally rendered. The ground floor room on the left of the front entrance originally possessed some fine panelling which was destroyed by fire in the late 1930s. The main staircase was also badly damaged at the same time and a new sympathetically designed staircase was installed at the same period. The moulded heads to the windows at the left of the front doorway appear to have been replaced in more recent times and no doubt these were also damaged by the fire.

Internally some interesting features are to be found, for instance in one of the old panes of glass to the kitchen window the name 'Joseph Constantine' has been scratched. Also in this room is a fine 17th century fireplace with a joggled keystone and a lintel on each side carved to imitate joggled voussoirs. In the utility room is an interesting beehive oven with a small store to the side of it and a late 18th century or early 19th century fireplace. The original stone staircase remains in the older part of the house and under the eastern section of the 17th century house is a fine barrel vaulted cellar. The later two storey section of the property, which is set back at the east end, contains a very finely preserved two-seater privy! The stone gateposts have some similarities with the original gateposts to Grassington House and the iron gate is quite fine.

The Batty family had a long association with Thorpe extending back from the Middle Ages until the mid 19th century. In the early 18th century William Batty (1688-1759) owned this property and no doubt he extended the house so attractively. Later his granddaughter Elizabeth lived here. She married the Rev'd Henry Wigglesworth, Vicar of Slaidburn, and they continued to use the house. Henry, it is said, kept a pack of hounds here and hunted in the surrounding countryside. When Elizabeth Wigglesworth either died or left the village, Robert Proctor bought the property.

Today there are only houses and barns in this village but, apparently, at one time there was an inn called 'Bridge End', but it has not been possible to determine in which building it was located if, in fact, the property is still standing.

Now walk the few yards up the hill to the east, beyond the Manor House, to view Rookery Cottage and its adjoining farm buildings.

This property (2), dates from the second half of the 17th century and possesses a fine four light mullioned window and 17th century doorway at ground floor level, and a two light mullioned window at first floor level on the south elevation. The elevation facing the lane has had later windows inserted in the 18th century and, together with the projecting porch, has been rendered in more recent times. The adjoining barn fronting on to the lane is probably 18th century and the buildings to the rear generally much later.

Now retrace your steps back down the hill in order to view Maypole Cottage, on the left, and beyond it Manor Barn.

Maypole Cottage (3), started its life as a dwelling and was later converted into a stable belonging to the Manor House, having many details similar to Manor Barn (4), and both probably being built at the same time. The circular headed doorway on the north elevation of Maypole Cottage was originally located in the west elevation under the middle window, and in the east elevation there was, formerly, the stable entrance. Behind is a nice little building with a 17th century doorway. Manor Barn, which may have been built on the site of an early water mill, is an extremely fine building with very old roof timbers, and a stone staircase on the east side giving access to the upper floor where religious services were held for many years from the end of the 18th century onwards. Initially local Methodists met in various houses in the village from about 1787 until the upper room of this barn was put at their disposal. Subsequently this building was used alternately by Methodists and Anglicans. Until a few years ago the pulpit used for these services was still in this barn. The building has copings and kneelers at each end, together with two stringcourses and a fine barn entrance on both the north and west elevations and, in the north gable, there is an elliptical window with a projecting stone surround and a dovecote over.

Note the nicely detailed and constructed bridges over the little stream, alongside the west elevation. Over the barn doorway on this elevation is a datestone inscribed 'BM:1697'. It is a very late 17th century building and possesses many features more reminiscent of the 18th century. The stonework is of an extremely high standard and, although constructed rather late on, it is just possible that this barn, Maypole Cottage and possibly also some of the other fine buildings in this village may have been built by one of the monastic stonemasons' lodges which was still in existence, perhaps having recruited and trained some younger apprentices.

The garden between these two buildings was originally laid out in the late 18th century by one of the previous owners of the Manor House, whose property it was at that time. It is still most attractive and well maintained today forming the garden of Maypole Cottage.

The Shelter erected by Wesley Rhodes

Continue along the village street in a southerly direction.

The next barn (5), has been granted planning permission for conversion into a dwelling house and some new stone window openings have already been inserted in the south gable wall. Attached to the front of this building is a small rustic shelter with a nicely graded stone flag roof, which could almost be regarded as a memorial to the late Wesley Rhodes. The shelter is now so much a part of Thorpe that it looks as though it has been here for centuries but it was erected by Wesley Rhodes for the benefit of two elderly men who lived in the village at the time so that they could sit here and enjoy the sunshine. It is customary for the daily newspapers for the village to be deposited here and those who have a regular order come and collect their papers here at their convenience. The village notice board is also located here, together with two seats,

The next building continuing south is Kail Farm.

Kail Farmhouse (6), probably dates from the second half of the 17th century, having a projecting porch with a nice two light mullioned window at first floor level and a nice doorway from this period in the north side elevation of the porch. New windows have been inserted in this frontage in the 18th and 19th centuries. The attached barn, which has an entrance, ventilation slits and a 17th century doorway, is probably contemporary with the rest of the building and the small barn to the left, now used as a garage, is probably of a later date.

Continuing in a southerly direction the next little building, across the field, is delightful.

This building, known locally as 'Meredith Cottage', and now used as a field barn (7), has two entrance doorways at ground floor level the right-hand one having a nice cornice. There is evidence of what has probably been a two light mullioned window at first floor level, and I would think that this structure dates from fairly late in the 17th century, perhaps having originally been the home and workshop of one of the shoemakers and his family!

A little further on is another building with some later timber structures adjoining it with corrugated iron roofs.

This building (8), probably dates from the end of the 17th century. Nearby is a barn adjacent to the road (9), which has many 17th century features including copings and kneelers to the west elevation, and evidence of a doorway from this period on the left under the barn entrance.

Continue further for a few yards and take the little unmade lane to the right.

Here is Steel's Lathe (10). Over a door in the east gable of this building is a finely carved lintel with short jambs, located above a transom. This stonework obviously came from a building of some importance and, in the top left-hand corner is carved the letter 'T' and in the top right-hand corner the letter 'B'. These initials may refer to Thomas Bayne who acquired Thorpe Old Hall in 1608. 'Steel' is not a local name, but this barn may be named after a family of this name who lived here in the early 19th century and may have used

this barn. This building has some watershot stonework and a fine barn arch to the north elevation with the inscription in the keystone 'GK' over '1890'. In the west gable there is a tablet inscribed 'IW' over '1798'.

Continuing ahead for a few yards turn right into the narrow, rather grassy, lane first pausing to look at the remains of a building in the adjacent wall to the right of a gate.

In my opinion this stonework and the rather hummocky area of land behind (11), is probably the site of Thorpe Old Hall which was demolished early this century, about which very little is known.

A little further on the left is Green's Barn.

This fairly small building (12), was at one time used as a house and it most probably dates from the 18th century. Opposite is the remains of another little building, in more recent times used as a garage, which probably dates from the 17th century.

A few yards further on, astride a slightly elevated site, is Crag Lea which was once known as 'Cumberland House'. This property (13), which dates from the 17th century, was excluded from the land and buildings that Wesley Rhodes purchased in the early part of the 19th century. The building, although much altered on the front elevation probably in the late 18th or early 19th century, has some fine chimney stacks, copings and kneelers at each end with a later extension at the south probably built in the 18th century, but sadly today roofed with corrugated asbestos. The chimney on the north gable has an interesting projecting semi-circular stack similar to the one at Conistone Old Hall. Note the fine 19th century railings, gate, wall and gateposts. For nearly twenty years Tom Kerkham, the well-known Dales artist, lived here until he died in 1986. Tom was born in Norfolk and trained at the Slade School of Art.

Beyond, set back behind a nicely kept raised garden is Crispin Hall (14), which was originally known as 'The Rookery'. When Wesley Rhodes bought the estate there was an old three storey house here which he largely demolished in 1920, rebuilding the present fine building which was designed by Mawson & Hudson a firm of Bradford architects. Part of the original property was retained and incorporated into the rear of the present structure. In the early 1980s Ronald and Mollie Rallings bought this property and gave it the present name since St Crispin was the tutelary saint and patron of shoemakers, who is said to have supported himself by working as a shoemaker, at the same time spreading the gospel.

Adjacent to the drive of Crispin Hall is Stable Barn (15), which was converted into a dwelling house some years ago. It is a 17th century building with two entrances from this period still remaining on the front elevation.

Immediately to the north is a very small building (16), which was a former dovecote and is often known locally as 'Bull Hole'. It probably dates from the 17th century possessing some superb stonework. Beyond is Holly Tree Barn (17), again dating, I would say, from the late 17th century with a very fine gable elevation to the road which gives it the impression of once having been a chapel, but this is not so. It has copings and kneelers to the front elevation, together with a nice weathervane and an unusual datestone inserted between the first floor windows with a head with a face at the top and underneath 'W' over 'IH' over '1793'. The south elevation has a 17th century doorway and a fine barn entrance, which suggests that the front elevation may have been refaced and the windows inserted at the time of the datestone, perhaps this front portion for a period being a dwelling house.

The next property, end on to the road, is Holly Tree Farm (18), which was once known as 'Beverley House', with two cottages beyond known as 'Holly Tree Cottages'. The farmhouse is a fine Regency building with nice fluted stone surrounds to the windows and very slim columns to both the entrance doorway and the ground floor Venetian styled windows. There are nice simple stone quoins, copings and kneelers to the roadside gable. In addition there is a plinth and also a half-moon shaped window in the gable. Internally the lower flight of the staircase is constructed in stone and there is a cellar under part of the property. The second of the cottages probably dates from the 18th century, the first having a nice 17th century doorway and a three light ground floor window to the right dating from the 18th century, and a smaller window above of the same date. Note the nice cobbles here between the highway and the entrance steps.

To the north are two cottages, the southern one being known as 'Sunny Bank' and the other 'Sunny Side' (19). Sunny Side appears to date from the 17th century with simple 18th century stone mullioned windows inserted later. Sunny Bank would appear to be a little later having what could be a very early 18th century doorway at the southern end.

Holly Tree Barn

107

The next building, set back in a croft, is Elbolton Croft Barn (20), which probably dates from the 18th century having a most interesting lintel over the main barn entrance comprising a joggled keystone and a large single stone on either side.

Now continue walking northwards keeping to the left of The Triangle.

On the hill in the field behind the post box there was once a bell that was rung to summon people to worship at the Parish Church in Burnsall. This is still known locally as 'Bell Hill'.

Just beyond on elevated ground are the remains of a former house (21), where two trees are now growing and there is a small timber building behind.

Further on is the barn below Hardy Grange Farm (22), which has a nice 17th century barn arch, a lean-to projecting portion and a doorway from this period at the front. This was once partly used as a dwelling and on the north gable there is a flight of stone steps leading to a doorway of this period. Almost adjoining is Hardy Grange Farmhouse (23), probably also dating from the 17th century but it has been superbly refronted, probably in the late 18th century with watershot stonework. The barn alongside the entrance to this farm (24), possesses some very old roof timbers and also probably dates from the 17th century.

The next property, set back from the road, is known as 'Stoneycroft' (25). Originally this building was known as 'Featherstonhough House' and it probably dates from the early part of the 18th century.

Now continue northwards, crossing Thorpe Lane and continuing for about two hundred yards pausing just before a small stone building on the right.

Here to the left you will see a section of wall (26), which has obviously once formed a part of a building. This is said to be all that remains of some early fortifications erected a very long time ago to help to repel the Scots. However, it is interesting to note that the Scots never discovered Thorpe Village and the same applies today, for many visitors to the area are completely unaware of its existence. When I came here in July this old stonework, and the nearby sections of walling were a blaze of colour with the many beautiful wild flowers which included herb robert, spinning cranesbill, stonecrop, sowthistle, Yorkshire fog grass, bladder campion, rat's tail plaintain, meadow grass and Welsh poppies.

Now retrace your steps back towards the village noting the fine new barn on the left, designed to National Park standards and completed in 1998.

On the left just beyond Thorpe Lane is Blackburn House Barn (27), with a dovecote in its south gable, which probably dates from the late 17th century. Blackburn House (28), is a superb example of a 17th century dwelling with a number of fine mullioned windows which probably date from about the middle of the century, two fine chimney stacks and an interesting plinth adjacent to the road and also on the north elevation. I have a strong feeling that this house might have been built upon the site of an earlier Medieval timber framed building. Part of the garden wall on the roadside, immediately beyond the house, appears to have once been a part of an earlier building.

Continue downhill back into the village bearing left.

The first block facing The Triangle is Hardcastle House Barn and adjoining it Hardcastle House (29). The barn dates from the 17th century and the window at an upper level, being 18th century with a mullion, suggests that this building might have been partly used as a dwelling at one time. Hardcastle House has been refronted again probably in the latter part of the 18th century with rather fine projecting stone quoins.

The next building (30), is one of the real architectural gems of Thorpe, being a delightful mid 17th century barn. It has a most unusual projecting entrance porch detail with corbels more akin to the design of some of the 17th century fireplaces, of which there is an excellent example in Grassington at No 1 Rathmell Fold. For many years this entrance porch was in a dilapidated state, but was carefully restored in the early 1990s.

Finally, the extensive range of adjoining farm buildings again probably date from the late 17th century (31). There is a fine barn entrance and a number of other interesting features.

We are, of course, now back at the starting point.

Ramble No 6

From Hebden via Ranelands Farm, Hartlington Raikes and Skuff Lane to Burnsall, returning along the Dales Way passing Loup Scar

STARTING POINT: This walk starts in Main Street opposite the Post Office.

DISTANCE: Approximately three and a half miles.

TIME REQUIRED: Two and a half hours, but extra time should be allowed if you are going to look at the buildings and other features in Hebden on the first part of the walk, and similarly the buildings and other features in Burnsall Village.

TERRAIN: For this walk it is essential to have suitable footwear since part of the footpath between Ranelands Farm and Burnsall is through gritstone country and can be very wet in places. After leaving the valley of Hebden Beck the path climbs fairly gradually up to Ranelands Farm and then more steeply towards Hartlington Raikes. The next section of the route descends very steeply in places. The path from Burnsall to Hebden along the River Wharfe is relatively level, with a short steep climb back into Hebden Village.

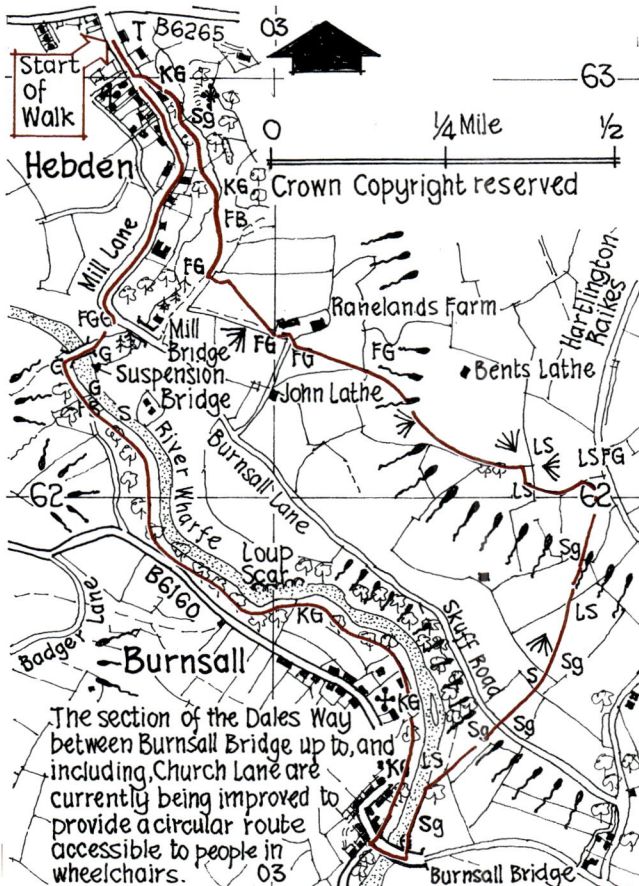

Crown Copyright reserved

The section of the Dales Way between Burnsall Bridge up to, and including, Church Lane are currently being improved to provide a circular route accessible to people in wheelchairs.

Attractive features of this walk are the fine extensive and changing views of Upper Wharfedale on the section of the path from Ranelands Farm to Burnsall and in contrast the delightful river scenery on the return, being amongst the most beautiful on the section of the Dales Way between Bolton Abbey and Grassington.

Proceed in a southerly direction along Main Street. A few yards beyond the former school on the left, pass through the kissing gate signposted 'Hebden Suspension Bridge $^1/_2$ Hartlington Raikes 1$^1/_2$'.

FOR INFORMATION ON THE BUILDINGS AND OTHER FEATURES TO BE SEEN HERE REFER TO THE CHAPTER DESCRIBING A WALK AROUND HEBDEN VILLAGE.

The first part of the path, which is setted, drops steeply down to run alongside Hebden Beck. No doubt the kissing gate and this footpath were made by the owners of the former Hebden Mill, further down the valley, as a short cut for their workers who lived in this part of the village.

Just beyond the footbridge, leading to the

house across the beck, cross over the gated stile and continue ahead.

The old workings across the valley are the remains of a trial level dating back to lead mining days in the latter part of the 19th century. Although it was driven almost one and a half miles underground, it never yielded any lead.

On the left, before passing through the next kissing gate, you will see the old lodge, or reservoir, which was built to provide water power for the old Hebden Mill lower down this little valley.

Pass through the kissing gate and over the footbridge.

The nearby fish farm known as 'Yorkshire Salmon', which is a salmon hatchery, was established in 1982.

Former Hebden Primary School

Ranelands Farm

Looking down from the footbridge the valley of Hebden Beck is very beautiful dominated by Burnsall and Thorpe fells behind.

The path goes between two old trees and across a small stone slab bridge, then across the track leading to the downstream part of the fish farm, and up towards a footpath signpost. Take the path straight ahead signposted 'Hartlington Raikes' leading up the rough track.

The correct path is through the stone stile with steps up to it in the wall to the left, which is sometimes blocked up with stones by the local farmer at lambing time to stop the lambs going through.

Pass through the metal gate and follow the wall round to the left for a few yards to a further stile through which the path shown on the Ordnance survey map passes. Near this stile is a footpath sign pointing across the field to a track and gate between the farm buildings and a group of trees. Pause as you approach the metal gate.

Over to the right there is a fine view dominated by Burnsall and Thorpe fells, and at the right-hand end the three reef knolls, Kail Hill then the pointed top of Stebden Hill in the middle and Elbolton to the right. Behind there are excellent views of Upper Wharfedale and in the bottom of the valley the cottages of the former Hebden Mill can be picked out and beyond the River Wharfe

lined with the lovely horsechestnut trees. Further to the right some of the buildings of Hebden Village are visible and beyond the valley of Hebden Beck with its rocky escarpment, partly the result of quarrying.

Pass through the gate into the farmyard.

Ranelands Farm has a barn at the left-hand end with a datestone inscribed 'A:CF 1790' together with a coping and kneelers to its western gable. Note the fine weathervane with a cow on it and the word 'Ranelands' underneath. The farmhouse has simple stone mullioned windows and 'watershot' stonework to its south elevation and probably dates from the latter part of the 18th century. In view of the stone quoins which are clearly evident it is likely that both the barn and the farmhouse were once both freestanding, being joined together at a later date.

Pass through the double metal gates across the farmyard and follow the footpath sign straight ahead up the grassy field to a slight depression.

This depression may be the line of an old cart track.

The path now climbs steeply and gradually veers over towards the high gritstone wall to the right.

Bents Lathe Barn appears on the skyline ahead.

Pass through the metal gate and continue alongside the wall on the right to the footpath sign following ahead along a track in the grass.

It can be very wet and boggy near this gate at times.

The path goes slightly right uphill across the meadow.

As you climb up look back at the fine view with the River Wharfe snaking around far below. The barn to the left known as 'Bents Lathe' probably dates from the early part of the 18th century having a lean-to portion at the left-hand end and a coping to its west elevation.

Our route now heads towards the gritstone wall to the right where you will see two trees on the skyline, which are very close together and a footpath sign to the right of them. At the trees the path runs alongside the wall past a gate for some distance to a ladder stile on the right.

It can be very wet near this stile. Since this is the highest point on the walk pause to admire the superb view in every direction. Ahead to the south-east is Simon's Seat, which is 1,544 ft high (485m), and to the right of Raikes Farm is another reef knoll, also known as 'Kail Hill' and sometimes as 'Hartlington Kail' to distinguish it, which hides the village of Appletreewick from our view. Beyond is a glimpse of Ilkley Moor, then the forests on the edge of Barden Moor followed by Burnsall and Thorpe fells which reach 1,661 ft (506m) at their highest point. To the south-west Stebden can just be seen and below it the green reef knolls known as Kail Hill and Elbolton. Next is a glimpse of the Bowland Fells in the distance followed by a fine view of Upper Wharfedale and further right Grassington and Hebden moors. In the far distance on the extreme right Great Whernside 2,310 ft high (704m) can be seen.

Cross the ladder stile and follow alongside the wall on the left to another ladder stile.

Hereabouts we are just on the border of the gritstone and the limestone and you will see in this field that the wall over to the right (west side) has a gritstone bottom and a limestone top. Before crossing the next ladder stile you will get the first glimpse of the old village of Burnsall with a bit of the bridge being visible at the left and the top of the church tower to the right.

Cross the ladder stile and continue ahead alongside a post and wire fence on the right.

This section of the path can be very wet at times signifying that we are still on the gritstone.

Cross the ladder stile, to the left of a gate, on the right.

Ignore the ladder stile to the left of a gate, in the wall over to the left in front of the property known as 'South View'.

Head instead straight forward towards the right-hand side of the third large tree from the right. Pass through the gated stile and proceed ahead to a ladder stile, just to the left of the point where the wall disappears over the skyline.

Over to the right, down the hillside, is an attractive barn in a woodland setting probably dating from the early 18th century.

Cross this large field to a gated stile to the right of the far corner.

Note the predominance of limestone in this wall indicating that we are once more back in limestone country, and the way in which the stile, although repaired in recent times, is constructed in gritstone.

After crossing this stile the next one, although again much repaired in recent times, is a good example of a stile which is constructed in gritstone in a limestone wall.

Here there is a signpost to Burnsall.

Continue ahead down the steep hill with great care making for Burnsall Bridge.

From here there is an excellent view of Burnsall Village as you descend the hillside with the river winding its way down Wharfedale.

Pass through the gated stile crossing Skuff Road to a further gated stile, then following the path down the steep grassy slope towards the river to a ladder stile. After crossing it the path follows alongside the River Wharfe to a further gated stone stile, then on to a gate and a flight of stone steps leading up on to the bridge.

The approach to the bridge is part of an earlier structure which probably dates from about 1600. However, it is interesting to note that there has been a bridge here since 1275. Near the steps note the stone built into this part of the structure which reads as follows: 'This bridge was repaired at the charge of the West Riding 1674'. Take account of how well the steps are worn giving some indication of their antiquity.

At the top of the steps turn right and cross the bridge.

Here we join the Dales Way.

On the south parapet of the centre arch is a plaque which reads as follows: 'West Riding - Burnsall Bridge re-erected September 1884'. Observe how wide the river is here.

FOR INFORMATION ON THE BUILDINGS AND OTHER FEATURES TO BE SEEN HERE REFER TO THE CHAPTER DESCRIBING A WALK AROUND BURNSALL VILLAGE.

At the end of the bridge take the footpath around the corner on the right signed 'HebdenMill 1 Grassington Br 3'.

The backs of the old buildings on the left whose gardens run down to the river are interesting, terminating with the attractive little Methodist Chapel.

After passing through two kissing gates you will see the former Grammar School on rising ground to the left.

This school was founded by Sir William Craven as a grammar school for the boys of Burnsall Parish. Its main frontage is still the same as when it was built nearly four hundred years ago. The single storey extension built out towards the river was erected in 1964 and designed by Mary Wales and Barry Rawson.

Note the next building with a five light mullioned window at its northern end adjacent to a gate and a footpath sign, leading into a rough track known as 'Rectory Lane'. Burnsall Parish was originally divided into two medieties with two incumbents until 1829. This property, now known as 'Wharfegate' which was enlarged about 1820 was the rectory for the Second Mediety.

The next section of the river is very beautiful.

After climbing slightly and passing through a kissing gate there is a fine view of Loup Scar to the right.

Note how the river has cut through the limestone.

The next section of the path is very attractive and soon there are glimpses of Hebden Village across the river and the Hebden Suspension Bridge comes into view ahead.

Cross over a stone stile entering a little woodland and pass over a footbridge, after a stepped path joins from the left, proceeding to a further gate. After passing through another gate the path turns sharply right to cross the bridge signposted 'Grassington and Hebden'.

The river is very deep where it passes under the bridge. Note the stepping stones below the bridge. The age of the stepping stones is not known, although in the Middle Ages there was a ford nearby. After the partial destruction of Burnsall Bridge in the great flood of 1883, there was a need for a link between Hebden and Burnsall and so a temporary bridge was erected. However, there was soon a demand for something more substantial and a few years earlier William Bell, Hebden's local blacksmith, had built a suspension bridge at Netherside Hall. After inspection of this bridge, by some of the local people, Bell was commissioned to build a similar bridge which he did for the sum of £87. This was built by subscription with additional help from the Duke of Devonshire. William used scrap metal obtained from the Hebden Moor Lead Mines, with hollow cast iron columns at each end nine feet in height and nine inches external diameter, supported upon masonry blocks. However, the cast iron columns did not come from the lead mines but the wire rope did. In 1936 this bridge was damaged in another great flood, that probably surpassed that of 1883, and the County then rebuilt it at a slightly higher level. Prior to 1936, this bridge had a central support, the remains of which can still be seen in the river, and it wobbled about quite a lot and thus became known amongst local people as the 'Swing Bridge'.

Here we leave the Dales Way.

Continue ahead to a gate between a wall on the left and a line of pine trees on the right. Cross the field to a gate to the right of a field gate then turning left on to the surfaced road. The road climbs steeply into the village and the starting point is soon reached.

A Walk Around Burnsall Village

The origin of the name Burnsall is attributed to that of an Anglo-Saxon headman named 'Brunolvi' or 'Bryni' from which the first syllable is derived, the second syllable having come from 'halh' meaning 'nook of land' from which we are to believe that this was 'Brunolvi's' nook, or corner, of land. It is likely that people first settled here during the colonisation of Upper Wharfedale by the Angles in the early part of the 7th century. William I granted the Manor of Burnsall to the Norman baron Robert de Romille and in

1315 Edward II granted William de Hebden and his heirs for ever all the demesne lands of Burnsall and other nearby estates. Later through marriage the Manor of Burnsall came into the possession of the Tempests of Bracewell, who in turn sold it to John and Thomas Proctor of Cowpercotes who, after holding it for only a year, disposed of it to Henry Tempest of Broughton in 1556, whose family have retained the manor down to the present day.

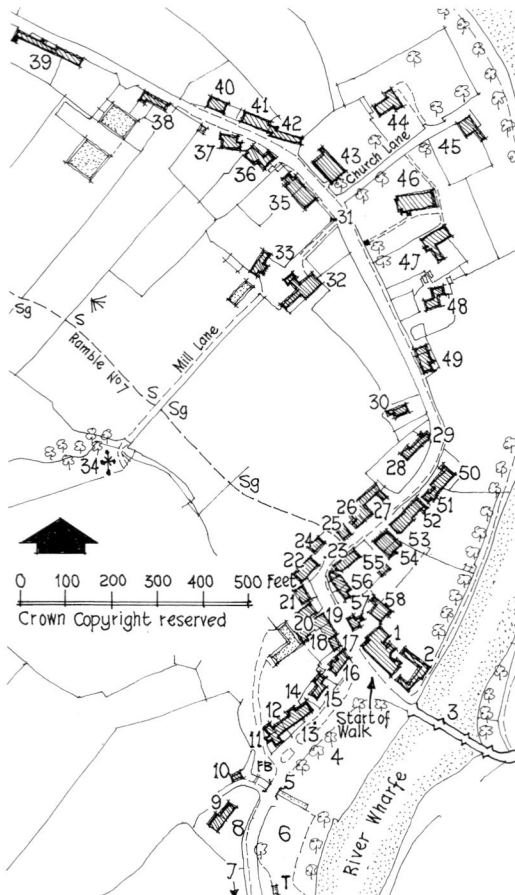

0 100 200 300 400 500 Feet

Crown Copyright reserved

This walk starts outside the Red Lion Hotel. It is likely that there has been some sort of accommodation on this site for many centuries, since before a bridge was built there may have been either a ferry or a ford. When the river was in spate this would have been a convenient place for people to stay until the waters receded.

The Red Lion Hotel (1), was known either as the 'Bridge Tavern' or 'Bridge End Tavern' until the early part of the 19th century. The present building dates from the late 17th century, although it has been much altered and extended over the years.

The properties Nos 1–5 Riversyde (2), were partly converted and partly rebuilt in the mid to late 1970s, being formerly stable buildings and a tea room belonging to the Red Lion Hotel. About the same time the attractive new car park to the rear of the Red Lion Hotel was laid out.

Burnsall Bridge (3), is a fine structure with three main arches spanning the river and a smaller arch at each end with cutwaters between. It is first recorded that there was a bridge over the river at this point in 1275 and it is likely that the bridge at this time would be a simple timber structure dating from even earlier times. About 1609 it is recorded that Sir William Craven, about whom more will be said later, was building a stone bridge and it is likely that the long approach on the east side, which bears a plaque that reads as follows: 'This bridge was repaired at the charge of the West Riding 1674', was part of the structure that he built. In the great flood of January 1883 much of the bridge was washed away and the part spanning the river beautifully faced in ashlar stonework was rebuilt in 1884 on the original pier foundations of the earlier three-arch bridge. This previous bridge had already been severely damaged some years earlier, in 1827, and had been repaired at the time by Mr Wade of Skipton. Mr Anderton from Skipton undertook the reconstruction, extending the abutments to add an extra arch at each end and there is a plaque in the south parapet of the centre arch recording this, the cost of the work being £8,000.

Now walk across the attractive expanse of grass known as 'Burnsall Green' (4).

The four sycamore trees bordering the Green were probably planted towards the end of the 19th century and it is thought that there has been a maypole here since Medieval times. However, at the time I was writing this chapter there was no maypole since the present one had rotted at the bottom and become unsafe! However, I was assured that it would be back again in time for the famous Burnsall Sports and Fell Race.

Whilst crossing the Green look across the river and the flat fields beyond.

In the distance you will see Calgarth House, which is said to date back to Medieval times. However, the present structure which largely has its origins in the 17th century, with 19th century alterations, has been in ruins for very many years and today has quite a large tree growing within its walls. It is said that there was once a mill here but there is no trace of this now.

At the southern end of Burnsall Green bear over to the right to join the road at Joy Beck Bridge where Joy Beck today forms the southern boundary of the Green.

Joy Beck Bridge (5), bears the date 1858 crudely carved on the end of one of the copings. It was built following the raising of the road approaches with materials from a house which was demolished near the Church. Prior to this Joy Beck ran across the road, which was especially dangerous in icy weather. It had a considerable flow of water at times until abstraction by Bradford Corporation Water Works higher up on Burnsall Fell to augment the flow of water into their reservoirs on Barden Moor.

Beyond Joy Beck is the entrance to the car park (6).

There has been a car park here since about 1920, and prior to this the land would have formed an extension to Burnsall Green. The car park was much improved with planting of trees and and the provision of new toilets about 1970, and the barrier mechanism was installed about 1990.

Now walk a few yards up the steep hill to view the Fell Hotel.

This hotel (7), was built shortly after the railway to Grassington was opened in 1902, in order to take advantage of the tourists who came to both Grassington and Bolton Abbey by train for holidays. However, unfortunately the railway to Grassington had a relatively short life, but with the great increase in the use of the motor car and the growth in the tourist industry in the Dales, this fine hotel in its superb location is a great asset to this part of Upper Wharfedale.

On the left as you walk back down the hill are two old properties.

These are known as Nos 1 and 2 Bunkers Hill (8), and probably date from the latter part of the 18th century. Up the rather overgrown grassy lane which goes off on the left just before Joy Beck, is the site of the village Pinfold, or Pound (9), which was located within the area of the present garden of the lower cottage on Bunkers Hill. Note the ancient stone slab bridge on the upstream side of Joy Beck Bridge. The little barn (10), on the north side of this track also appears to date from the 18th century.

Now cross Joy Beck Bridge in order to view the properties overlooking Burnsall Green.

The first pair of houses, end on to the road and known as 'Nos 1 & 2 Riverside (11), were built about 1983 with stone from demolished buildings, and stand on the site of a small garage and petrol pump. Also on this site is a nicely designed single storey garage with a corrugated asbestos roof linking Riverside with the next properties.

Adjoining are two properties (12), the first of which is a house and the second a shop. These were built as a mill known as 'New Mill' in 1804 and replaced an older mill on the same site.

Nearby on the grass verge is one of the three attractive structures housing a compensation tap (13), provided by Bradford Corporation Water Works in return for taking water from Joy Beck following the construction of their first reservoir on Barden Moor, Lower Barden Moor Reservoir known locally as 'Low Dock' which became operational in 1860.

Behind is Wharfe View Tea Rooms (14), which was for many years a single storey timber building. This Tea Room, where visitors will get a warm welcome, was rebuilt about 1990 being carefully designed to fit in with the adjoining buildings.

Clematis Cottage (15), the next building, probably

dates from the latter part of the 18th century and was greatly extended in the late 1970s. Beyond are two properties known as 'Wharfe Cottage' and 'Bridge House' (16), which are thought to have both been built about 1830. Bridge House has been refronted at a slightly later date now being quite an impressive building.

Now go around the corner to the left.

The next building is Meadowcroft Barn (17), which probably dates from the late 18th century and was converted into a house in the 1960s. Adjoining is a house known as 'Meadowcroft' (18), dating from about the same period.

Beyond is the Post Office and Village Store (19), which was built for retail purposes in 1904 on the site of a barn. The next building is Holme Barn (20), which was partly converted into a dwelling house in the early 1990s. Conistone House (21), is probably a late 18th century building which was refronted in the first half of the 19th century, having a front door which is distinctly Victorian!

At right angles to Conistone House is Holly House (22), and an adjoining building to the left.

Holly House appears to date from the late 18th century and the section to the left is the former 'gas house' for Conistone House. Early in the 20th century some of the more affluent residents installed acetylene gas lighting in their homes, but this was only possible where they had nearby outbuildings capable of accommodating the carbide and water cylinder. An example of this equipment from the Anglers Arms at Kilnsey can be seen in the Grassington Museum.

On the roadside in front of the next building is the Holly House Corner compensation tap (23), housed under an attractive stone arch with an old stone trough below so that animals could also drink here.

Beyond is Holly House Barn (24), around which the public footpath to Thorpe used to pass. This path was diverted in the early 1990s to run along the north-eastern edge of this site with a new wall being constructed on the left-hand side of the footway. The barn appears to date from the latter part of the 18th century. Croft Cottage (25), probably dates from the late 18th century.

Next is Rose Cottage (26), which dates from the second half of the 17th century having a nice two light mullioned window at ground floor level in the south-west gable and the remains of an early two light window, which has lost its centre mullion and has had a later window inserted, in the lean-to section at the rear. The entrance doorway on the front elevation is probably very early 18th century with a simple stone projecting porch. At each side of the door is an 18th century three light mullioned window. As the Wesleyan membership in Burnsall increased services were held in this cottage from about 1795 until 1832.

Valley View (27), may originally have been a slightly later extension to Rose Cottage, initially being a barn. The buildings on the north-east side of Valley View, which today form part of the guest house, stand on the site of the buildings belonging to James Clark & Sons, Joiners, Cabinet Makers, Wheelrights, Undertakers and Blacksmiths. Young Richard Clark who came here from Linton in 1840, founded the family business which continued for over a century. A number of items in the Church made by various members of the family bear testimony to the quality of their work. Especially worthy of mention is the oak furnishing in the Lady Chapel made by Norman Clark. This business ceased in 1992 and the north-east and north-west walls of the old buildings were largely retained in the most attractive redevelopment of the site to form guest house and garage accommodation in 1993 to the designs of Andrew Forman.

Colton Croft (28), set in an attractive garden is probably late 17th century, having a nice doorway on the front elevation dating from this period with an interesting hood mould made out of slates, but the property has been much altered in the 18th century having a two light mullioned window to the right of the front door. This building was originally two cottages and if you look over the garden wall you will see the path leading to the former door to the middle cottage, which has now been converted into a window. Colton Cottage (29), was no doubt built at the same time having a two light 18th century mullioned window at first floor level. There is a chimney stack between the two properties that is 17th century in design.

Behind is Croft Cottage (30), again dating from the latter part of the 17th century and having a nice

doorway with a hood mould, although the remainder of this building has been much altered probably in the first half of the 20th century.

Now continue along the footpath going slightly uphill. On the left opposite to the Churchyard is Mill Lane, which is a private road.

On Mill Lane Corner is the third compensation tap (31), provided by Bradford Corporation Water Works housed in an attractive arched recess. On the left in Mill Lane is a barn and farm complex known as 'Stable Loft' (32), the whole probably dating from the late 17th century. The barn contains many nice ventilating slits and also a nice doorway on the south-west elevation. The single storey extension on the south-west side was built in the 1920s.

Across the lane is another barn (33), which appears to date from either the very end of the 17th century or early in the 18th century.

It is interesting to note that across Joy Beck at the end of this lane is the site of the Manor Corn Mill (34), which is first documented in 1260. A little way upstream and in the trees which are mainly ash, are the remains of part of the dam which enclosed the mill pond, or lodge, which provided the water to drive the waterwheel. The mill on this site later became known as 'Burnsall Mill'. In 1802 it changed over to cotton spinning and in 1825 it became a saw mill, finally in 1864 being sold by Sir Charles Tempest to Bradford Corporation Water Works to enable them to extinguish the water rights.

Now continue along the main village street.

The first block of property on the left known as 'Colton House' and 'Fell Grange' (35), was all originally one house and dates from the second half of the 17th century having a number of very fine mullioned windows on the north-east elevation. Colton House was considerably altered internally in 1965 under the guidance of Mary Wales, architect. At one time the upper floor of Fell Grange was one large room used as a dormitory to accommodate the 'haytime men' who came here each year from Ireland to help with haymaking. On one occasion there were thirteen people sleeping here. There are three fine chimney stacks that appear to date from the 17th century, together with copings and kneelers to each gable. The south-west elevation has been largely refenestrated in the 18th century, the new windows having nicely detailed moulded stone surrounds. Beyond is a 17th century barn (36), with three nice doorways from this period in its south-east gable.

A few yards further on the property known as 'Skuff View' (37), is a delightful old house that was once an inn. It has a nice 17th century doorway on the south elevation and what have originally been two four light 17th century mullioned windows to the left of the south entrance doorway, with a continuous hood mould over the two windows. These windows both now have only the centre mullion remaining with nicely designed later windows inserted. To the right of the door is a two light mullioned window which has been blocked up and, to the right of this, a further doorway that has been made into a window with what appears to be 'H' inscribed above. At first floor level there are two three light mullioned windows both of which, at some time, have lost one mullion. Near to the south doorway, in the very attractive and well-kept garden, is an old well beautifully preserved and complete with timber barrel at the top, which probably dates from the latter part of the 17th century.

Continuing along the road we come to The Cottage (38), dating from the 18th century and having a number of three light and one two light mullioned windows and a nice little projecting porch on the south-west elevation. The last block of property on this side of the road is a very long group of buildings known as 'Oat Croft' (39), probably dating in the main from the second half of the 17th century. On the south-west elevation there is at ground floor level one 17th century two light window remaining which has now lost its centre mullion, with an 18th century Georgian sliding sash window inserted. It would appear that the centre part was the original farmhouse with a barn at the south-east end probably converted into part of the house in the 1920s. A shippon at the north-west end was partly converted into a holiday cottage in the 1950s. The attractive porch on the north-east elevation was added in the late 1940s or early 1950s and the original barn entrance remains on this elevation at the northern end. This

elevation has some 18th century mullioned windows.

Now retrace your steps back in a southerly direction, taking great care on account of the traffic that goes very fast at times, in order to view the properties on the other side of the road.

The first property is known as 'The Little House' (40), which was originally a granary and was converted into a house in 1986. It was extended westwards, virtually doubling its size, in the mid 1990s. Beyond is a fine barn (41), which probably dates from the late 18th century having a very nice archway to the south elevation with finely cut voussoirs to the segmental arch. Adjoining is another barn (42), which probably dates from the 17th century or perhaps earlier, being in a very poor state of repair. It is said that this building was once a tithe barn.

A few yards further on is Burnsall Village Hall (43), which is probably both one of the largest and most attractive buildings of its type within the whole of the Yorkshire Dales National Park. The original building, which is to the rear of the four gabled section fronting on to the road, was built by Messrs Bland & Hargraves of Burnsall and opened in 1909, being erected on glebe land purchased from the rector. In 1914 the extension fronting on to the road, comprising a reading room and a kitchen was officially opened, the whole being carefully designed to fit in with the character of the church and the nearby school, having many similar details to the latter including mullioned windows, copings and finials. A further extension at the northern end was added in 1992. Note the extremely fine entrance to the porch, being in the Tudor style complete with spandrels and hood mould.

Now turn left down Church Lane in order to view the two rectories.

On the left is the present Rectory (44), which was divided into two properties in 1988, the older western section now being known as 'Rectory Cottage' and the Victorian section to the east being the present Burnsall Rectory. The north elevation of Rectory Cottage appears to date from the late 17th century. On the ground floor to the left of the door is what appears to have been a two light mullioned window with a Georgian window inserted and, above it, a smaller window which may have been a two light mullioned window at one time. There is also a tall staircase window to the right of the entrance door, this having a pointed arch. There is a chimney of 17th century design to the western gable and the south elevation has been substantially altered in Victorian times. The Victorian east wing, which is the present rectory, was added by the Rev'd William Bury soon after he came to Burnsall in 1839.

On the opposite side of church lane is the former rectory of the Second Mediety today known as 'Wharfe Gate' (45), which appears to date from the late 17th century. The west elevation has a simple doorway with a pediment over and on either side is a two light mullioned window. At the north end of this elevation is what has obviously been a two light mullioned window with a hood mould and, above it, what appears to be a coat of arms upside down with a moulding around the top three sides, which is in fact the Arms of the Fitzhughes family who were Patrons of the Living for many years. A rather chunky five light mullioned window on the east elevation was apparently moved from the west elevation after this building passed out of church ownership. An outside stone stairway leads to the upper chambers that may have been haylofts and latterly were used as a bothy for the rectory gardener.

Parish Church of St Wilfrid

Now retrace your steps back along Church Lane for a few yards, taking the little gate on the left leading into the Churchyard, in order to view the ancient Parish Church of St Wilfrid (46).

The present Church is probably built upon what has been a religious site for many centuries. It is likely that the Anglian settlers may have erected a preaching cross here in the 7th century. St Wilfrid, the patron saint of Burnsall was born in Northumbria in 634 and, after training for the priesthood, was made Abbot of Ripon in 661 and appointed Bishop of York five years later. During his long ministry he inspired the replacement of wooden churches by stone ones and it is very likely that there was an early stone building here.

Looking now at the north elevation of the Church the stonework to the North Aisle of both the Nave and the Chancel, which is random rubble, appears to me to be quite old and could be part of a much older building. In the west bay of the North Aisle, before the Tower, there is evidence of an old doorway which has been blocked up and intrudes into the area of the later window. The windows are all Perpendicular in style and the Tower, together with the western bays of both the North and South Aisles, all having fine plinths and faced in ashlar stonework, are an excellent example from this period of architecture.

The Tower is very similar in design to a number of other towers in the area including Skipton, Bingley, Kildwick, Gargrave, and Arncliffe. It could be that they were all built by the same group of stonemasons, since it was quite usual in Medieval times for groups of stonemasons to move around and carry out work in different parts of the country. Similarly, no doubt the Early English sections of both Beverley Minster and Lincoln Cathedral, which have distinct similarities in their design, would both have a number of men working on them from the same guild of stonemasons. The West Front of Beverley Minster is said to have been built by stonemasons from Somerset.

The windows to the North Aisle of the Chancel and those of the Clerestorey are, in my opinion, quite sophisticated in their design for the Dales and could have been altered at the time of one of the restorations, perhaps the one carried out by

John Varley in the 1870s. However, there is no clear evidence of this upon inspection of these windows from the interior of the Church.

Now walk along the path along the east side of the Church.

The lower stonework of the East Elevation, with three projecting pilasters, appears to date from the Norman period and the East Window is a nice example of Perpendicular work. The East Windows of the Aisles probably date from about 1300. Near the path, adjacent to the East Window, stands a cross of Portland stone dating from the early 1930s, which is easily identified by its beautifully carved Roman lettering. This marks the grave of Phillip Dawson and his wife of Hartlington Hall. This memorial is of particular interest since it was carved by Eric Gill, whose fine Perpetua and Gill Sans typefaces frequently feature in our lives. Eric Gill carved the Stations of the Cross in Westminster Cathedral and St Cuthbert's Church in Bradford. The War Memorial that he carved in Portland stone at Leeds University depicts 'Christ Driving the Moneychangers from the Temple'.

Follow the path round on to the south side of the Church.

Some of the stonework in the South Aisle may date from the earlier church and the windows are good examples of the Perpendicular period. The Porch is Victorian and the stone seats inside appear to be supported upon some earlier tracery.

Now have a look inside this beautiful old building.

Although it is said that the Nave and Chancel were in the main built about 1520 and the West Tower a few years later, my own feeling is that the Nave and Chancel arcades may well be rather earlier possibly dating from the Decorated period. On the west side of the entrance is a plaque worded in rather quaint English recording that the Church was repaired and 'butified' at the expense of Sir William Craven in 1612. The fine circular Font, mounted upon a square base, dates from Norman times and the nearby stones from Saxon crosses were found during excavations under the Tower in the late 1880s.

There is no mistaking that the Victorian restorers have been here since the rather incongruous Chancel Arch, although well detailed, gives me

quite a shock at first each time I enter this building! It is inscribed 'Glory to God in the highest and on earth peace good-will to men' and probably date from the 1880s. The nice oak screen at the entrance to the Chancel dates from 1891 and the figures of Christ and Our Lady and St John, designed by Sir William Milner of Parcevall Hall, date from 1935. The oak panelling behind the Altar is in memory of Robert William Smith BEM, Churchwarden and local Sub-postmaster for many years who died in 1961. The Pulpit is Jacobean with handsome baluster feet. The other items of special interest are all in the North Chancel Aisle. On the east wall is a fine Alabaster panel depicting the 'Adoration of the Magi', which was unearthed during a restoration in 1859 and may have been part of the reredos to an altar in Medieval times. Two hog-backed gravestones were found locally dating from Viking times. One is preserved here and the other is on loan to the Craven Museum in Skipton. Also of note is the Saxon cross, the stones of which were found during excavations in this part of the Church between 1876 and 1888.

On leaving the building walk up the path towards the Lych Gate.

Note the rather fine doorway on the west elevation of the Tower giving access to the Ringing Room and the Belfry. The original six bells were cast by Dalton of York in 1790 and recast in 1853. After being unringable for almost a century the bells were retuned in 1986 by John Taylor and Company of Loughborough, and rehung in a new metal frame now forming a most delightful ring of bells.

Parcevall Hall

Roughly in the middle of the section of the Churchyard on the left is the tombstone of Billy Bolton, the Dales Minstrel. Over to the right, near to the wall bordering on to Church Lane are the Village Stocks. On the right of the path, near a tree, is a tall stone cross marking the grave of Sir William Frederick Victor Mordaunt Milner, who died in 1960.

Sir William, who was born in 1893, was the only son of the Right Honourable Sir Frederick George Milner and Lady Adeline and on the death of his father, in 1931, he became 8th Baronet of Nun Appleton. In 1711 the Nun Appleton estate was purchased by Alderman William Milner, a cloth merchant of Leeds, who had served as Mayor of the City, but the estate was sold by William's father in 1897. William Milner went up to Christ Church, Oxford but his university education was interrupted by the outbreak of war, when he served in the 1st Lothians and Border Horse, but he was subsequently awarded a pass degree (Batchelor of Arts) in 1919 and an MA in 1934. While in London in the 1920s he got caught up in the Anglo-Catholic movement and met Father Hope Patten, Vicar of Great Walsingham in Norfolk, who was intent upon restoring its Medieval shrine. In 1927, after making frequent visits to Wharfedale, and, like so many of us, falling in love with the area he purchased Parcevall Hall a derelict 17th century longhouse on a bleak hillside near Appletreewick, lovingly restoring and extending it. At the same time, since he was so tall, lowering the floors in the original house making the 17th century fireplaces look rather odd! He also laid out extensive landscaped and terraced gardens such that today it is one of the most beautiful and peaceful places in the whole of the Yorkshire Dales National Park. With his knowledge of architecture, which is admirably displayed in his

work at Parcevall Hall, he went into partnership with Romilly Craze, a London architect, the firm being known as 'Milner & Craze'. They designed the Shrine Church in Walsingham, part of which

Lych Gate

was completed in 1938. In addition they were involved in over five hundred church projects throughout the country, including three in Hull. St Martin's, inspired in its design by the Norman style of architecture and consecrated in 1939, on the west side of the City is a church that I frequently attended in my boyhood. In more recent times Mary and I have from time to time attended services at another church they designed, St Alban's in North Hull which follows the Anglo-Catholic traditions, when visiting my parents in Kirk Ella.

A few yards further on we come to the Lych Gate.

This ancient structure was carefully moved to its present location in 1858 due to an extension to the Churchyard. In more recent times, in 1987, it was restored in memory of Norman Clark. It is fairly unique as far as the operation of its gate by weights is concerned, there being only three others elsewhere in the country working on the same principle. In 1745 there is an item in the churchwarden's accounts for the repair of the Lych Gate, which probably dates from about 1700.

Now walk down the road to the left for a few yards. The fine property set back is Burnsall Grammar School.

Burnsall Grammar School

This delightful old building (47), whose elevation has remained unchanged since it was built nearly four hundred years ago, is almost like a manor house. Two storeyed with an asymmetrically placed gable porch, it has fine mullioned windows, a plinth and stringcourse together with copings and finials. There is another similar outstanding Grammar School building in Slaidburn, but it was built over a hundred years later. A stone tablet over the entrance to the Burnsall building is inscribed: 'William Craven Alderman of London Founder of this Schoole Ano dm 1602'. William Craven intended this school to be used by boys from Burnsall Parish, which in the 17th century covered a large and very scattered area and so, from the beginning, it was necessary for some pupils to be boarders. This building continued as a grammar school until 1876. It was then called Mr Stead's School and at this time there were still several boarders. In the late 1930s the dormitories still remained on the upper floor divided by oak panelling, but this partitioning which has many initials and dates carved upon it by the former boarders, has been largely reused and rearranged to form an attractive flat for the headteacher. Similarly there are also many initials and dates scratched on the small panes of glass to the former dormitory windows. In 1902 the school became the responsibility of the County Education Authority. A new extension at the rear, designed by Mary Wales and Barry Rawson was opened in 1966 and the former 'Master's House' at the north end of the building was converted into a school kitchen, office and storeroom on the ground floor with the staff room and educational storeroom above. It was at this time that the headteacher's flat was created.

William Craven, the benefactor, was born in Appletreewick in 1548, and little is really known about his family. About 1561 he went to London to be apprenticed for seven years to Robert Hullson, who was a prosperous member of the Merchant Taylors Company. William continued to work for Robert after the end of this apprenticeship, who later left his prosperous business to him in his will. It is not known exactly when Robert died, but in 1594 the Merchant Taylors elected William Warden of their Company. In 1600 William was elected Alderman of the Bishopsgate Ward and he remained an Alderman of the City of London until

his death. In 1601 he was chosen to be Sheriff of London, and on the accession of James I he was knighted on the 26th July, 1603. Seven years later, in 1610, William Craven, now Sir William, the boy who had left his native Appletreewick fifty years earlier, was joyfully acclaimed the Lord Mayor of London, the highest civic honour in the kingdom. Eric Lodge in his 'History of Burnsall' writes as follows in relation to the death of Sir William Craven on the 11th August 1618 and his burial in the Church of St Andrew Undershaft: 'So departed a great Englishman, who, having climbed the ladder of success and won the esteem and respect of his peers tasted the joy of sharing his rich rewards with those in need, and through his bequests enshrined his name in the annals of Dales History'.

Continuing downhill the next building is Wharfe View Farm (48).

This building probably dates from the latter part of the 18th century, having a fine semi-circular headed Regency styled staircase window on the north elevation. It would appear that the front elevation has been refaced in the early 19th century with watershot stonework and very pronounced projecting stone quoins. The extension to the rear was probably built in the early part of the 20th century.

Beyond is The Coach House and Wharfe View Cottage (49), which were built at separate times. Wharfe View Cottage would appear to be slightly older, perhaps dating from the latter part of the 18th century with an extension at the southern end. The Coach House is architecturally very attractive, probably dating from the early part of the 19th century and originally providing stabling with some residential accommodation. There are three nice windows at first floor level of Regency design and a matching doorway at ground floor level; the former stable entrance having been attractively converted into a window.

Ahead is Burnsall Methodist Church (50).

This building with its spire forms an attractive feature at the bend in the road, having been described as 'The Most attractive Methodist Church in the Dales'. A number of foundation stones were laid in 1901 and the building was officially opened in 1902, having been designed by

James Hartley, a Skipton architect. The next building known as 'High Croft'(51), is the former Wesleyan Chapel, which was erected in 1840 on land previously belonging to Manor Cottage. It was converted into a dwelling house in 1968. Note the plaque built into the boundary wall on the left inscribed 'Wesleyan Methodist Chapel erected in the year 1840'. The stone surrounds to the flower bed in the garden, laid in the form of a quatrefoil, are from former window arches in this building.

Beyond is an interesting group of three cottages, namely, Manor Cottage, The Nook and Woodbine Cottage (52), which appear to date from the latter part of the 17th century. The middle property, today with a plaque inscribed 'AD 1880' over the front door and the plaques inscribed 'Bland' and 'Place' in the two side gables, is obviously the oldest section having been freestanding with the other cottages added on later. The datestone would appear to have been installed at the time of Victorian alterations including the projecting bay window.

Adjoining is the Manor House Private Hotel (53), which started its life as a Liberal Club built by John Atkinson Bland, a public spirited man, to provide recreational amenities for the men who were rebuilding Burnsall Bridge at the time. After the departure of the last construction workers John Bland hoped that the building would be used as, in effect, a village hall but he was probably rather ahead of his time and this never happened. A few years later John Bland's eldest son, Robert, added two extra storeys to the building converting it into a guest house which has done much over the years to enhance the tourist industry in Burnsall.

Set back on the adjoining site is the former Police House (54), which is typical of many such buildings erected in the late 1950s or early 1960s throughout the former West Riding of Yorkshire, in this instance being constructed of secondhand stone. The next property is Cobbler's Cottage, formerly known as 'Rosedene' (55), being a rather

nice little building dating from the late 17th century with copings and kneelers to each gable and one two light mullioned window surviving at first floor level.

Turning the corner, the next block comprising Corner Cottage, Howgill House and Ivy Cottage (56), probably dates from the 18th century, although Howgill House has been much altered on the front elevation in the very late 18th century or early 19th century with new stonework and stone quoins at the left-hand end. Ivy Cottage has nice 18th century mullioned windows, and the front door itself with six panels may date from Georgian times.

Beyond is The Barn (57), which probably dates from the early part of the 18th century, the original barn entrance having, I would think, a much later stone arch. This property has changed its use a number of times from house to shop and back again, since it was originally converted in the late 1970s.

The last property set back is known as 'Riversyde' (58). This is a delightful mid 17th century house which has a four light mullioned window remaining at ground floor level and, what has been another four light window to the left of it which has now lost two of its mullions. Above are three windows which were originally two light mullioned windows, today having Yorkshire sliding sash windows inserted. The northerly projecting section to the rear appears to date from the 18th century.

We are now back at the starting point outside the Red Lion Hotel.

Old Wesleyan Methodist Chapel

Ramble No 7

From Burnsall crossing Badger Lane and passing between
Kail and Skulberts hills to Thorpe, returning along the
Dales Way

STARTING POINT: This walk starts outside the Red Lion Hotel.

DISTANCE: Approximately three and a half miles.

TIME REQUIRED: Two and a half hours, but extra time should be allowed if you are
going to look at the buildings and other features in Burnsall on the first part of the walk,
and similarly the buildings and other features in both Thorpe and Hebden villages.

TERRAIN: For this walk it is essential to have suitable footwear since this ramble in its
entirety is through limestone country where exposed rock can be very slippery in both wet
and icy weather. The path climbs gradually from Burnsall and then more steeply where it
passes between Kail and Skulberts hills on the way to Thorpe. We then pass along a narrow
macadamed walled lane, which descends fairly steeply in places. After crossing the B6160
main road we follow a bridleway which descends abruptly from time to time to join the
Dales Way, just below the Hebden Suspension Bridge. The path along the River Wharfe is
relatively level, apart from a short climb at Loup Scar.

Attractive features of this walk are the fine views back over Burnsall and the valley
beyond, dominated by Simon's Seat. After leaving Thorpe extensive views open out
both up and down the dale and across to Grassington Moor where the lead mines
chimney can be clearly seen.

Proceed in a north westerly direction
along the narrow footpath on the right-
hand side of the road in order to face the
oncoming traffic.

**FOR INFORMATION ON THE BUILDINGS
AND OTHER FEATURES TO BE SEEN HERE
REFER TO THE CHAPTER DESCRIBING A
WALK AROUND BURNSALL VILLAGE.**

Holly House Corner compensation tap

Where the road bends sharply round to
the right be especially careful, and then
look for the footpath sign a few yards
beyond the water trough. The very narrow

pathway is actually located between Croft
Cottage and Rose Cottage and is not very
obvious, the footpath sign marked 'FP to
Thorpe' being partly obscured by a tree.
Pass through the little gate, up a few steps
and through a gated stile leading into a
little meadow.

This section of the path has been diverted in
recent times, since originally it went around two
sides of a barn and then through a stile,
immediately to the south of the electricity
substation.

The path continues in a fairly straight line
through attractive meadows, passing over
a series of stiles some of which are gated.

Note especially the second gated stile, with
steps up to it, which has very old and worn
projecting steps and is a very good example
of a nicely constructed gritstone stile in a
limestone wall.

Pause at the fourth stile, which is
another fine gritstone stile in a limestone
wall, to look back at the fine view of
Burnsall Village.

Above the village is the forest on Barden Moor,
to the left of this is Simon's Seat and over to the

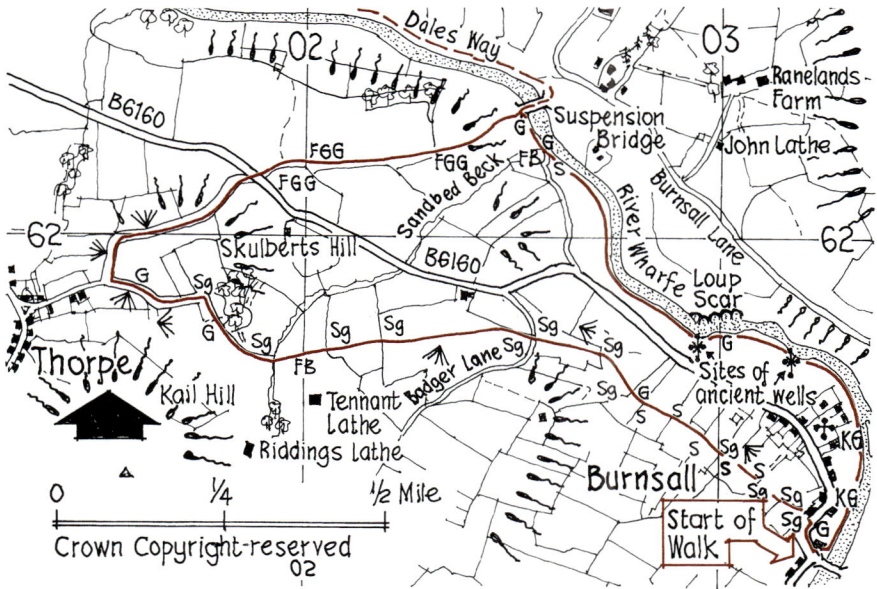

Crown Copyright-reserved
02

right Burnsall Fell comes into view. Standing on the top steps of this stile and looking ahead a whole series of stiles on the path beyond can be seen.

Eventually we cross a stile.

A few yards to the left along this little lane down in the trees is Joy Beck on the other side of which the Manor Corn Mill, first documented in 1260, is thought to have been located. A little way upstream can be seen the remains of part of the embankment which enclosed the mill pond, or lodge, which provided the water used to drive the waterwheel. The mill on this site later became known as 'Burnsall Mill'. In 1802 it changed over to cotton spinning and in 1825 it became a saw mill, finally in 1864 being sold by Sir Charles Tempest to Bradford Corporation Water Works to enable them to extinguish the water rights.

Now go through a gate in a post and wire fence, which forms the other boundary of Mill Lane, continuing to a gated stile in the corner of the wall ahead.

Here there is a footpath sign.

Bear up the hill to the right passing under the electricity wires, then climbing fairly

steeply up a more abrupt little hill to a gated stile located about a third the way along a wall over to the right, near three large trees.

After passing through this stile superb views open out ahead.

We soon reach Badger Lane, crossing it via two gated stiles.

Note how this little lane is sunken well below the level of the fields on either side which indicates its great antiquity. It was probably once quite an important route and the roadway has gradually been worn away with horses and wheeled traffic struggling up the steep gradient over the centuries.

The path now continues alongside a wall to the right following the electricity poles for a short distance and then veering off to the left, heading towards two large trees. It then bends round slightly heading for the right-hand end of a line of four trees that now appear ahead.

From here there are fine views to the left of Thorpe Fell with its dark gritstone walls and further right Kail Hill which is much greener with its lighter limestone walls.

125

After passing through a gated stile the path drops down to a further gated stile and Tennant Lathe comes into view to the left.

This is a 17th century barn which has had more than one extension added to it in recent times.

We now drop down to cross a little footbridge over a stream, made of two old railway sleepers. After passing through a gated stile the path follows ahead uphill alongside a wall on the right towards a woodland.

Note the barn to the left behind three dead elm trees, which is known as 'Riddings Lathe' and probably dates from the 18th century. Over to the right from this point Dowgill Lathe, a very small barn, will be seen.

After climbing uphill alongside the woodland, pass through the gate in the short timber fence. The path now climbs quite steeply to run alongside the wall to the left round to a gated stile giving access on to a narrow walled track known as 'Kail Lane'. A few yards ahead where this track widens slightly pause, in order to look back at the delightful view.

We have now almost reached the summit of the little pass between Kail and Skulberts hills.

Looking back at the fine view you will see over the woodland Simon's Seat and below it the other very green Kail Hill near Appletreewick, often known as 'Hartlington Kail' to distinguish it, and to the right Earl Seat and further right the forest on the slopes of Barden Fell can just be seen. Even further right rising up from this lane are the slopes of Kail Hill, one of the green hills which, in effect, hide Thorpe Village from the rest of the world!

Continue ahead passing the little plantation on the left pausing at the summit of Kail Lane a few yards further on.

Over to the left from this point is a fine view of Thorpe Fell on the left and Stebden Hill with its pointed top in the middle, and beyond Elbolton.

After passing through a gate we come to a junction with a macadamed lane.

In the summertime there is a fine display of wild roses on the wall opposite.

If you would like to see the old village of Thorpe, which has many unusual and fascinating buildings, continue leftwards for a hundred yards or so, then return to this point.

FOR INFORMATION ON THE BUILDINGS AND OTHER FEATURES TO BE SEEN HERE REFER TO THE CHAPTER DESCRIBING A WALK AROUND THORPE VILLAGE.

Turn right on to the narrow surfaced walled lane. Just beyond the first tree pause to look over the wall on the left at the fine view.

In the bottom of the valley you will see Threshfield Village and to the right of it Grassington, backed by Grass and Bastow woods and above them the long mass of Old Cote Moor between Littondale and Wharfedale. Further right, over the belt of trees, Buckden Pike will be seen and beyond near the next tree Great Whernside can just be seen peeping up over the skyline.

Soon the lane bends sharply round to the right gradually descending.

Pause again here to look at the fine view across Wharfedale. The red roofs of some of the buildings which have been retained from the former Grassington Hospital are clearly visible and above them the new houses that have been erected here can be picked out. Further to the right the valley of Hebden Beck will be seen and behind Grassington Moor and the chimney at the Grassington Lead Mines.

Along this section of the lane meadow cranesbill and later harebells grow in profusion during the summer months.

As the lane starts to drop more steeply down towards the main road Hebden Village comes into view ahead. Cross the main B6160 road.

Note the old stone finger signpost at the junction on the left. On its left side it is inscribed 'To Thorpe'. On the right-hand side it is inscribed 'To Burnsall' and 'To Linton and Kilnsey'.

Pass through the small gate to the right of the field gate signposted 'BW to Hebden'. Continue ahead towards the tree on the right to pass through a further gate to the right of a field gate. The path now continues downhill keeping fairly close to the wall on the right.

From the next section of the path there are fine views of Simon's Seat, Earl Seat, the forests on the slopes of Barden Fell and further right Burnsall Fell. Below Simon's Seat and Earl Seat is Appletreewick's very green Kail Hill.

Pass through the next gate to the right of a field gate, where there is a bridleway sign.

Here ramblers are requested to follow the waymarker posts.

The grassy path now drops down fairly steeply towards the trees near the river, keeping an electricity pole immediately to the right.

The Hebden Suspension Bridge soon appears in the trees below.

The path makes to the left of the suspension bridge past some stones immediately to the right, which at one time must have formed a stone wall.

From here there is a superb view of the River Wharfe and the suspension bridge below with the Hebden Beck running in near the stepping stones, a number of which are missing.

Pass through the gate first turning left on to the Dales Way if you would like to have a look at Hebden Village, otherwise turn right in order to continue this ramble.

The age of the stepping stones is not known, although in the Middle Ages there was a ford nearby. After the partial destruction of Burnsall Bridge in the great flood of 1883 there was a need for a link between Hebden and Burnsall and so a temporary footbridge was erected. However, there was soon a demand for something more substantial and a few years earlier William Bell, Hebden's local blacksmith, had built a suspension bridge at Netherside Hall. After inspection of this bridge, by some of the local people, Bell was commissioned to build a similar bridge which he did for the sum of £87. This was built by subscription with additional help from the Duke of Devonshire. William used scrap metal obtained from the Hebden Moor Lead Mines, with hollow cast iron columns at each end nine feet in height and nine inches external diameter, supported upon masonry blocks. However, the cast iron columns did not come from the lead mines but the wire rope did. In 1936 this bridge was damaged in another great flood, that probably surpassed that of 1883, and the County then rebuilt it at a slightly higher level. Prior to 1936, this bridge had a central support, the remains of which can still be seen in the river, and it wobbled about quite a lot and thus it became known amongst the local people as the 'Swing Bridge'. If you do go across this bridge note how deep the water is in the river below.

FOR INFORMATION ON THE BUILDINGS AND OTHER FEATURES TO BE SEEN HERE REFER TO THE CHAPTER DESCRIBING A WALK AROUND HEBDEN VILLAGE.

Continuing the ramble pass through the gate into a little woodland, cross the footbridge and then the stile ahead, where a stepped path joins from the right.

The next section of the path is extremely beautiful and note, especially in the summertime, the lovely wild roses on the hillside to the right.

After passing through a more wooded area known as 'Low Bank Wood' we soon reach Loup Scar.

Here the river has cut through the limestone in a most dramatic way. Note to the left of the path, just before the start of Loup Scar, against a tree with large post near it, the remains of an old stile. The footpath must have gone much nearer to the river at one time.

The path crosses a small stone slab bridge, where the ground is usually extremely boggy to the right, and bends round to climb steeply up to a gate.

Close by this stone slab bridge is the site of the ancient St Margaret's Well and possibly the well was fed by the stream causing the boggy ground today.

Pause before the gate to look at Loup Scar and the river below. Note the interesting folds and twists in the various layers of rock. This is one of the most lovely sections of the River Wharfe and one day in the early 1930s a chapel choir came here in the evening after they had been on a char-a-banc outing to Grassington. Sitting here above Loup Scar they sang all they knew including very appropriately 'Rock of Ages'.

After passing through the gate the next section of the path is stepped and then runs alongside the river.

Be sure to look back at the fine views of the rocky gorge.

Soon the path becomes narrow alongside the river with a concreted section.

A short distance beyond the concreted path, close by the river, is the site of the ancient St Helen's Well. The next section of the river is very beautiful.

After passing through the kissing gate the path bends round to the right.

Here there is an island in the river that has been formed within living memory.

Pass through another kissing gate adjacent to Burnsall Chapel, a fine building with a spire which will be seen to the right. A short distance further on pause near the sign on the right which reads 'Manor House Private Hotel'.

Here you will see the remains of the old boat house on the right and on the left the little jetty in the river which appears to have had some repair work carried out upon it in recent times. Rowing boats were available for hire on this stretch of the river from as early as 1899 and this activity continued until shortly before the Second World War, being revived for a short time more recently.

A few yards further on turn right at the bridge back to the starting point.

Burnsall Bridge

IAN GOLDTHORPE

A Walk Around Conistone Village

Conistone was formerly known as 'Cunestone' which undoubtedly means 'King's Town'. The de Hebdens were the principal land owners in this village during the Medieval period since there was very little monastic land here, apart from one house and a pasture for five hundred sheep. During the 15th century the Manor passed, by marriage, to the Tempest family who, in 1568, sold it for £500 to Alexander Rishworthe, of Heath near Wakefield. In 1575 Rishworthe sold the Manor to John Kaye of Oakenshaw for £700, except for one property with its land which he had already sold to John Battie, its occupant. In 1583 Kaye sold the whole of the Manor to the twenty seven tenants, fourteen of whom didn't live in Conistone at the time. No doubt most of the houses then would be of Medieval timber framed construction, and perhaps a few of cruck construction, with wattle and daub infill and thatched roofs. Then gradually as these people, the first freeholders or their descendants became more wealthy, some becoming yeoman farmers, they gradually rebuilt the properties in stone, or encased the existing buildings during the 17th century. They often inserted datestones with their initials, some of which we shall see in the course of our walk.

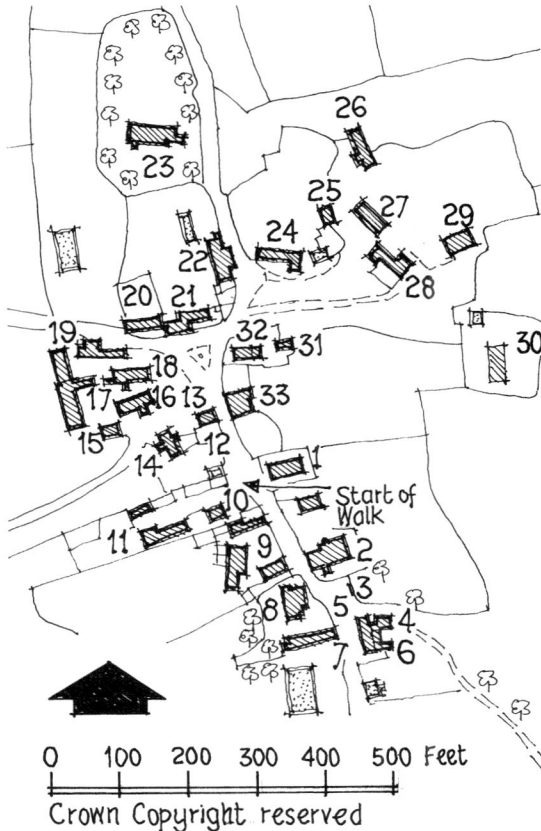

129

This walk starts from the area used for car parking opposite Conistone Hostel and Chapel. Cross the road to view this former chapel.

This building (1), was originally built as a Wesleyan Methodist Chapel and has an 1885 datestone. This Chapel ceased to be used for services in the mid 1960s.

Continue in a southerly direction and the next building on the left is Conistone Old Hall (2).

Conistone Old Hall

This building has many similarities with Tophams Farm at the other end of the village and probably dates back to about 1630. In the very early 1990s a very careful restoration of the building took place when the original single storey projecting porch to the south elevation, with a datestone inscribed 'RC' over '1657' which stands for R Constantine, was demolished and replaced by a beautifully designed and constructed two storey porch incorporating the original datestone. At the same time a late 19th century rear extension, adjacent to the road, was demolished and the new garage block to the rear was erected. There is an interesting semi-circular projecting chimney stack to the rear which is unusual in this part of the Dales and much more akin to Dentdale and parts of the English Lakes. A very delightful new stone porch was added to the rear elevation at the time of the recent restoration. There are nice 18th century moulded stone surrounds to three ground floor windows to the south elevation. For many years this old building was divided into two properties.

Adjacent to the front of Conistone Old Hall note the three drinking troughs (3), in front of the wall

to the left. These are obviously of great antiquity and the water here usually flows, except in times of extreme drought.

Beyond is a very interesting block of property. First go up the little lane to the left known as 'Pasture Gate'.

Leyland Cottage (4), was originally a separate property with an independent living apartment above, probably for a farm worker and the fine external stone steps giving access still remain. This building possibly dates from the mid 17th century and there is evidence of two doorways from this period in the north elevation, one under the staircase landing. There is also evidence of a semi-circular headed window at first floor level which has been blocked up.

The cottages fronting on to the road, namely Leyland House and Close Garth (5), again date from the 17th century having a projecting plinth and in the southern gable end the remains of mullioned windows. The two porches have both been added in recent years. Behind, at the southern end, is another little cottage (6), dating from the 17th century with three light mullioned windows at both ground and first floor level still surviving, although in each case one mullion has been removed. In the wall to the rear of this cottage is a very good example of four Bee Boles, which probably date from the late 17th or early 18th century.

Now cross the road to look at Hemplands Barn.

This fine barn (7), probably dates from the latter part of the 17th century. There are two 17th century doorways to the north elevation and an 18th century window towards the rear at an upper level indicating that at one time residential accommodation may have been provided here for a farm worker. The stonework to the two barn entrances probably dates from the late 18th or early 19th century.

Hemplands Farmhouse (8), has a stringcourse and

a datestone over the door inscribed 'RW 1694' which stands for Richard Wigglesworth. This house contains a fine 17th century fireplace with joggled voussoirs. There is a nice 18th century doorway to the west elevation together with a number of windows from the same period. In addition there is a semi-circular headed late 18th or early 19th century staircase window to the east elevation.

The next group of buildings on the left going northwards is known as 'Conistone Fold' (9).

This property originally comprised two barns and a shippon. The barn on the left has a datestone inscribed 'D' over 'EH' and the date '1864'. The D stands for Dawson. This is an interesting example of a Victorian barn with its hammered sandstone quoins and door openings picked out in a constrasting stone with a slate roof. The barn to the rear on the right probably dates from the early part of the 18th century and adjoining it is an old building with a monopitch roof and some late 17th century doorways. What was the largest building to the rear, a former shippon, was converted into a house in 1987. It has some interesting ventilating openings at the left-hand end, the remainder being nicely restored with new mullioned windows, complete with drip moulds to the ground floor and an 18th century styled entrance door. This work was carefully carried out by Melvin Jarvis of Skipton.

Immediately to the north, set back behind a yard area is a small barn.

This barn (10), has two late 17th century doorways partly walled up to form windows.

The property behind known as 'The Cottage' (11), was a small building much extended, probably in the 1980s with a new adjoining garage at the east end built in the mid to late 1990s. The barn on the right of the drive appears to date from the late 17th or early 18th century.

Proceeding northwards in a few yards we come to the Pinfold, or Pound (12), on the left.

This is where stray animals were kept until claimed by their owners. It would be here before many of the stone walls in the locality were built. Adjoining, on the north side, is Pinfold Barn (13), which

probably dates from the late 17th or early 18th century.

Behind Pinfold Barn is the Old Barn (14), which dates from the 17th century since there are some old doorways remaining from this period. This is a most excellent example of a very careful conversion of a barn into a dwelling which was carried out in 1978 to the designs of Mary Wales for which the scheme was awarded a Civic Trust Award for the North East.

Behind The Old Barn is the original 'Old School' (15), where the parents had to pay for their children to attend the lessons. It is now a garage and was originally built in the 18th century.

Renshaw Farm House

Renshaw Farm House (16), is the next building overlooking the little Village Green and originally formed part of a complex of farm buildings. The oldest part of the house dates from the early part of the 17th century, possibly about 1634. There is a massive fireplace with incised joggled voussoirs, comprising a centre keystone and a large stone at each side. There is also another fireplace with a single stone lintel, shaped and chamfered with corbel-like supports on stone jambs. Over one of the fireplaces is a datestone inscribed '1697 WS'. There is an interesting stepped three light mullioned window at first floor level in the east elevation overlooking the Village Green. The entrance doorway has a stepped lintel and an inscribed plaque '1705' over 'F' over 'GS' and a symbol in the middle like a tree. The 'F' in this datestone apparently refers to the Fawcett family who were in residence here at this time. There are some more mullioned windows in the rear extension. In addition there is what has been a three light mullioned window at first floor level with only one mullion left, the remains of a two light mullioned window at ground floor level together with 17th century doorways at both ground and first floor level, one above the other. This property was very carefully restored to the designs of Andrew Fisher in the early 1990s.

Behind is West View Barn (17), which originally comprised two barns dating from the 17th century. This is an extremely fine range of buildings with four barn archways. There are datestones over two doors, one is inscribed '1637 JL' and on the other '1627 JL' which probably stand for John Leyland. These two barns were converted into one dwelling to the designs of Andrew Fisher about 1993.

On the right going down to West View Barn is Renshaw Cottage (18), which in more recent times was used as a barn. However, since it contains a fine 17th century fireplace at least part of this building must have been used for residential purposes when it was first built. The rear portion is a drying house, or kiln, dating from about the same time. This building was carefully converted into a dwelling in the early 1990s to the designs of Andrew Fisher.

Beyond and adjacent to the road to Kilnsey is Tophams Farm (19), which has a fine 17th century fireplace. The western portion was originally a barn which was converted into a garage with a flat above at the same time, both these schemes being to designs prepared by Alan Dodd.

Across the road is Holme Farm (20), which is now divided into two dwellings. It probably dates from the late 17th or very early 18th century but has been very much altered externally.

Adjoining Holme Farm is Maypole Cottage (21), which appears to date from very early in the 18th century, although since it has copings and kneelers to each gable it could be slightly earlier. There are some nice three light 18th century mullioned windows to the front elevation and this building was latterly the Post Office before Conistone lost this service. The extension at the eastern end was built in the late 1980s.

Continue around the corner into the road leading to Kettlewell.

On the left is another property known as 'Leyland House' (22), which was originally a slaughter house. It has on its east elevation a doorway which came from a barn in the village, now demolished, which has over it the inscription 'IT 1697' and what looks like a Yorkshire rose in the middle. The initials probably stand for John Tennant. On one of the stones forming part of the right-hand door jamb is carved 'LB 1791'.

Proceed northwards along Kettlewell Road past the cattle grid entrance to Leyland House for a few yards to a nice iron gate on the left.

This old gate with an ancient stile to the right, with a flight of four steps leading up to it, give access to what could rightly be described as 'Upper Wharfedale's Best Kept Secret'. This is Conistone's ancient Church of St Mary (23), on the site of which Christians have worshipped for over one thousand years. Sadly this very old building is overshadowed by the much better known Church of St Michael at Hubberholme with its Norman West Tower, ancient arcades and Rood Loft dated 1558, of which there are few remaining in the country, others being at Flamborough in Yorkshire, one in Wiltshire and another in Norfolk.

In 1846, when Conistone Church formed part of the large parish of Burnsall and the Vicar, the Rev'd William Bury, lived at Chapel House Kilnsey, this Church was much restored and partly rebuilt to the designs of Sharpe and Paley, architects. At this time a new Chancel and South Porch were added together with a new Belfry, all in the Norman style. At the same time a new Vestry was added on the north side having an East Window from the earlier Church with two triangular headed lights with a chamfered mullion.

As you approach the entrance to the Church note the two 18th century chest tombs on the right of the path. The first which has weathered rather badly is inscribed: 'Here lieth the Body of Richard Constantine who departed this life September the 15th, 1746 and in the 63rd year of his Age. Jane ye wife of the above Ric.d died Fbr. ye 21st 1755'. The more southerly tomb has an incised line and roll moulding to the top slab and lettering which has been sharply cut is well preserved: 'Here lieth the Body of Thos. Son of Jonathan & Margaret Constantine who died Fbr. ye 25th 1745 in the

18th Year of His Age. The above Margaret died Janr. ye 28th 1927-8. Also the Body of the above Jonathan who died May 17th. 1768 Aged 73'. Henry Constantine was one of the tenants who bought his holding after 1583 and may have lived at the Old Hall before it was rebuilt.

As you enter the porch note the fairly new outer entrance door inscribed: 'Dr Robert Keighley Hon. Curate 1979-1989'. Mary and I knew Robert very well and I attended his funeral service here, when this little Church was packed to capacity and he was buried in the north-east corner of the Churchyard. He was born in Swaledale in 1913 and, after qualifying as a doctor, spent many years of his life working as a general practitioner near the University of Leeds. He married Jacqueline, another doctor, and they both later became lay readers in the Church of England. After retirement Robert was ordained and they both came to live at Chapel House Lodge near Kilnsey. They were both enthusiastic members of the Upper Wharfedale Field Society and led many walks, Robert serving as President of the Society for two consecutive terms, the only member to have done so in recent years!

The interior of the Church is most pleasing and striking. However, there is considerable uncertainty regarding the dates of the arches leading into the North Aisle. The two western bays, with semi-circular arches and heavy square pillars, are thought to be pre-Conquest, possibly Saxon, dating from before 1066. The two eastern bays with octagonal piers are thought to be Early English, in all probability dating from about 1220. Both the Font and the Vestry Window are Norman, but could be Saxon, and so this Church, almost without doubt, is the oldest building in Craven.

The oak pews were installed in 1957, being hand carved by Thompson of Kilburn. Have a look for the mouse which is carved on each pew! On the front of one of the pews is the following inscription: 'The pews in the Nave were given by Mary and Robert Haughton Tomalin to the Glory of God and in beloved remembrance of their parents Jane & Thomas Horner of Bordley and Thostle Nest Farm, Conistone; and Addy & Frank Tomalin of Long Buckby, Northamptonshire, and Kettlewell, 1957'. The Choir Stalls have some linen-fold panelling and the Pulpit is inscribed: 'To the Glory of God and in memory of George and Rebecca Horner 1898'.

At the West End of the Church, on a pier supporting the western arch, is a nicely carved box with the short inscription: 'Remember the Poor'.

Note the poem above which reads as follows:

To the potholers lost in Mossdale Cavern.

Parish Church of St Mary – ancient North Aisle arcade

They gently sleep, those brave young hearts and true,
No more their feet must tramp the dewy grass;
No more they'll seek, the cruel dangers new,
Or hear the moor birds warning as they pass.

The rock rose gleamed upon their upland way,
And swiftly kissed their eager hapless feel,
And life to them was one long beauteous day,
Nor dreamed they of the fate they were to meet.

Sleep sweetly on ye lads of valiant worth,
All honour due, nor do we seek to blame;
But God still rules with mighty hand this earth,
And we must bow and ever bless His name.

This was written by Olive Pratt, who lived in Grassington, after she became blind and well illustrates the dangers involved in this popular sport. These six potholers, who were aged between 17 and 26 years, came from the Leeds area and were killed in 1967. Their families have erected a memorial in their memory, which is located in the Churchyard on the right as you approach the gate.

Note the two old bells on the floor at the west end of the Church, one dated 1664.

After leaving the Churchyard turn right and then left into the little Village Green in a few yards.

The block of property on the left (24), comprises two cottages which probably date, in the main, from the 18th century. The first cottage was for many years Conistone Post Office. The second property known as 'Greystones' has a projecting block at its eastern end with a four light mullioned window at both ground and first floor level and a barge board to the gable above. This extension appears to date from the 1920s or early 1930s and may have been converted from an existing barn.

Beyond, and behind, is a property known as 'The Gurling' (25), which was converted from a barn in 1980. Behind, up a drive, is a former barn (26), which was converted and extended in the late 1970s. A further extension was added to the designs of Barrie Birch.

There are two cottages facing down the green (27). The left-hand property could have originally been a separate dwelling linked to the adjoining house at a later date. The right-hand cottage known as 'Town Head' has a 17th century

doorway and to the right of what has been a three light mullioned window.

The white property with a barn attached at the left-hand end, known as 'Ghyll Foot' (28), probably dates from the late 18th century. To the left of the right-hand ground floor window there is evidence of an earlier doorway. Behind is the former Conistone School, now known as 'Old School House' (29), which was opened as a school before 1850 and was closed in 1948. After being used as a barn for about ten years the building was enlarged and converted into a dwelling.

Across the track is a property now known as 'Ebony House' (30), which was built in the 1970s to replace a timber holiday cottage. Initially this house was called 'The Rise'.

Now walk back towards the maypole in the centre of the village, noting the seat on the Village Green on the left.

This seat was made by John Ely in memory of Walter Hebden (1937-1988), who was a headmaster in Bury St Edmunds and brought many school parties to the Dales. This was his favourite spot.

The first little building on the left is a former barn (31), probably dating from the 18th century which is now used as a garage for Hemplands Cottage.

Adjacent is Hemplands Cottage (32), which dates from the 17th century. This property was once two cottages and contains a fine 17th century fireplace with a centre keystone and a curved lintel on each side incised to represent voussoirs. In another room there is a delightful smaller stone fireplace with the dates '17' and '22' and a carved motif in between rather like a heart. There is a nice three light mullioned window at both ground and first floor level at the east end of the south elevation.

To the south of Hemplands Cottage is Hemplands Barn (33), which is an interesting building which probably dates from the 17th century. There is evidence that part of the building once may have comprised living accommodation.

Now walk a few yards in a southerly direction back to the starting point.

Ramble No 8

From Conistone along Kettlewell Road and Scot Gate
Lane then southwards along the Dales Way, returning
through Conistone Dib

STARTING POINT: This walk starts from the area used for car parking opposite
Conistone Hostel and Chapel.

DISTANCE: Approximately two and a half miles.

TIME REQUIRED: One and three quarter hours, but extra time should be allowed if you
are going to look at the buildings and other features in Conistone Village either on the first
part of the walk or at the end of the walk.

TERRAIN: For this walk it is essential to have suitable footwear since the last part of the
path through Conistone Dib is narrow, steep and very rough. After leaving Kettlewell Road
it is a long climb, which is fairly steep in places, up to the Dales Way. The section along the
Dales Way is relatively level. The path leading down into Conistone Dib is grassy but fairly
steep in places. The last part of the walk leading back into Conistone is through a narrow
limestone gorge which drops down steeply in places and is very rough.

Attractive features of this walk are the extensive views of Upper Wharfedale, including
Littondale to the north-west and Cracoe and Rylstone fells to the south. There are
also spectacular views from the Dales Way looking down into the fine limestone dale
known as 'Conistone Dib'.

Proceed in a northerly direction, bearing
right at the maypole and continuing ahead
into Kettlewell Road passing the vehicle
restriction sign.

**FOR INFORMATION ON THE BUILDINGS
AND OTHER FEATURES TO BE SEEN HERE
REFER TO THE CHAPTER DESCRIBING A
WALK AROUND CONISTONE VILLAGE.**

Conistone Church

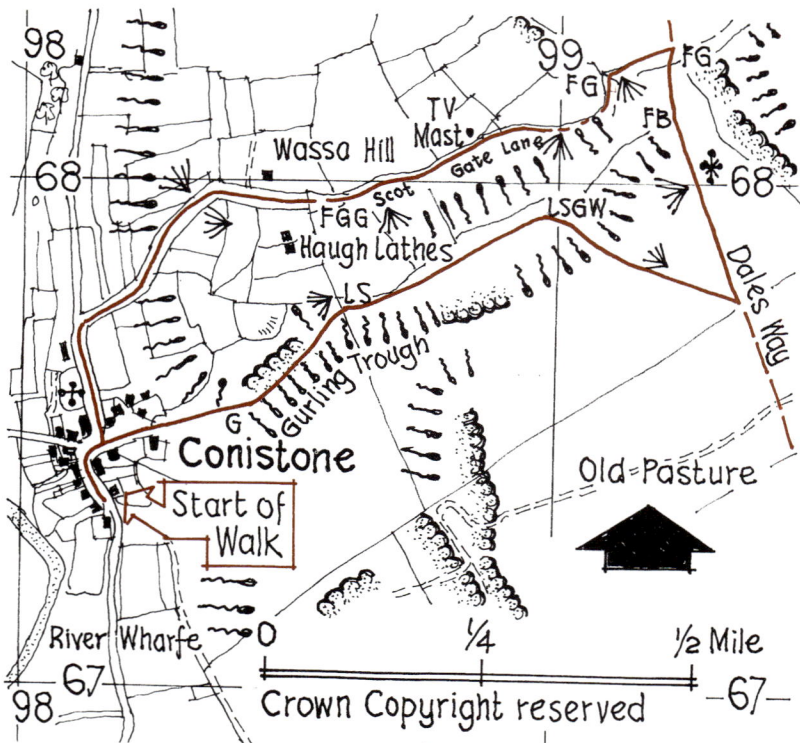

Look for Conistone Church on the left probably dating back to pre-Conquest times, with its attractive iron gate, and to the right of it, an old stile with a flight of steps. Also take note of the nearby old limestone wall on the right covered with moss from top to bottom.

At the boundary sign marked 'Conistone' take the lane off to the right with the footpath sign 'Middlesmoor II', and the sign on the left which states 'Bridleway only. Strictly no right of way for motor cycles and cars'.

The lane soon becomes unsurfaced and stony.

As the track begins to climb it becomes well surfaced with an extremely fine wall on the left. Where the road bends round to the right, and there is a gate on the left pause.

Here look back at the superb view of the valley below with Kilnsey dominated by the cream painted Tennant Arms Hotel backed by Mastiles

Lane climbing up over the moors. To the right the scene is overshadowed by Kilnsey Crag and below the River Wharfe can be clearly seen. A number of new tree planting schemes are also visible straight ahead.

Looking through the gate on the left there is a magnificent view of Littondale going off leftwards and Kettlewell backed by Buckden Pike straight ahead. This part of the road and other more steep and difficult sections have been surfaced to give better access to the television mast.

Continue ahead along the road.

Looking through the next gate on the left is a fine barn with a lean-to right-hand section, probably dating from the early part of the 18th century.

Where this section of surfaced road stops pass through the small metal pedestrian gate to the right of the main gate, proceeding ahead on the rough track known as 'Scot Gate Lane'.

136

Looking through the next gate on the right there is a fine view below of the little valley known as 'Conistone Dib'. As the track zig-zags around to meet the wall on the left there is a good example of a 'creep hole', or 'cripple hole', just near where the road again becomes surfaced. Creep holes are used to allow sheep and lambs to pass from one side of the wall to the other without larger animals being able to do so.

At the next bend, just below the TV Mast, where the road takes a sweep round to the right, you will see the line of the original highway close by the stone wall on the left.

At the TV Mast the road flattens out and is unsurfaced again.

A short distance beyond the TV Mast the line of the old road can again be clearly seen going through the grass to the right. There is some fine limestone scenery hereabouts. Note the further creep hole in the wall on the left, just before the road starts to climb again.

From here there is a further fine view of the limestone dale to the right leading down to Conistone Village. At the next bend there is another very tall creep hole on the right - the sheep hereabouts must have been much larger!

The path now bends sharply round to the right leading to a gate. Pass through the gate and continue ahead to join the Dales Way.

The Dales Way, which crosses our track is clearly marked by the footpath and bridleway signpost. Look to the right at this point at the fine view dominated by Cracoe and Rylstone fells in the distance, and you can just see above the nearer hills the tops of some of the trees in Bastow Wood.

Leave Scot Gate Lane descending a grassy bank leading down to a gate with a sign 'please shut the gate'.

The Dales Way descends quickly to cross a stone slab bridge. On the right is an alternative path, passing over a ladder stile, leading back to Conistone.

Nearby, to the left, along the next section of the path are the remains of Romano-British settlements.

Continue ahead noting the superb vews to the right of the dry limestone valley leading back down to Conistone.

The path becomes grassy and relatively level as it crosses the moorland.

At the ladder stile in the wall ahead signposted 'FP Grassington', take the footpath leading back down to the right into a little valley signposted 'FP Conistone'.

Here we leave the Dales Way.

As the path starts to descend there are fine views ahead looking up Littondale, with the distinctive summit of Old Cote Moor on the right. In the hollow to the left of the path is a fine example of an old dewpond.

As you enter the valley pass through the gateway to the right of a ladder stile and bear left down the little dale, again signposted 'Conistone'. The grassy path gradually descends until a wall and ladder stile are reached.

From here there is a fine view as this little dale becomes more rugged, with the fells beyond dotted with clumps of trees.

After crossing the ladder stile the grassy path continues for about three hundred yards to a point where there are three cairns.

The considerable limestone screes on each side of the valley at this point are impressive. This area is known locally as 'Gurling Trough'.

Our route now becomes much more stony as two more cairns are reached and then descends steeply through a narrow gorge. This gradually opens out, with trees on the right, as the edge of the village is reached.

The path has obviously been the bed of a river at one time and, as you reach the village, you descend a small rocky escarpment which may once have formed a waterfall, although some quarrying in this vicinity has taken place in more recent times.

A little further on pass through the gate back into the village. Continue ahead bearing left at the maypole back to the starting point.

The early name for Kilnsey was 'Kilnesse'. The word 'kil' means Celtic chapel and 'nesse' is Norse for a protuberance or jutting piece of land. In the 12th century Kilnsey became by gift a sheep grange of Fountains Abbey, and for four hundred years sheep were reared here for the production of wool. After the Dissolution Henry VIII sold the Fountains lands, including Kilnsey, to Sir Richard Gresham, the financier. Later the Wade family acquired Kilnsey Old Hall and in the 17th century Lady Anne Clifford stayed here overnight with the Wades on several occasions.

This walk starts outside the Tennant Arms Hotel and it is interesting to note that in White Beck on the opposite side of the road mimulus grows in profusion.

The cream painted section of the Tennant Arms Hotel (1), probably dates from about 1840, the left-hand section being much older with evidence of a blocked up 17th century window at first floor level. The present windows on the front elevation of this more ancient part date from the late 18th or early 19th century.

Turn right down the little lane at the south end of the hotel.

On the side elevation of this building there is evidence in the gable wall of the front section of a blocked up mullioned window, and in the linking piece a 17th century doorway. The rear block, with its gable fronting on to this lane, has a number of mullioned windows in the side and rear elevations, one which was formerly a two light mullioned window with a Georgian window inserted. There is

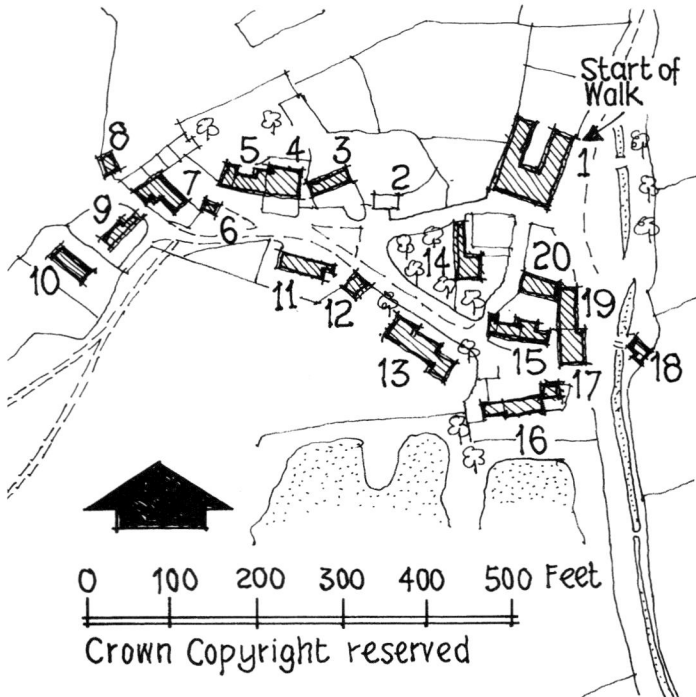

Start of Walk

0 100 200 300 400 500 Feet

Crown Copyright reserved

also evidence of a plinth to the earlier section of the building and the gents toilet boasts a two light mullioned window!

A few yards further on is what may be the remains of the Pinfold or Pound on the right (2), where stray animals would be kept until claimed by their owners. However, earlier maps seem to suggest that there may have originally been some small buildings on this site.Beyond on the right is Crag Cottage (3), which dates from the 17th century. This originally had two four light mullioned windows at ground floor level, one with a hood mould. There are more mullioned windows at first floor level and an additional window has been inserted later at ground floor level, possibly in the early part of
the 19th century.

The next property known as 'Old Hall Farm' (4), is probably a 17th century house doubled in width in the 18th century. To the rear there is a datestone over a window inscribed '1628 EE' and a semi-circular headed late 18th century staircase window. Old Hall Cottage, the adjoining property (5), was initially built as a dairy, with accommodation above for a farm worker. Much of the ground floor was obviously converted to residential use a long time ago since to the rear of this property is also a fine semi-circular headed late 18th century staircase window. The lean-to barn at the end of this block is probably rather later in date.

In front of the block that we have just looked at is a little building known as 'The Gatehouse' (6), with a blocked up three light mullioned window similar to the windows at Threshfield Old Hall and a doorway with spandrels above. This building dates from monastic times and, although only a part of the original structure, may have been built

The Gatehouse

in the 14th century but it could be as late as the middle of the 15th century.

Behind is Kilnsey Old Hall, architecturally the most important building remaining in Kilnsey today.

The oldest part of this building (7), is probably the south-west wing which contains two Tudor styled fireplaces, one at ground floor level and one at first floor level both with single curved stone lintels and what appears to have been a beehive oven to the side of the upper fireplace. The

Kilnsey Old Hall

building was originally three storey possessing a number of very fine mullioned windows, including two six light ones with hood moulds. The south-east gable has a plinth together with a coping and kneelers capped with carved finials. Under the landing to the external stone steps on the north-east elevation is a very fine 17th century doorway, probably as fine as anything to be found in the whole of Wharfedale as regards the quality of its detailing and carving. Above is another much simpler 17th century doorway, the outstanding ground floor doorway having a datestone over it inscribed '1648 CW', standing for Christopher Wade who owned the property at this time and was the son of Arthur Wade of Bordley. It has been said that Christopher built the hall using stone from the old monastic buildings, but in my opinion much of what we see today may have originally been built by the masons employed by the monks of Fountains Abbey, although being modified and altered many times over the centuries. The fine doorway with his initials, doubtless installed by Christopher Wade in the mid 17th century, in many ways looks to me to be much more recent than many of the other fascinating features of this building. The superb roof timbers are almost all original and of great age and even in the early 1980s some of the decorated plasterwork had still survived.

Sadly this beautiful building has been used as a barn and for storage purposes since about 1800, and the barn entrance on the north-east elevation probably dates from the late 18th or early 19th century. Whitaker was able to inspect the

Doorway at Kilnsey Old Hall

decorated plaster about 1800 and stated that the pattern was one of leaves and flowers. In his book 'Upper Wharfedale' by F W Houghton published in 1980 Mr Houghton writes as follows about the interior of this building: 'Under a blocked up window (query of the great room) a stone label about six feet long and nine inches deep with the figures '16' at one end and '22' at the other with the initials '?W' in the centre. Under this label is a faint diamond shape on the plaster with another item in the centre. We puzzled over this and wondered about heraldic 'fleur de lis' and 'pomegranates'. Later thoughts put us on to another suggestion: the Wade family arms were

a 'saltire' with four 'escallops' so perhaps our diamond shape was a segment of the family's blazon'. Behind Kilnsey Old Hall are some walls which are obviously the remains of further monastic buildings.

Now continue up the hill alongside Kilnsey Old Hall noting the interesting piece of limestone pavement, once used as a gatepost and still possessing part of a hinge.

Where the road bends sharply round to the left is another little building (8), which is currently held together with metal braces. This building has a nice doorway with spandrels and doubtless, in my opinion, may date back a very long way. It has been suggested that perhaps this could have been used as a small chapel during monastic times.

Now retrace your steps back down the hill.

On the right is Monks Cottage (9), which probably dates from the 18th century, although it has been much restored and skilfully extended in recent times with the gable wall angled for traffic reasons. The property beyond known as 'Mastiles Garth' (10), was built in the late 1980s.

Continuing along the road the next property on the right is Old Hall Barn.

This house (11), was converted from a barn in 1992. An additional small barn beyond (12), was converted into a garage for this property at the same time.

Continuing ahead we now enter the section of road known as 'The Green' located on the south side of the small Village Green.

Next we come to a delightful little scheme of four cottages (13), which was built by the Sanctuary Housing Association to the designs of Robert Groves in 1997.

The property opposite known as 'Glenholme' (14), dates from the 18th century. Here it is interesting to note that when he retired Dr Walter Hibbert came to live in this house and he was over one hundred years old when he died in 1978. The next two properties known as 'Pear Tree Cottage' and 'Rose Tree Cottage' (15), appear to date from the 18th century, each having an interesting small moulded cornice over the doorway.

Cottages built by the Sanctuary Housing Association

Opposite is a block of three houses known as 'Smithy Cottages' (16), the lower part of the right-hand property being originally the smithy, probably at one time with living accommodation above since the steps remain. The whole of this block, which comprised in addition barns, was converted into three dwellings in the 1970s.

We now join the main road turning left.

On the corner of this junction is the former Anglers Arms (17), which dates from the 17th century and was a farm as well as an inn. It ceased to be a public house in the 1930s but continued as a farm for some years afterwards. On the front elevation there is a fine doorway at the north end and a blocked up entrance where the mounting steps are, both dating from the 17th century, although the rest of this frontage was much altered by the insertion of new windows in the 18th century. There are also two 17th century windows remaining on the rear elevation and over the main entrance is a datestone inscribed 'O' over 'HE' and the date '1768'. Inside, behind the blocked up doorway on the front elevation is a fine Georgian bookcase very similar in design to the one at Grassington House. There is also a nice window seat with 18th century detailing.

This building is important historically since it is here that Dr Petty and Tom Lee had been drinking before the doctor was murdered on his way back to Grassington, whilst passing through Grass Wood. In the evidence it was stated that there had been an altercation between the two men and others within the hostelry that evening. This former inn is now known as 'Anglers Cottage'. The little building opposite, across the stream (18), was originally the brewhouse and laundry for the Anglers Arms.

The two adjoining cottages known as 'Anglers Nook' and 'Anglers Barn' (19), have a datestone inscribed '19 RDM 88' which stands for Robert Dixon Metcalfe who rebuilt the property at this time and whose family live there now. A barn stood on this site which was used by the Anglers Arms for farming. The barn roof fell in during the 1980s and the stone and slates were used to construct these new properties. The building behind (20), was originally a coach house at the lower level, now operating as a blacksmith's, with a joiner's shop above approached from the raised lane behind and probably dates from the 18th century.

In a few yards we are back to the starting point outside the Tennant Arms Hotel. However, I think that in concluding this chapter mention should be made of Chapel House, which is situated about one mile down the dale from Kilnsey Village. There has been a building on the site of Chapel House since about the 12th century. The house and surrounding land were owned by Fountains Abbey until 1539, being part of Kilnsey Grange. Part of the present buildings date back to the 17th century and the Georgian front part of the house was built by John Tennant, in 1783, after a fire.

Ramble No 9

From Kilnsey along Mastiles Lane and footpath to Bow Bridge, returning on footpath from Conistone Bridge

STARTING POINT: This walk starts outside the Tennant Arms Hotel.

DISTANCE: Approximately two and a quarter miles.

TIME REQUIRED: One and a half hours, but extra time should be allowed if you are going to look at the buildings and other features in Kilnsey on the first part of the walk, and similarly the buildings and other features in Conistone Village.

TERRAIN: This is the shortest walk described in the book and also one of the easiest. Provided you have suitable footwear it is perhaps a suitable walk for fit, but less experienced, ramblers to tackle. The initial climb up out of Kilnsey, although steep in places, is not very difficult and is easy to follow. From Scarth Cote to Bow Bridge the path presents no problems, the remainder of the route being very flat and easy to follow.

Attractive features of this walk are the fine views of Upper Wharfedale from Mastiles Lane and on the return journey, the spectacular view of Kilnsey Crag with the little village of Kilnsey nestling at its foot.

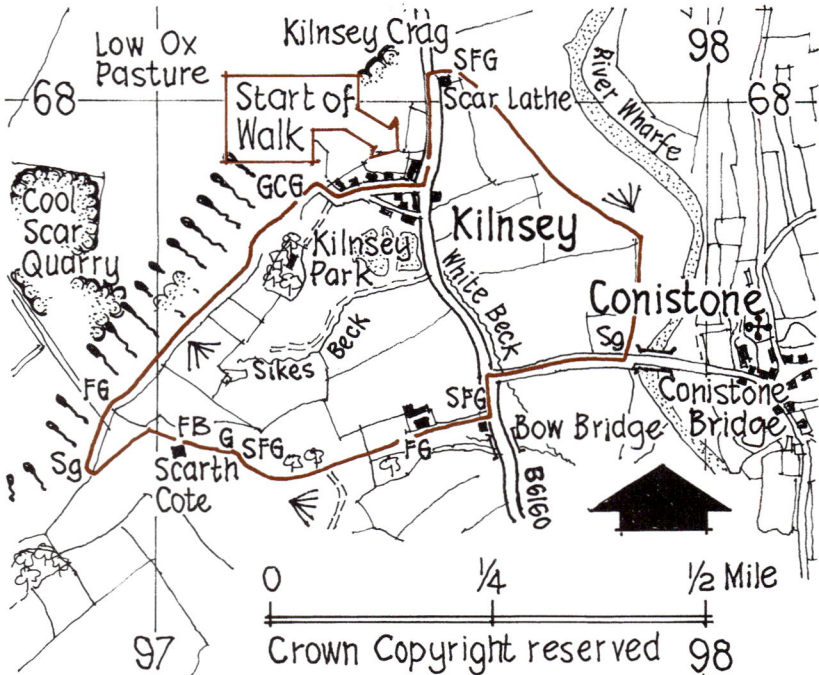

Tennant Arms Hotel and Crag, 1969

At the southern end of the Tennant Arms Hotel turn right up the little lane which is marked near the bus stop with a sign 'Unsuitable for motors'. At the junction with the wider road in the centre of the village bear right.

FOR INFORMATION ON THE BUILDINGS AND OTHER FEATURES TO BE SEEN HERE REFER TO THE CHAPTER DESCRIBING A WALK AROUND KILNSEY VILLAGE.

Where the road starts to climb at the 'S' bend note Kilnsey Old Hall on the right.

At the top of the village pass through the gate to the left of the cattle grid and continue ahead up Mastiles Lane.

This was originally a main road for monastic traffic and was marked by wayside crosses at several points along its length, although today only the bases of some of these crosses remain.

Pause as you come abreast of the trees to the left to look back at the fine view of Kilnsey Village, Kilnsey Park & Trout Farm and beyond, across the valley, Conistone Village and to the left of it Conistone Dib. Further to the right Grass Wood is clearly visible.

Nearby, within the woodland, is located an old property dating from the 17th century originally known as 'Windy Arbour' and now called Hatchery Cottage.

About 1980 Kilnsey Park & Trout Farm was established, which is very well worth a visit. At this time the lakes were dug out utilising a spring which bursts from the limestone producing a spectacular flow of pure crystal-clear water. It is interesting to note that this water supply has been used for various purposes over the centuries. In Medieval times it was used by the monks of Fountains Abbey, who owned Kilnsey Grange, to supply their stew-ponds where they reared their fish. Early in the 20th century it was used to generate electricity for the village before the arrival of the National Grid, and the water turbine stood on the site presently occupied by the trout farm toilets. Many of the local properties still receive their water supply from this spring.

A few yards further on, still alongside the plantation to the left, the road widens out on the right and there is what appears to be a concrete base with a metal pipe embedded in it.

This is where the old production plant and loading bay for Cool Scar Quarry was located until the early 1960s when it was removed inside the works. Hereabouts bird's foot trefoil and wild thyme grow in profusion.

Where the macadamed road bears off to the right up the hill continue ahead on the unsurfaced track, which is the continuation of Mastiles Lane signposted 'Bridleway Malham 5½'.

The surfaced road leads into Cool Scar Quarry, which has been in continuous operation since it started in 1945. It takes its name from a nearby Limestone scar and produces an extremely pure material known as 'Cove Limestone'. It is known as a 'keyhole quarry' since the very narrow entrance largely screens the quarry behind, which was granted planning permission in 1987 for a very limited amount of expansion again for a certain period of time.

Pause here to look at the fine view to the left, where you will see a nice old barn in the bottom of the little valley probably dating from the late 17th century. Behind is Grass Wood and beyond to the right Thorpe and Cracoe fells will be seen.

In the middle, and slightly to the right, you will see a large area of new tree planting.

After passing through a metal gate look out for a recess in the wall to the left some two hundred, or so, yards further on. Here take the gated stile, which has no footpath sign, following a faintly marked grassy path which descends towards the corner of a wall ahead. At the corner of the wall the path turns sharp right descending further to cross an ancient limestone clapper bridge, passing behind some ruins and an old pinfold.

The ancient farm complex known as 'Scarth Cote' dates from Medieval times, formerly belonging to the monks of Fountains Abbey. It comprised two farm houses and a smaller house, and from 1456 until the end of the 17th century these two separate farmhouses were occupied throughout by members of the same two respective families. In 1972 the foundations of these properties were excavated by Arthur Raistrick and the Friends of the Craven Museum in Skipton, when pottery dated between the 14th and 17th centuries was found.

IAN GOLDTHORPE

Hatchery Cottage

Pass through a gate in what appears to be a temporary fence, then cross the line of the new water supply pipeline laid early in 1998 to pass over a stile to the left of a metal gate, continuing ahead on the right-hand side of a stream to follow down the little valley.

The view ahead from this point is very attractive.

Our route soon becomes a well defined grassy path and after a short distance is a clearly defined track as we approach a gate. After passing through the gate the track runs alongside some fairly new farm buildings on the left with an older building behind. The main B6160 road is quickly reached after passing a single storey dwelling on the right known as 'The Bungalow', which was built in the 1930s. Pass over the stile, to the left of the gates which are often locked, turning left along the main road for a few yards, preferably walking on the right-hand side to face the traffic.

The path along which we have just walked has a sign 'FP to Coolscar.'

Turn right at the road junction where there is an array of signposts marked 'St Mary's Church, Pony trekking centre and Conistone $\frac{1}{2}$'. Close to the junction we cross White Beck.

White Beck frequently has a lot of water in it which comes mainly from Sikes Beck, which flows through the Kilnsey Trout Farm with additional water from a series of springs just beyond Kilnsey Crag. This stretch of the road does very occasionally flood. Note the two openings in the wall on the right, before the 'Conistone' sign is encountered, which have been constructed to enable the water on the road to drain back into the river through the field. These are not 'creep' or 'cripple' holes for the sheep.

At the beginning of the bridge take the gated stile on the left marked 'FP to Scar Lathe opposite Kilnsey Crag'.

This stile is unusual in having a specially designed little metal gate with a spring.

FOR INFORMATION ON THE BUILDINGS AND OTHER FEATURES TO BE SEEN IN THE

NEARBY VILLAGE REFER TO THE CHAPTER DESCRIBING A WALK AROUND CONISTONE VILLAGE

Descend the six steps leading on to the footpath, but before continuing ahead look back to view Conistone Bridge.

This very long structure, was all built at the same time being faced in ashlar stonework. It is similar in design to a number of other bridges in the Yorkshire Dales National Park and beyond including Arncliffe and Slaidburn, all of which probably date from the late 18th century. There are three main arches with cutwaters between, together with three smaller subsiduary escape arches. At the eastern end is a bridge of two arches spanning the former course of the river, which was rebuilt in 1816 by Bernard Hartley Senior. The first bridge on this site, which was constructed in timber, was erected in 1190 to give access to and from Fountains Abbey. In 1588 Diana Wade of North Cote gave an oak tree to assist with the rebuilding of the bridge. Note the low floodbank alongside the river. From this section of the walk there are fine views ahead of Kilnsey Crag and to the left of it Kilnsey Village dominated by the cream painted Tennant Arms Hotel.

The path goes in a northerly direction soon running alongside a wall on the left.

The large field through which we are passing is used for the Kilnsey Show on the first Tuesday after each August Bank holiday. It is one of the largest and oldest agricultural shows in Yorkshire and marked its centenary in 1997.

This flat area of the valley was once a glacial lake and in Medieval times reeds for thatching were grown here.

From the corner of this wall the path heads off in a north-westerly direction keeping to the right of the corner of the next wall to pass around the corner of the third wall. Our route now goes on the north side of Scar Lathe to pass over a stile to the right of three gates.

Scar Lathe probably dates from the 18th century.

Turn left on to the B6160 road preferably walking with care on the right-hand side, alongside White Beck, in order to face the oncoming traffic. The starting point at the Tennant Arms Hotel is soon reached.

A Walk Around Arncliffe Village

The name of this village means 'eagle's rock, or cliff' and the settlement is probably of Anglian foundation. Just over half a mile to the south on Blue Scar are the remains of an important Iron Age settlement. In the 14th century, probably on the site of the former Arncliffe Mill, there was a corn mill owned by the canons of Bolton Priory. Wordsworth in his poem 'The White Doe of Rylstone' calls this dale Amerdale, which is still retained in the name 'Amerdale House', now Amerdale House Hotel, and also in the name of the new village hall. From the mid 1600s onwards the Hammond family gradually acquired land in Arncliffe and beyond, as well as in Wharfedale, and there were no heirs to inherit the estate when Mrs Nellie Hammond, the last of the family line, had also inherited an estate in Horton in Ribblesdale, died late in 1954. The estate was left to Major Michael Maude with the request that he incorporated the name 'Hammond' into

his own name which he did. The land and holdings at this time included most of Arncliffe Village although a few buildings had already been sold off including, for instance, the sale of The Falcon and a little later Bridge End House to the Miller family many years earlier. Therefore, in effect, Arncliffe could possibly be described as an 'estate village'.

This walk starts at the piece of spare ground adjoining the river bank on the north side of the road between Arncliffe Bridge and the boundary wall of the Churchyard, where it is possible to park a small number of cars.

Cross the bridge and continue a short distance to the 'T' junction turning left to view the property known as 'Old Cote'.

This fine yeoman farmhouse (1), has a 1650 datestone with the initials 'ISMS' and an interesting staircase turret to the left of the projecting two storey porch. The fine hood mould and

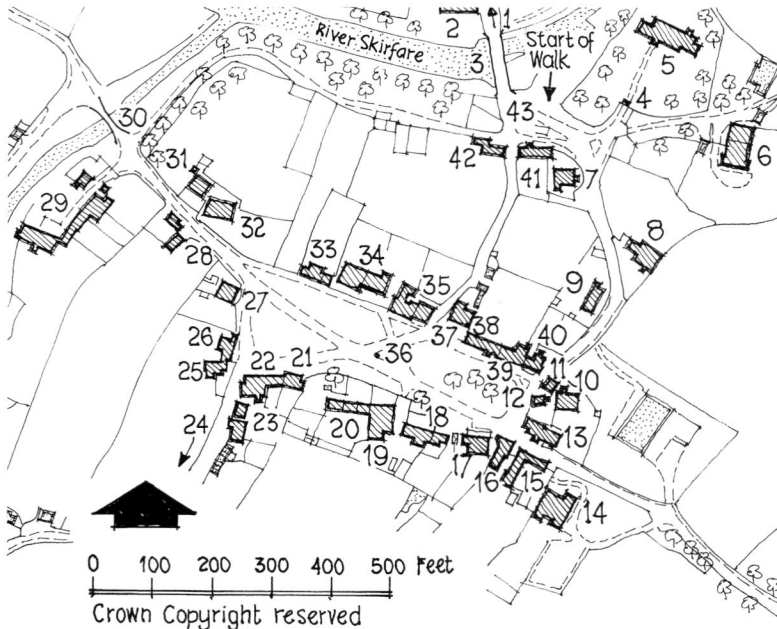

0   100   200   300   400   500 Feet

Crown Copyright reserved

stringcourse to the left extends over two mullioned windows, a four light and a three light. The right-hand extension was probably built in the late 1920s. There is a well weathered finial over the porch and a stepped three light window at first floor level.

Arncliffe Bridge (3), is very similar in design and construction to Conistone Bridge but having two main arches and a smaller arch at the southern end, with cutwaters between, is architecturally in my opinion much more pleasing, being located in a most attractive setting. Faced in ashlar

Old Cote

Now retrace your steps back towards the village. On the right, just before the bridge, is Bridge End House (2).

This building dates from the 17th century and at the far end of the rear elevation, at ground floor level, is the remains of a window from this period. No doubt the fireplace inspired the Rev'd Charles Kingsley when he wrote his famous book 'The Water Babies' but tradition says that Kingsley came to Bridge End and met the woman who was the model for his Mrs-do-as-you-would-be-done-by, and that, at the end when Tom comes to wash himself in the river and go with the water babies, Kingsley visualised the place as the pool in Cowside Beck. The rear windows with their simple mullions are 18th century, but the more precise mullioned windows with hood moulds to the south elevation suggest that this was remodelled somewhere between 1820 and 1840. No doubt the rendering covers up some interesting features! Note the nice iron gates to both the front and rear of this house with a letter 'M' worked into the design, which probably stands for the Miller family. Formerly this was the house where the senior members of the Hammond family lived in their later life.

stonework, it probably dates from the latter part of the 18th century. Hereabouts coltsfoot, the giant bellflower, meadowsweet and sweet cicely are to be found along with some young willow trees beside the river bank.

Bear left at the end of the bridge and left again in a few yards in order to view the Lych Gate and the Church of St Oswald.

The attractive Lych Gate (4), has a plaque high up inside on the left which reads as follows: 'The Lych gate was erected by a former Vicar as a thankoffering for 80 years of Life (1851-1931). Laus Deo'. The 'former Vicar' was Canon W A Shuffrey who wrote several authoritative books about Littondale and the surrounding area.

Roughly halfway along the path to the Church some yards away on the left is the grave of Bishop John Arthur Thomas Robinson, former Bishop of Woolwich, who died on 5th December 1983 and who wrote the book 'Honest to God'. Beyond the seat, in a lower section of the Churchyard near the river, are many of the graves of the Hammond family and also of the Gill family who worked for them over very many years.

Arncliffe Church (5), stands on the site of an earlier church dating from Norman times and a bell given by Prior Whixley of Fountains Abbey, about 1350, indicates that the first church had a tower. All burials originally took place here and there was a corpse way over the fell from Upper Wharfedale. About 1500 the second church was built of which the West Tower is the only remaining part. Except for the tower the Church was completely rebuilt in 1796 and the roof, made from lead from local mines, was replaced by one of slate. When Archdeacon Boyd, who wrote the first part of the book 'Littondale Past and Present', came here as Vicar in 1835 he is said to have been horrified at the ugly 18th century part of the building. Shortly afterwards he set about remodelling the Nave in the Perpendicular style to the designs of John Dobson. The stained glass in the East Window, made by Wailes, was installed in 1847. High up on the left in this window are the Arms of University College, Oxford, who were probably Patrons of the Living at this time since William Boyd was a Junior Fellow of this College. The Nave was further improved about 1840, probably with the Victorian external stone facing being added together with a completely new Chancel. Internally, in the Nave, it is possible to see where the original Georgian windows were located. In addition there is a fine George III painted Coat of Arms dated 1797 and a 15th century Tower Arch. On the right-hand side of the Tower Arch is an illuminated list on the wall of the Amerdale men who were mustered for the Battle of Flodden Field in 1515. Before the present framed copy, which has been very artistically carried out, was placed here, the old list which it has replaced also used to show the daily rate of pay for each man levied. Overall, I think that this is a most pleasing building in a setting surpassing that of almost any other church in the Yorkshire Dales. In the late winter the Churchyard here is a white carpet of snowdrops.

Now retrace your steps back through the Churchyard and the Lych Gate turning left down the drive passing between the stone gateposts, signposted 'FP Hawkswick', in order to view the Old Vicarage (6).

This is a fine building with interesting Palladian windows to the west elevation. It dates from the latter part of the Georgian period, since the box frames are set behind the stone window surrounds being built about 1770 and carefully extended on the south side to match the original building a

century later. There is a plaque on the west elevation of the building with the name 'Tennant' and the date, part of which is missing. On the north side of the drive are the derelict remains of the Coach House of the 19th century vicars, later made into a milking parlour for Mrs Thorman, the last vicar's wife who farmed the glebe land.. A planning application for conversion to residential use has been refused on appeal, but the building may still be used for agricultural purposes. A number of years ago when parishes in the area were amalgamated the Vicarage was put on the market and subsequently carefully restored and divided into two houses the southern section being known as 'Old Vicarage' and the northern section as 'The Vicarage Cottage', both today having an attractive garden.

Now retrace your steps back along the drive bearing left to join the road.

Opposite is a fine building (7), with the date '1894' over the entrance. This was built as the Reading Room which was opened in 1895. After being closed in the late 1950s it was converted into a house now known as 'Glen Holme'.

A little further on to the left is Arncliffe Church of England Primary School (8).

This attractive little building stands on the site of an earlier building and was erected between 1858 and 1860 as the Arncliffe National School. The rather unfortunate flat roofed extension was erected in the late 1960s and this school now serves the whole of Littondale. How nice it would be if the small extension could be faced in its entirety in stone with a low pitched roof covered in either stone flags or slates; perhaps even to mark the Millennium!

Just beyond on the right is Amerdale Hall (9), which is well used for many different social events by the residents of Littondale as a whole. It was built in the 1980s to the designs of Robert Groves and is a good example of a modern building carefully conceived and planned to fit in with the character of the village. It has very thin secondhand slates on the roof.

The north elevation of Carr Farmhouse on the left (10), is very evident ahead dominated by its fine semi-circular headed Regency staircase window, so typical of buildings of this period in the Dales.

IAN GOLDTHORPE

Amerdale House Hotel

However, this property with kneelers and copings to each gable dates from the 17th century and there is evidence of a window from this era on the ground floor at the left-hand end. The south elevation has been refaced in the late 18th or early 19th century with a form of watershot stonework.

The first building fronting on to the road (11), has a 17th century mullioned window at first floor level and probably originally comprised a barn with some living accommodation. Adjoining is a barn (12), adjacent to the front of Carr Farmhouse which was obviously once a dwelling. On its south elevation it has an interesting plaque inscribed 'P' over 'I : S' over '1728'. At first floor level is what has obviously originally been a 17th century two light mullioned window and at ground floor level there is a later three light mullioned window. In my opinion this building dates from a few years earlier than the date on the plaque.

Now leave the Village Green turning left in order to view Amerdale House.

The large barn on the corner of the road (13), which has a fine projecting porch on its south elevation, probably dates from very early in the 18th century.

Amerdale House (14), is the substantial square block a few yards further on the right with an attractive garden to the east. This is the house where members of the Hammond family lived until 1954, comprising the original property at the rear dating from the late 18th century with a new Victorian front which they added in 1872. There is a very fine semi-circular headed Regency staircase window to the west elevation. Although the house is said to date back to Elizabethan times there is no evidence of this in the present structure, the stone vaulted cellars only dating from the 18th century.

We now retrace our steps back into the Village Green in order to view the buildings which surround it.

Immediately to the west of Amerdale House is a fine range of buildings (15), again dating from the latter part of the 18th century. Note the interesting ribbed surrounds to some of the windows.

The first building fronting on to the Green is Mitton Cottage (16), which probably dates from the 17th century since there is evidence of an earlier opening at the west end of the front elevation, and also a blocked up opening in the west gable wall. Elm House (17), is a good

149

example of the use of watershot masonry, having an attractive projecting porch with two nice corbels, the property dating from the late 18th or early 19th century.

Beyond is a block of property comprising a cottage and, adjoining it to the west Castle Farmhouse (18), dating from the late 17th century. The entrance doorway dates from this period and the window at first floor level and slightly to the right has obviously at one time been a two light mullioned window, now with a Georgian window inserted which has probably lost some of its glazing bars over the years. To the right of the entrance at ground floor level is a three light 18th century mullioned window, and the other windows appear to date from the late 18th century. Note the tree in front of this block of property which was planted to mark the Silver Jubilee of Her Majesty Queen Elizabeth II June 1977.

Following westwards along the south side of the Village Green we now come to Castle Barn (19).

This fairly large building appears to date from the latter part of the 18th century possessing some nice stone quoins and two circular forking holes at an upper level. However, at ground floor level windows with concrete surrounds have been added in much later times. The adjoining cottages and barn known as 'Castle Yard' (20), appear to date from the late 17th century since the window openings once formed mullioned windows with Georgian windows inserted later, and there is a Victorian vertical siding sash window in the opening to the left of the entrance to cottage No 2. The cottage adjoining The Falcon known as 'Ferndale' (21), probably dates from the late 17th century since there is evidence of some blocked up windows and some very small windows, which help to confirm its antiquity. The lean-to portion at the front is a much later addition.

Adjoining is The Falcon (22), which was at one time known as 'The Leg of Mutton'. This building appears to date from the latter part of the 18th century having a fine semi-circular headed staircase window in its east elevation. However, it has obviously been much altered in Victorian times, the front door being a fine example from this period.

Now walk down the lane at the side of The Falcon.

Immediately to the rear is a property known as 'West View' (23), which dates from the latter part of the 17th century, the almost adjoining property beyond being slightly later dating from the early 18th century.

Continue two hundred yards, or so, further along what soon becomes a rather grassy lane passing the telephone exchange to view Botany End (24). This building originally comprised a group of mill cottages dating from Regency times, which was converted into one dwelling in the 1920s, probably by Arnold Pace, a York architect. The end result is, I think, quite fascinating.

Now retrace your steps back to the Village Green.

The barn to the left (25), adjacent to the west gable of the Falcon and where the gents toilet is located, probably dates from the late 17th or early 18th century. Adjoining is High Green Cottage (26), which is probably of a similar date. Prospect House (27), located at the road junction has a fine view down the Village Green. It dates from the late 18th century having fine stone quoins and a stringcourse below the first floor windows to the front elevation which also has watershot stonework. The mouldings to the front door and the shutters inside the front windows are Georgian in design.

Turn left leaving the Village Green.

Green Farm Cottage and the attached barn on the left (28), probably date from the second half of the 17th century. There is a finial to the south east gable and the elevation fronting on to the road has an interesting stepped projecting chimney stack; also there is evidence of some blocked up windows. Note especially the enormous stone quoins.

On the left just before the bridge is an interesting group of buildings (29).

The long two storey building to the rear, extending almost to Cowside Beck and today a dwelling known as 'The Mill', as mentioned previously probably stands on the site of a much earlier corn mill. The present structure is all that remains of the former Arncliffe Mill, which was actually five storeys in height on one elevation and was built in the late 18th century. In the 1820s it changed from a woollen mill to a cotton spinning mill and cloth was woven here until the late 19th century, when largely on account of transport difficulties the business was transferred to Colne. The cottage on the right of the entrance drive known as 'The Gatehouse', which still has the old entrance for waggons to pass through visible on the front wall, with its copings and kneelers could date back as far as the late 17th century. The properties on the left including Mill Holme were probably built as mill cottages. The little building on the left, nearest to the road, is of particular interest and may date from the 17th century.

A few yards beyond is the old single arched bridge (30), which spans Cowside Beck. This is a most beautiful structure and Harry Gill (1865-1947) said in his notebook that it was built by the Petty family, financed by Mr Hammond, Mr Johnson and Mr (later Archdeacon) Boyd.

Now retrace your steps back towards the Village Green.

The first building on the left is Green Farm Barn (31), which probably dates from the mid 18th century although the steps and entrance at first floor level are very much later. Green Farmhouse (32), has an inscription over the front entrance 'T' over 'M:I:1730' most likely again referring to a member of the Tennant family. This building has an especially interesting range of 18th century tall two light mullioned windows with transoms on its south elevation. In the east end of the high garden wall is an interesting arched entrance with a rather nicely designed door, probably dating from the late 18th century.

The first building facing the Village Green is Blue Scar Farm (33), formerly known as 'Rose Cottage', which dates from the 17th or early 18th century, since there is evidence of early window surrounds which are probably part of previous mullioned windows. The windows now comprise modern frames based upon earlier Georgian designs. The east end gable wall of this building could have been raised and it may, therefore, have been an earlier cruck building. This cottage was for many years occupied by John Jowett, a shoemaker, who died in 1906 and was a member of the church choir for the whole of his married life. His family continued the same business here until the 1940s.

High Rylands (34), was built in 1871 by Mr Johnston of Eshton House on the site of an older house which stood further back and which he pulled down. The front doorway, inside the porch, appears to date from the 18th century and over the door on the rear elevation is a lintel inscribed what appears to be '1629 IS : '; these may both have been salvaged from the earlier building. There is a nice semi-circular headed staircase window over the doorway on the north elevation. The keystone to the archway of the adjoining Stable, or Coach House, is inscribed 'TMJ 1871'. The low iron railings which surmounted the stone wall in front of the main house have been removed, probably during the Second World War, although a fairly simply designed iron gate still remains. The very nicely designed railings and gate in front of the Coach House are probably fairly new, but fit in extrememly well with the overall character of the village.

The Old Pump

The next two cottages adjoining the little lane (35), known as 'Low Rylands', are probably late 17th century remodelled in the 18th century. There is evidence of shutters to the inside of the windows dating from the Georgian period. The simple entrance doorway to the left-hand cottage has a small moulded cornice above supported by a tiny corbel at each end. Before he rebuilt High Rylands Mr Johnston owned these two cottages, one of which was used as a shooting box, and there was a stable and coach house behind. Mr Johnston used to shoot with Mr Hammond every August. Later this property was used as the Schoolmaster's House.

Nearby on the Village Green is the Old Pump (36), which probably dates from the late 18th century, although it has some early 19th century characteristics and still contains some of the original mechanism. During the Second World War it had a wide white band painted around it fairly low down, so that it could be more easily seen by the traffic with its dimmed headlights at night in the intense darkness. How nice it would be if this delightful feature in the middle of this beautiful Village Green could be restored in time to mark the Millennium. Perhaps, at least, a new handle and spout to match the original design could be put back and, of course, if it could pump water again so much the better!

The fine house at the right of the little lane known as 'Lane Top' (37), is in my opinion by far the most attractive building overlooking the Village green. In the tympanum above the delightful entrance doorway is the date '1736', but the remainder of the inscription has weathered rather badly apart from a letter 'T' which is still decipherable. However, the property with its kneelers and copings could date back to the 17th century and doubtless the rendering to the front elevation may be hiding some useful clues!

The next rather long building comprising a barn and a shippon (38), has a plaque over one of the doorways inscribed '1677' over the initials 'TFA', and has an interesting porch. Adjoining is the Post Office building (39), which probably dates from the 17th century since there is evidence of an earlier blocked up opening on the front elevation at ground floor level. Plane Tree Cottage (40), probably dates from the late 18th century and it was at one time occupied by a Mr Peacock who had a very large family of nineteen. Some years earlier it was a joiner's shop with a saw pit located on the Green outside.

Now retrace your steps back to Lane Top turning right into the narrow winding lane.

Soon ahead you will get a glimpse over the wall of Buck Laithe (41), a former barn probably dating from the late 17th or early 18th century. It was attractively converted into a dwelling house to the designs of Howard Riley in the early 1990s. On the left at the end of this little lane is Smithy Cottage (42), which appears to date from the early part of the 18th century. It has an interesting projecting flag porch over its entrance and the projecting portion at the western end was the original smithy.

The final point of interest on this walk is what appears to be a small partly walled garden (43), on an island of land on the north side of Buck Laithe. This was the village Pinfold, or Pound, where stray animals were kept until claimed by their owners, and it would be here before many of the stone walls in the area were built.

Lane Top

Cross the road back to the starting point.

Ramble No 10

From Arncliffe to Kettlewell over Middlesmoor Pasture
then passing Gate Cote Scar to Hawkswick, returning
along riverside footpath

STARTING POINT: This walk starts at the piece of spare ground adjoining the river bank on the north side of the road between Arncliffe Bridge and the boundary wall of the Churchyard, where it is possible to park a small number of cars.

DISTANCE: Approximately six and a half miles.

TIME REQUIRED: Four and a half hours, but extra time should be allowed if you are going to look at the buildings and other features in Arncliffe Village on the first part of the walk, and similarly the buildings and other features in both Kettlewell and Hawkswick villages.

TERRAIN: This is the most difficult and strenuous of all the walks described in this book, and should only be attempted by ramblers who are fully equipped and have had previous experience of walking on the fells. The first part of the path climbs very steeply and extreme care should be taken on the limestone rocks at all times, and especially in either wet or icy weather. The remainder of the route up to the summit on the boundary of Middlesmoor Pasture is a long steady uphill path followed by a similar descent down into Kettlewell, the last part being especially steep. The path from Kettlewell to Hawkswick involves a long steady climb up to its summit followed by a delightful grassy path leading down into Hawkswick. The largely flat route back to Arncliffe alongside the River Skirfare has many delightful sections.

Attractive features of this walk are the superb and very extensive views, not only of Upper Wharfedale and Littondale, but far beyond and for this reason a fine clear day should be chosen if at all possible.

Cross the bridge taking the footpath at the end on the right marked 'FP to Kettlewell' passing through a gated stile.

FOR INFORMATION ON THE BUILDINGS AND OTHER FEATURES TO BE SEEN HERE REFER TO THE CHAPTER DESCRIBING A WALK AROUND ARNCLIFFE VILLAGE.

Note Bridge End House on the other side of the road whose fireplace is thought to have inspired the Rev'd Charles Kingsley when he wrote his famous book 'The Water Babies'.

From this path, especially in the winter months, there is a fine view of the West Tower of Arncliffe Church which is built in the Perpendicular style of architecture. Note that ramblers are requested to keep to the wallside since this meadowland provides winter food for stock.

At the end of this short path climb up the nine steps and pass through the gated stile. Cross the road and continue on the path signposted 'FP Kettlewell' passing through another gated stile.

Arncliffe Church

The barn on the hillside to the left probably dates from the 18th century. As you approach the next stile note the two 'creep' or 'cripple' holes, one of which is partly blocked up, allowing sheep and lambs to pass from one side of the wall to the other without larger animals being able to do so.

Pass through the stile noting the remains of an older stile to the right. The path now starts to climb steeply and we quickly reach the fine trees of the outlying woodland which are mainly ash.

Pause here and look back towards Arncliffe, of

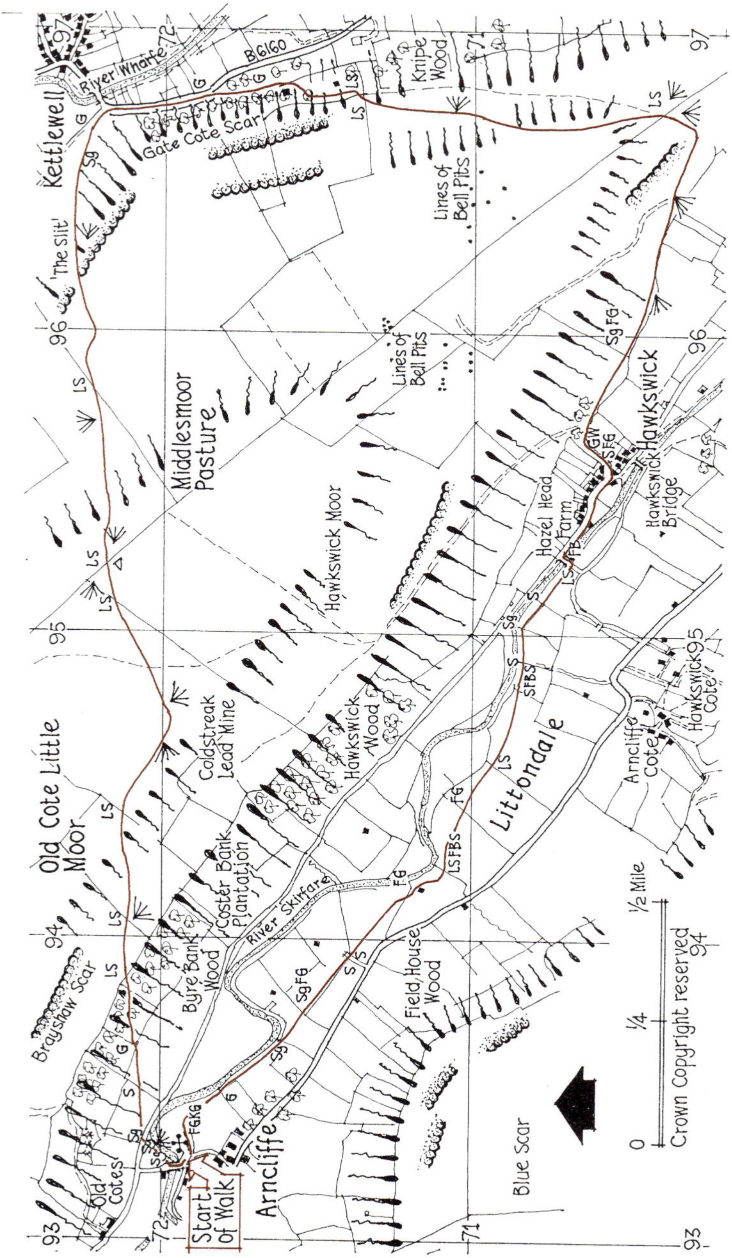

Kettlewell

River Wharfe

B6160

Knipe Wood

Gate Cote Scar

'The slit'

Lines of Bell Pits

Middlesmoor Pasture

Lines of Bell Pits

Hawkswick

Hawkswick Moor

Hazel Head Farm

Hawkswick Bridge

Coldstreak Lead Mine

Old Cote Little Moor

Hawkswick Wood

Littondale

Hawkswick Cote

Arncliffe Cote

Coster Bank Plantation

Byre Bank Wood

River Skirfare

Braishaw Scar

Field House Wood

Blue Scar

Old Cotes

Start of Walk

Arncliffe

0   ¼   ½ Mile

Crown Copyright reserved

which little can yet be seen due to its wooded setting, and behind can clearly be seen the steep road zigzagging up hill to Darnbrook and Malham Tarn. Note the lines of earlier roads in the grass to the left.

At the edge of the woodland we pass through a gate in a fence. The path through the trees is fairly easy to follow and as it becomes rocky it turns sharply round to the left climbing steeply up to a ladder stile at the top edge of the wood. After crossing the ladder stile the path goes off to the right soon bearing slightly round to the left to climb the hill, and after crossing a small stream climbs more steeply to cross another ladder stile.

Here note the fine view down Littondale with Simon's Seat just peeping up on the extreme left and, over to the right, the long range comprising Burnsall, Thorpe, Cracoe and Rylstone fells. On reaching the heather pause again to look at the fine view, both up and down the valley, and what will probably be the last glimpse of Arncliffe Village now far below. Pause again at the footpath sign since here we are partly on the gritstone and partly on the limestone. The Old Cote Moor range which we are crossing is essentially limestone with a gritstone capping.

The path soon passes through a gap in a rather decrepit wall and continues ahead over the moor towards a signpost on the skyline.

On the next section of path there are the remains of what appears to have been a short section of wall on the left and a long heap of stones a few yards along on the right. If you look across from the heap of stones to the caravan site at Hawkswick Cote across the valley, in between on the hillside you will see the remains of Cold Streak Lead Mine. Lead was mined in this area from as early as 1692 until the middle of the 19th century.

At the footpath sign pause again to look back at the superb view of Littondale. The path now bears left up the hillside and the top of the next ladder stile can just be seen on the skyline.

Looking back from this point on a clear day it is possible to see, on the distant moors to the right of Rylstone Fell, the windmills at the Wind Farm

on Ovenden Moor near Halifax.

The path soon becomes rather boggy.

On the left are the remains of a sink hole. At the time I last did this walk, in August, there were a lot of individual yellow flowers in the very wet sections which may be marsh fleawort, although I understand that this is a fairly rare plant!

After crossing the next ladder stile the path veers away from the wall on the left to the ladder stile on the summit of the ramble, which is 1,600ft (490m) above sea level. Note the old worn stone stile to the

New Bridge at Kettlewell

left. Pause here to admire the fine view in each direction.

Ahead is Great Whernside 2,310ft (704m) above sea level. Looking along the top of the wall to the right Simon's Seat 1,544ft (485m) comes into view. Further right looking down Wharfedale Ilkley Moor will be seen, and still further right Grass and Bastow woods appear in the bottom of the valley dominated by the long range of Burnsall, Thorpe, Cracoe and Rylstone fells. Beyond are the distant moors in the Haworth area. Looking now due west the long high ridge of Fountains Fell 2,191ft (662m) is easily picked out, being so named since all that vast area of wild moorland originally belonged to the monks of Fountains Abbey. Plover Hill 2,231ft (680m), being the northern end of the Pen-y-ghent Range, appears beyond. Going·further right, at the head of Littondale, Whernside 2,419ft (736m) which is now Yorkshire's highest mountain will be seen, since Mickle Fell which formerly had this distinction was moved into County Durham in 1974 at the time of local government reorganisation. Looking north-westwards along the line of the wall is Old Cote Moor Top 1,991ft (607m) and across Upper Wharfedale, almost due north, is Buckden Pike 2,302ft (702m). Between Buckden Pike and Great Whernside the ancient Tor Dike can just be picked out on the skyline, so altogether quite a panorama!

After crossing the ladder stile the path gradually descends.

Soon Starbotton and Kettlewell villages come into view far below. Looking down towards Starbotton you will soon see the remains of some lead mine workings.

We soon cross a low limestone escarpment and the path then traverses a fairly boggy section of ground leading on to a nice grassy green path. Our route now descends more steeply.

Note here the superb views looking up Wharfedale, being a fine example of a 'U' shaped glacial valley with a very flat bottom! Pause at the top of the next limestone escarpment to admire the fine view of Kettlewell below.

Pass through the narrow little rocky limestone gorge, known as 'The Slit', with great care and then follow the steep path down to a gated stile. At the footpath sign bear right on to the bridleway soon passing through a gate leading on to the road.

FOR INFORMATION ON THE BUILDINGS

AND OTHER FEATURES TO BE SEEN HERE REFER TO THE CHAPTER DESCRIBING A WALK AROUND KETTLEWELL VILLAGE.

Bear right on to the main B6160 road.

Note the seat at the back of the little green with its own little concrete bridge, inscribed 'In loving memory of Verney Stott and his wife Dorothy'.

In two hundred yards, or so, leave the road taking the footpath on the right signposted 'FP Hawkswick 2m'. In a few yards leave the grassy track that goes straight ahead to a disued quarry, instead bearing right at the footpath sign where the path starts to climb steeply. Where the paths split it is better to take the higher one, both being quite good and joining a little further on. Pass through the next gate and continue ahead steadily climbing. Eventually the path leaves the woodland and climbs steeply around an 'S' bend past a ruined building, then going through a gap in a wall to continue its steep climb alongside the woodland on the right. At the top of the woodland the path goes through an opening in another wall, to the left of a ladder stile, and climbs steeply to a further ladder stile below the southern end of Gate Cote Scar. The path continues to climb steeply zigzagging past a cairn and across the limestone escarpment. From the next section of the path there are fine

GOLDTHORPE

A quiet corner of Hawkswick

views across the valley of Scargill House.

This now famous Christian Conference and Holiday Centre has been modelled upon Lee Abbey in North Devon. Originally a country house, which still survives in the centre of this fine complex and whose last owner had a biplane which he landed on the flat grassy area between the limestone escarpments, above and to the right of the buildings. This Centre was the inspiration of a few dedicated Christians, including Dr Donald Coggan then Bishop of Bradford, in the mid 1950s. When the property came on the market they very quickly raised enough money to purchase the house and immediate grounds deep in the hill country of what was once part of the ancient Kingdom of Northumbria. Here in former times the Brigantes tribes defended their homesteads and clashed with the Roman invaders. Later the Anglo-Saxon farmers brought their skills and their language, their customs and their culture and centuries later, in another generation, the rugged lead miners toiled and helped to add many stone cottages to the delightful friendly villages set in outstanding countryside that we see today.

The building work to adapt the original house for its new use was started in 1958 and the Official Opening took place in June 1959. Scargill House is run by a dedicated Christian Community and it is a most moving and memorable experience to take part in a service in the famous Chapel which together with the rest of the scheme was designed by the well-known architect, George Pace of York. The Chapel, which is architecturally one of the finest buildings erected in the whole of Britain in the 1950s and 60s was listed as a Building of Special Architectural or Historic Interest by English Heritage in 1998.

After continuing on a long grassy path which steadily climbs we reach the ladder stile on the summit of this part of the ramble.

Note the older stile to the right.

Pause here to look at the fine view and note the sign which reads as follows: 'Please refrain from rolling stones down the hillside. This causes damage to people, livestock and property. Please keep to the footpath and keep dogs under control'.

As the path descends Hawkswick Village soon comes into view and there are fine aspects back down Wharfedale with Grass and Bastow woods and behind Burnsall, Thorpe, Cracoe and Rylstone fells and ahead fine views up Littondale. Just beyond a short setted and paved section of the path a green track goes off to the right.

This gave access to the old Bell Pit lead mines which operated in the 17th century. Note how deep this track has been cut into the hillside due to heavy traffic continually wearing away the road surface.

After a long grassy descent with superb views of Hawkswick and Littondale beyond we pass through a gated stile to the left of a field gate. As we approach the village there are some fine ash trees on the left and more ash trees on the right as our path becomes a walled lane. At the end on the right is a fine sycamore tree. Now pass through a gateway.

Note the small oak tree on the left with a notice worded 'This tree was provided by the National Park Authority and planted by the Parish Meeting in 1994 to Commemorate: Centenary of the establishment of Civil Parishes 40th Anniversary of the Yorkshire Dales National Park'.

A short distance further on cross over a stile to the left of a field gate, turning right into the village.

FOR INFORMATION ON THE BUILDINGS AND OTHER FEATURES TO BE SEEN HERE REFER TO THE CHAPTER DESCRIBING A WALK AROUND HAWKSWICK VILLAGE.

About one hundred yards beyond the village cross the footbridge signposted 'FP Arncliffe $1\frac{1}{2}$'.

Note the large square cantilevered slab of slate, just before the bridge, which supported an earlier footbridge which went diagonally across the river, having a centre support which rested on the large block of limestone in the middle of the River Skirfare.

At the end of the bridge turn right back towards the edge of the river to cross the ladder stile continuing alongside the river. The first section of the path is fenced and after crossing a stile the path follows

alongside the river crossing a series of stiles and a footbridge eventually veering away from the river and entering a very large meadow, which has a more recent post and wire fence dividing it. After passing through a field gate in this fence we come near to the river again crossing a ladder stile, a footbridge and another stile abreast of a barn across the road to the left.

This barn probably dates from the 18th century.

The path now passes a barn to the left to go through a field gate to the right.

This nice barn with a lean-to northerly section again appears to date from the 18th century. On the hillside to the right again can be seen the remains of the Cold Streak Lead Mine.

The path now goes leftwards across the meadow to pass through two very old stiles at the end of a short overgrown walled lane which may, at one time, have given access to the fine 18th century barn in the field to the right.

Note how the next section of the path has been raised up alongside the wall to the left and there is evidence of limestone in the grass, probably indicating that this was once the line of an earlier road, possibly the continuation of the walled lane.

Cross over the gated stile to the left of a field gate, where the path can be muddy at times. The path now bears slightly right towards a signpost at the beginning of a wooded section of the river crossing a gated stile.

The final section of the path which climbs quite high above the river is very beautiful. Before the next gate note the young aspen trees alongside the river bank.

After passing through the gate and crossing a meadow we pass through a kissing gate to the right of a field gate, then along the drive leading from the Old Vicarage back to the starting point.

A Walk Around Hawkswick Village

In the Domesday Book this village is named 'Hocheswic', which probably means Hauk's hamlet or farm. Other possibilities are that it could be so called on account of the hawks which originally infested the limestone cliffs in the district, or after a Viking adventurer who established himself here and gave the place his name. A further likelihood may be that it was derived from the German word 'hoch', being descriptive of the elevated nature of the site. As far back as the 13th century lead was dug on the nearby moors and fells and at the height of the lead mining era there were about forty dwellings in the village. In 1652 Hawkswick formed part of a forfeited estate and was purchased by Lord Lowther from William Middleton of Stockhead. At one time the Quakers are said to have had a secret printing press in this village.

This walk starts towards the southern end of the village on the opposite side of the road near a garden between Riverside Barn and Redmire, where there is a rough piece of ground suitable for the parking of about three cars.

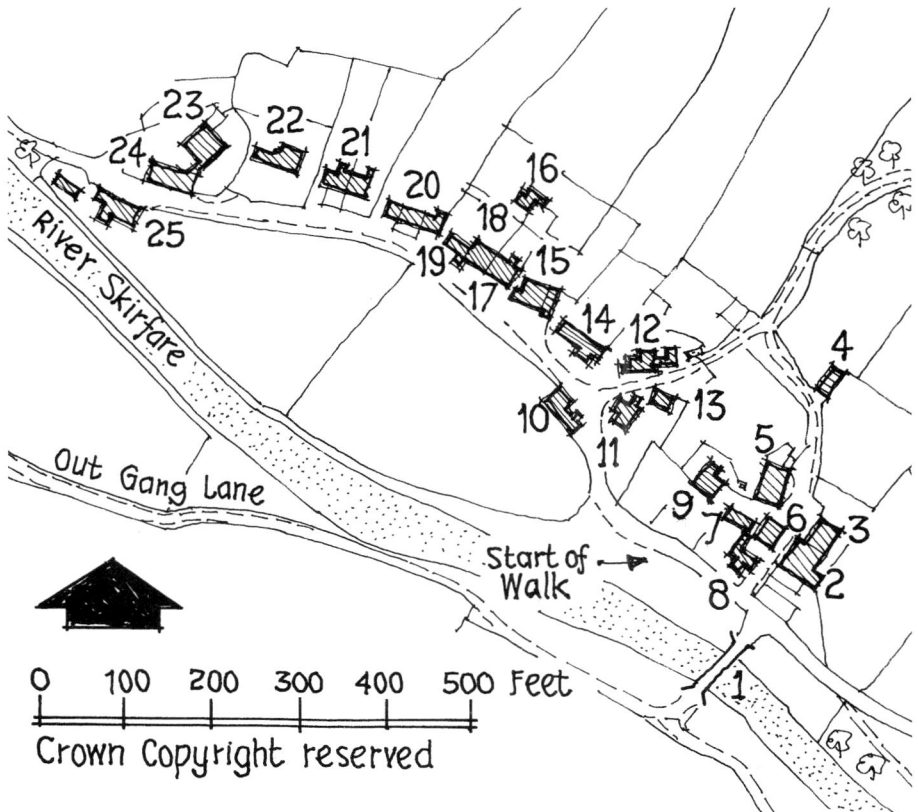

River Skirfare

Out Gang Lane

Start of Walk

0   100   200   300   400   500 Feet

Crown Copyright reserved

Walk a few yards along the road in a south-easterly direction turning right into Out Gang Lane in order to view the bridge (1).

There was a bridge over the River Skirfare at Hawkswick as early as 1175 but it may not have been in this location and would probably have been constructed in timber. The present structure dates from the early part of the 18th century and replaced a ford across the river at this point. This bridge is especially notable for having one of the widest carriageways amongst single span bridges in Yorkshire. However, the bridge over the River Ure at Aysgarth is a little wider and may well qualify for this title! Note the distinctive fluted coping stones to the parapets, which probably date from the early 19th century and may be the work of either Alexander Nowell or Bernard Hartley Senior. Hereabouts many wild flowers are to be found including coltsfoot, hairy willowherb, goat's beard, meadowsweet, spear-plume thistle and sweet cicely.

Now retrace your steps back to the main street turning left and immediately right into the unsurfaced lane.

A few yards along on the right is Old Hall Barn (2), which probably dates from the late 17th or very early 18th century and has been largely converted into residential use in more recent times, still retaining many interesting features.

Beyond, and adjoining, is Thackholme Farmhouse (3), which has inscribed on the lintel to the doorway on the north-east elevation 'I.T. 1788', which doubtless refers to a member of the Tennant family. There are some interesting 18th century three light stepped mullioned windows to the south-east elevation which were probably installed in 1788, although the building with its copings and kneelers to each gable may well go back as far as the mid 17th century.

The barn further along the lane, beyond the gate (4), probably dates from the middle of the 18th century and in my opinion the other nearby barns on the left of this little lane, namely nos (5), (6) and (7), although altered over the years, probably also date from the same period.

Now return to the main street turning right.

On the corner is Low Barn (8), which dates from the 18th century and was converted into a house about 1990 by David Claughton, a Grassington builder. Beyond is a property known as 'Redmire' (9), having some simple three light mullioned windows to the front elevation and most likely dating from the early part of the 18th century.

The road bears round to the right and on the left is an old building in a rather derelict state.

This is known as 'Frances Barn' (10), and probably dates from the 18th century. It is shortly to be converted into a dwelling to the designs of Robert Groves. Opposite is another barn (11), which appears to date from the 18th century and was nicely converted into a dwelling by Michael Critchley. It bears a datestone high up on the south gable wall inscribed 'Riverside Barn Rebuilt 1995'.

Now walk up the little lane to the right with a signpost 'FP Kettlewell'.

On the left is Strand House and adjoining it a barn now converted into an extension to the house (12), both dating from the 17th century. In the original house there is evidence of a two light mullioned window at first floor level dating from this period. At ground floor level there are two three light 18th century mullioned windows and an interesting little projecting porch comprising two stone flags, this latter being a characteristic of many buildings in Littondale. In the left-hand end of the barn there is evidence of what has originally been a two light 17th century mullioned window at both ground and first floor level, indicating that the barn probably contained some residential accommodation for a farm worker right from the time it was built. Internally the house possesses a 17th century fireplace with joggled voussoirs and a beehive oven.

Across the lane is the rear elevation of the property known as 'Riverside' (13), which probably dates from the latter part of the 18th century.

Now retrace your steps back down the lane bearing right.

The next property is Manby Barn (14), which is a delightful building dating from the 17th century. It obviously started its life as a smaller barn with a lean-to portion at the front, and was a few years later extended at each end. There are two nice

Manby Barn

17th century doorways and a superb stepped three light mullioned window with segmental arches at first floor level at the northerly end. The whole was most sensitively converted into a dwelling house to the designs of Barry Rawson about 1990.

Beyond is a building known as 'The Cottage' (15), which has a datestone over the front door inscribed 'B+T 1864'. This property appears to date from the 18th century and the front windows may have been altered in 1864. On the rear elevation is a nice semi-circular headed staircase window which probably dates from Regency times.

Now walk up the little lane at the westerly end of The Cottage.

At the top of this lane on the left is a property known as 'The Field House' (16). This was originally a barn dating from the 18th century. It was converted into a dwelling in the early 1940s and much of the building work was carried out by Italian prisoners of war who were billeted in The Bailey at Skipton. They built the monopitched single storey extension. Faintly scratched into the lintel over the doorway in the extension appears to be 'P.O.W. 1945' and underneath four names which, sadly, it is now impossible to decipher with any certainty.

Now retrace your steps back down to the main street turning right.

The first property is Borrins Cottage (17), which

probably dates from the 18th century and Borrins House (18), which adjoins it is older since there is evidence of 17th century mullioned windows to the rear. Both of these properties have attractive little projecting porches comprising two stone flags.

The adjoining barn (19), which has been nicely converted into a dwelling in recent times probably dates from the 18th century. The village post box is located here. Beyond is a pair of houses, now converted into one property known as 'Privet Cottage' (20), which may date from the 17th century since there is evidence at the eastern end of two small blocked up openings from earlier times, but it has been extensively altered in the 18th century. A small extension and a lean-to garage were very carefully added at the western end in the early 1990s.

Beyond are two properties known as 'Garris Cottage' and 'Garris House' (21), which appear to date from late in the 18th century. Garris Cottage has a nice Victorian door and an interesting small moulded cornice over the doorway.

Set in an attractive garden behind a high wall is Croft House (22), which probably dates from the mid 17th century, possessing on its south elevation one two light mullioned window and a number of similar three and four light windows. The rendering may hide some more interesting features!

Croft House

Beyond, facing down the village street and approached by steps and a fine gateway, is Hazel Head Farmhouse (23), which was rebuilt by Thomas Tennant after a disastrous fire. It has a datestone over the front door inscribed 'T.T. 1839'. The front elevation is extremely fine being faced in ashlar stonework with nice moulded Georgian styled surrounds to the windows, together with two stringcourses, one below the ground floor windows and one below the first floor windows. Internally there are some fine Georgian doors which may have been salvaged from the earlier house. The adjoining barn, fronting on to the road (24), has kneelers and a coping at the western end, and a datestone high up in the gable wall inscribed 'TT 1839'. In the early 1990s this building was converted into two dwellings known as 'Hawksnest' and 'Holme Barn' to the designs of Andrew Howcroft.

Opposite is a very fine building which was originally the Tennant's Coach House (25). Over the delightful entrance is a datestone inscribed 'T.T. 1840'. For many years the upper floor in this building was used for dances by the people who lived locally and, therefore, when it was converted into a dwelling house in the early 1990s to the designs of Robert Groves, the new owners quite appropriately decided to call it 'The Ballroom'. The garage immediately to the west was built at the same time as the other alterations were carried out.

Now retrace your steps back to the starting point at the eastern end of the village.

How nice it would be if this little rather untidy area, where visitors frequently park their cars, could be tidied up and made more attractive in quite a simple way. Perhaps chippings could be used to define the parking area, with boulders to mark the boundary and the planting of a few trees and shrubs would greatly enhance the locality entailing only moderate expenditure. No doubt this could be done by the local people who live in this most attractive village to celebrate the Millennium!

A Walk Around Kettlewell Village

The earliest record of Kettlewell is in the Domesday Survey of 1086 where the name is given as Ketelwell. The name is Anglian cetel wella, meaning 'a bubbling spring or stream in a deep valley'. In 1320 Kettlewell was granted a Charter in order that a market could be held each Thursday and so in a sense Kettlewell, like Grassington, could be described as a small town, its appearance in parts being much more urban in character than the other villages described in this book. At the time Kettlewell was granted its Charter it was divided into two manors, one of which belonged to Coverham Abbey and the other to the Earl of Westmorland. First, in 1534 the Dissolution of the Monasteries began, and the Coverham Abbey estates passed into the hands of the Crown. A generation later due to the Earl of Westmorland and his family, the Nevilles, being involved in the Rising of the North their estates were forfeited to the Crown in 1569. In 1628, Charles I granted the Manor to four London citizens, who in 1656 sold it to eight local residents who became known as the 'Trust Lords of Kettlewell'. This group, acting as trustees, then sold off the various properties to the tenants who became the first freeholders. It is interesting to note that many of the smaller buildings were used as miners' cottages in the 19th century and in 1838 there were five inns.

This walk starts at the National Park car park. On leaving the car park turn right for a few yards and on the opposite side of the road take the footpath signposted 'FP Lovers Lane & Stepping Stones', descending the seven steps in order to view the bridge known as 'New Bridge'(1).

This bridge is so named because the older downstream section, which has a fine set of masons' marks to be found upon it, was built in 1605 when the road high up on the west bank of the river replaced the original low level road known as 'Hawkswick Head Lane'. It was widened, probably in the late 18th century, about the same time as Grassington Bridge was increased in width roughly doubling its breadth.

Now retrace your steps back to the Garage (2).

Kettlewell Garage was largely rebuilt in the 1960s using interesting concrete blocks cast with pieces of limestone embedded in them, a type of block first developed by a small firm in the Peak District many years ago.

Note the block of five old toilets and small adjoining barn (3), across the road, probably dating from the early 19th century. The first block of cottages including The Cottage Tea Room (4), dates in the main from the 19th century but the tea room is much more recent dating from the 20th century. Adjoining is Dale House Hotel (5), which dates from Edwardian times and for many years was used as an annexe for accommodation for the Bluebell Hotel.

Cliff Cottage and the adjoining cottage (6), date back to the 18th century. Cliff Cottage has some watershot stonework to its front elevation and has carved in the lintel over the left-hand ground floor window the date '1864' and the initials 'GPT' in the lintel over the front door. The adjoining cottage has been rendered, probably in the 19th century and the garage at the east end is a very recent addition.

Continue ahead crossing Townfoot Bridge.

This bridge (7), is a most attractive little structure having similarities with Arncliffe and other Dales bridges and I would think dates from the latter part of the 18th century.

Nearby is The Racehorses Hotel (8). This large

Townfoot Bridge

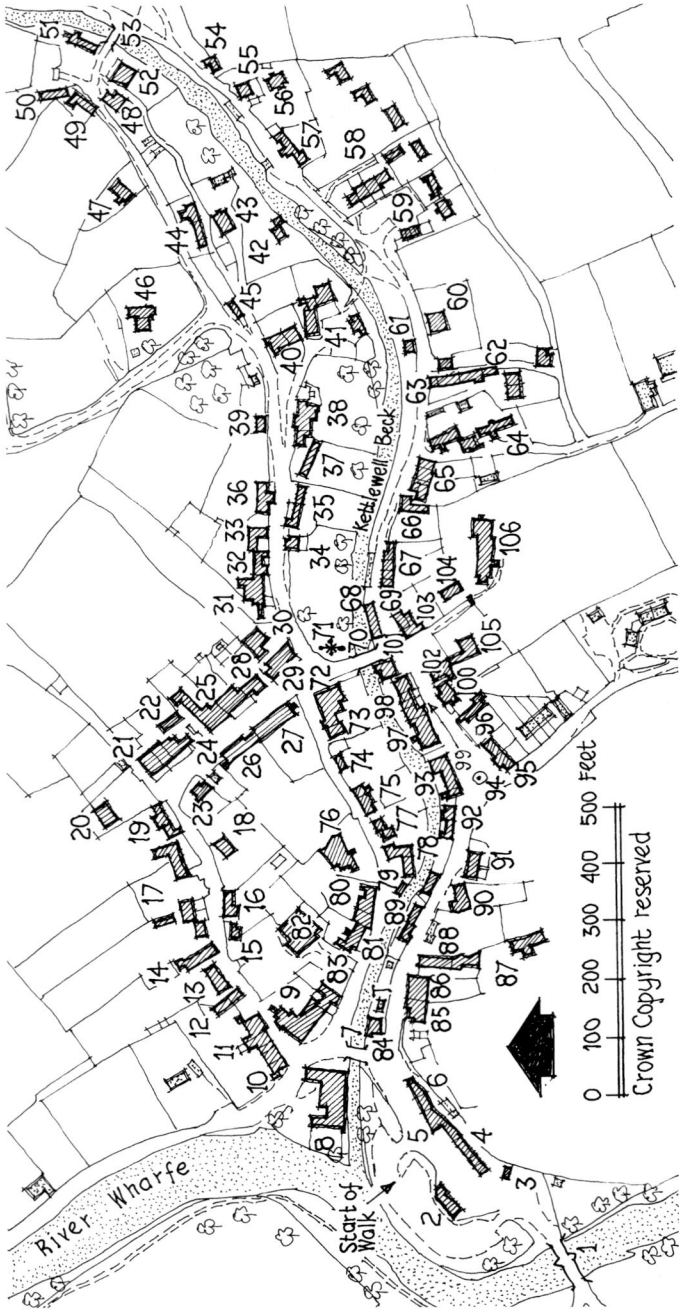

River Wharfe

Kettlewell Beck

Start of Walk

Crown Copyright reserved

0   100   200   300   400   500 Feet

164

block of buildings appears to date back at least to the 18th century and later, and started its life as stables belonging to the Bluebell Hotel where the tracehorses were kept. These horses were supplied by the Bluebell Hotel to provide the extra power needed to pull heavy loads up to the top of Park Rash. Therefore, this hotel should really be known as 'The Tracehorses Hotel'. The original part of the building dating back to the early part of the 18th century can be picked out in the front elevation.

Across the road is the Bluebell Hotel (9), being the original coaching inn which dates back to 1680 although there have since been many changes and extensions.

Now continue along the lane at the left-hand side of the Bluebell Hotel.

On the left are two properties known as 'Pennycroft' and 'Greystones' (10), which substantially date from Edwardian times. The adjoining properties known as 'Inglenook' and 'Eta Cottage (11), have been converted from old stable buildings formerly belonging to the Bluebell Hotel and dating from the early 18th century.

Rosemary Cottage (12), dates from the late 17th century having a nice entrance doorway with spandrels to the front elevation and evidence of earlier blocked up windows, but having been substantially altered in more recent times. There is evidence of a blocked up doorway with a small window inserted in the rear elevation. The front portion of this building was originally a barn.

Cam Laithe (13), appears to date from the second half of the 17th century, the left-hand section formerly being a barn added on slightly later, since the join is visible on the rear elevation. The mullioned windows were discovered since they had been blocked up and the porch was added, the overall restoration scheme being designed by Alan Dodd and carried out in the early 1990s.

Far Lane Farm (14), again dates from the 17th century but being much altered in the 18th century, comprising a farmhouse with a barn attached. The little cottage opposite (15), probably dates from the 18th century and has been rendered in the 19th century having a Victorian door.

Next is Prospect House (16), which in the main appears to date from Victorian times but there are

some 17th century mullioned windows to the rear of the eastern section of the building. The group of cottages opposite (17), were built in the early 1970s. Croft Cottage (18), was built in the 1980s.

Cam Cottage (19), has a datestone inscribed '1652 TR' over the front door and Cam Farmhouse, although dating from the 17th century, has been much altered in the late 18th or early 19th centuries, both properties having very Victorian front doors. Cam Lodge (20), is a good example of Victorian domestic architecture, with a rather nice slate roof; it probably dates from the 1860s.

Follow the road round to the right

Cam Cottages (21), originally comprising cottages and barns, appear to date from the early part of the 18th century although much altered in later times, No 1 having been converted fairly recently from a barn. Cam Fold (22), behind Cam Cottages has obviously been converted from a barn in recent times. Opposite is Jasmine Cottage (23), dating from the late 17th century although having been altered in the 18th century and later.

The garages (24), probably date from the 18th century. Whernside House, the Youth Hostel (25), appears to have a datestone over the door inscribed 'AS 1858', or it could be 1868, and it has been extended to the rear in recent times.

Opposite is Wharfedale House (26), which has a datestone over one of the entrances inscribed 'WC 1671'. This block which is now split into cottages overall probably dates from the 17th and 18th centuries. The adjoining property known as 'The Elms' (27), is a fine Victorian house with a beautiful south-west elevation, which has had stables to the rear dating, I would think, from the 1860s or 1870s.

Across the road is West Gate (28), which has a datestone over the door inscribed '16TC', but the remainder of the number is now illegible. It appears to have been altered in Regency times and rendered, possibly about the same time. The attached barn and the barns behind probably date from the 18th century.

The next building is The Vicarage (29), having a datestone over the nicely detailed front entrance inscribed '1661', although this could be incorrect since it is very difficult to decipher! This house has been extended in the early part of the 18th century and the front elevation much altered.

Turn left into the lane at the southern end of The Vicarage.

The barn (30), with a nice lean-to section at the front appears to date from the early part of the 18th century. Opposite, in the little meadow where the large trees now stand was formerly Kettlewell Mill (71), about which more will be said later.

Damside House (31), is a most interesting property dating from Regency times with a nice Georgian door and doorway with an inscription inscribed 'WDB 1815' on the lintel. Note the nice iron railings and gate. This building was once the home of Cutcliffe Hyne creator of Captain Kettle a late Victorian children's hero. This house and Damside Cottage are so named on account of the nearby reservoir, or lodge, which was formerly located in the meadow opposite in order to provide water power for the mill. The adjoining barn (32), may date back as far as the end of the 17th century.

Damside Cottage (33), appears to be contemporary with Damside House, or perhaps a few yards later, and the adjoining barn has the initials 'D' over 'WB 1835' carved in a plaque over the barn entrance.

Sunters Cottage (34), and Sunters Garth Farm (35), both date from the latter part of the 17th century, but Sunters Cottage has been much altered in the 18th century. The barn (36), also dates from the latter part of the 17th century with 18th century additions.

The Old Hall (37), is a delightful building with a fine range of mullioned windows to the south elevation. It would appear that the eastern end of the property with transoms to the five light mullioned windows dates from the first half of the 17th century, with the western section being added a few years later. Nearby are two barns (38), dating from the 17th and early 18th century.

Opposite is Croft Cottage (39), which appears to date from the 18th century but has been altered on the front elevation in the 19th century, having a very Victorian front door.

Now go down the little lane opposite.

The Old Hall

On the left is a block known as 'Green Lee' (40), which has its origins in the 17th century, although much altered in the 19th century together with a further nice extension near to the macadamed lane probably dating from the 1920s.

Beyond on the left is Kiln Hall Farm (41), which has a nice inscription over the door '1660 TC' with a rather interesting motif between the date and the initials, the 'T' probably referring to a member of the Tennant family. There are some interesting remains of three light mullioned windows on the front elevation, which in most cases have lost a mullion. The adjacent barns appear to be contemporary with the farmhouse.

Now retrace your steps back to the surfaced lane turning right. In a few yards bear right down another unsurfaced driveway.

Down by the side of Kettlewell Beck is a bungalow known as 'Burnside' (42), which appears to date from the 1930s and has been added on to the Generating House for Kettlewell's former electricity supply. This supply was started in 1913 and continued until the early 1950s when mains electricity was brought here. The Generator, which was powered by water from Kettlewell Beck, was not on the same scale as the project in Grassington and only produced enough electricity to provide one electric light in each property.

Chestnut Cottage (43), dates from the late 18th century having been altered in the 19th century. The three cottages including Renar Cottage and Long View (44), date from the 18th century with later alterations.

Now retrace your steps back again to the macadamed lane turning right.

Note the former joiner's shop (45), at the road junction which probably dates from the 18th century.

High up on the hillside to the left, adjacent to Coverdale Road, is Kettlewell's former school (46). The first reference to a school in Kettlewell is about 1660. In 1861 a committee was formed to raise money for a better qualified schoolmaster but most of the members were Wesleyans and the Vicar found little agreement between himself and them and so, in 1867, he started a separate fund to rebuild the school which was by this time far too small. The money was fairly quickly raised and this building was erected and the old school was pulled down in 1875. It was registered with the National School Society, but the villagers were unhappy about its location and withdrew their support and, so within a year, it closed and was never reopened. For many years this building was used as a hostel and in 1976 was converted into two dwellings known as 'Dalesview' and 'The Old School House'. At this time a floor was put in to make it two storey and a single storey extension was added on at the front. Following the closure of this building the school was carried on in a hired room in the village, when there was an average attendance of about fifty children. In 1883 the Education Department compelled them to form a School Board and build a Board School, this being the building just outside the village at the side of the road to Starbotton.

Continuing north-eastwards along the road we soon come to Meadowcroft (47).

This property has a datestone inscribed '1929' over the entrance door. Beyond, on the right, is Fell Foot (48), which appears to date from the 18th century but has been much altered in more recent times.

We now enter a pleasant little square with a green, this part of Kettlewell being known as 'Town Head'.

Ladycroft on the left (49), may have its origins in the 18th century, but it has been very much altered, probably in the 1920s. Beyond is Townhead Cottage (50), which may date back to the 17th century having a nice battered projecting chimney stack, but it has been much altered in recent times. A modern lintel bears the inscription 'EG 1731'.

The two cottages opposite, known as No 1 and No 2 Town Head (51), appear to date from the 18th century, but have been much altered in later times. To the south is the former Kettlewell Methodist Chapel (52), which bears a plaque inscribed 'c 1860'. However, it was actually built in 1835 when lead mining was the dominant industry. This Chapel was closed in 1987 and shortly afterwards it was converted into two cottages known as 'Chapel Beck' and 'Chapel Fell'.

The bridge over Kettlewell Beck (53), is a very pleasing structure which probably dates from the latter part of the 18th century. About a quarter of a mile further up this little valley (Grid Reference 975728) on the bank of Cam Gill Beck a smelt mill had been established before 1669. The mill closed in 1887, but was kept in good condition until 1942, when it was blown up by the army. The mill chimney, however, had already been blown down in a gale in 1893.

It is interesting to note that this chimney was located high up on the hillside well above the Park Rash road and having an underground flue. If you go on to the Coverdale Road to a point about 100 yards beyond the last of the line of trees on the right-hand side, where there is a small gate on the left, the route of the flue can easily be picked out. It did not go up from the smelt mill in a straight line and the section below the road will be seen to have a distinct curve round to the right.

Cross the bridge turning right into the little lane leading back into the village.

Abreast of the former Methodist Chapel graveyard on each side of Kettlewell Beck can be picked out the concrete abutments which formed the door for the electricity undertaking. The wall on the south-east bank extended out well beyond the middle of the beck with a groove at the end to accommodate timber boards. On the other bank was a concrete pillar with a similar recess, thus allowing a series of boards to be slotted in to impound the water. The reason for this arrangement was on account of silting up and so periodically the boards were removed so that the reservoir could easily be cleaned out.

The first building on the left is a little barn (54), which probably dates from the early part of the 18th century. Beyond is Ghyll Cottage (55), which may have its origins in the 17th century, but it has been much altered in the 18th century and later. Behind is Moorlands (56), which would appear to date from the 1930s.

A little further on is Hawbank (57), which may date back to the latter part of the 17th century, but it has been much altered in more recent times. Some old worn steps remain which at one time may have given access to accommodation for a farm worker over a barn. There is evidence of a projecting semi-circular chimney stack in the westerly gable and the garages are quite new.

Looking across the beck Burnside (42), can be clearly seen linked on to the former electricity generating building. Note the concrete piers in the beck, which supported the pipeline which carried the water to drive the generator.

Behind Hawbank are three detached properties known as 'Craiglands', 'Willow Bank' and 'Heathlands' (58), which were built between 1980 and the early 1990s, using cast blocks similar to those used for Kettlewell Garage. Langcliffe Garth (59), mainly comprises local authority housing built in the 1960s and now almost all in private ownership.

Continuing in a westerly direction we come to Langcliffe Country House (60), which has a datestone inscribed '1700' over its front door. If this is a genuine datestone then this building has been much altered in Victorian times. Across the road is a cottage (61), which has been converted from an 18th century barn. The front part of High Fold (62), has been made out of a barn which appears to date from early in the 20th century. The block to the south at the end of the garden has been converted from an 18th century barn.

Beyond is Wears Fold (63), comprising a block of three cottages dating from the latter part of the 17th century, but much altered in the 18th century. There are some mullioned windows and one 17th century doorway remaining and at the south end a new section has been added on, probably in the 1970s. The adjacent Langcliffe Cottages appear to date from the 1920s.

Now walk down the little lane on the left.

The four cottages known as 'Cowslip', 'Clover', 'Coltsfoot' and 'Buttercup' (64), were nicely converted from 17th century barns in 1987. Beyond is Fold Farm which is architecturally and

Fold Farm

historically one of the more important buildings in Upper Wharfedale. Note that it has a much steeper roof pitch than most other Dales buildings, since it started its life as a late Medieval (15th century) four bay timber framed single storey open hall structure which would have had a thatched roof and wattle and daub infilling between the wooden members. Many fragments of the timber framed building remain including several roof timbers and it is possible that this residence may have been built by a wealthy yeoman connected with the textile industry in the Calderdale area.

This house was probably encased in stone in the 17th century, at the same time being extended at each end with the addition of a semi-circular stair turret on the east elevation. There are two late 17th century stone fireplaces at ground floor level.

Retrace your steps back to the main lane, noting Fold Cottages (65), before turning left.

Fold Cottages appear to date from the 18th century with later alterations. Eller House (66), dates from the latter part of the 18th century, but has been much altered in the 19th century having an entrance from that period. Note the Victorian gateposts and wall together with the iron railings and gate.

The next block of four cottages including Sunnydale (67), appears to date from the 18th century although it has been built in phases. Almost opposite is Kings Court (68), which was converted from barns in the early 1990s. Lilac Cottage (69), was converted from a barn in the late 1980s.

Fold Farm as it may have appeared in the 14th century

Turn right crossing Kettlewell Bridge.

Kettlewell Bridge (70), is almost identical in design to the bridge in Threshfield Village and was built about 1820 by Alexander Nowell. On the right just beyond the bridge, where there is today a group of tall trees, stood Kettlewell Mill (71). The first mention of a building on this site is in 1265, which would be a corn mill. In 1656 the Mill was let in two portions, one of them to the Bolland family who held it until 1805. At this time the import of cheaper wheat and the changes in the economic structure brought the useful life of the local corn mills to an end. The Mill, therefore, changed its use to the manufacture of cotton, but by 1822 this operation had ceased and long before the end of the century the buildings had been pulled down. This ended several hundred years of activity on this site with peasants, miners, White Canons, and the Lords of Middleham Castle together with the Trust Lords of Kettlewell all being concerned with it.

Opposite is Kettlewell Post Office & Village Store (72), having a fine Victorian entrance doorway bearing the date 1877. The part of the building near to the bridge is older and in the front are some nice Victorian railings.

Now turn left into the lane alongside the Post Office.

Knipe View Cottage (73), has obviously once been a chapel having a stone high up inscribed 'Jubilee 1863', although there would have originally been more wording. Brook House (74), is probably a fairly early Victorian building although the overhanging gables suggest that it may have been altered early in the 20th century.

The former Barclays Bank building and Hideaway Cottage (75), probably have their origins in the 17th century, the Cottage having its main elevation to the rear facing south. Note the lintel over a ground floor window with the initials 'IH' and what appears to be a bird carved crudely in the stonework. Opposite is Wharfeside (76), a fine Victorian house dating from the middle part of the 19th century with a recent extension at the north-east end. The barn (77), dates from the early part of the 18th century with a lean-to garage section set back, which is much later in date.

Beyond is The Cornershop Tea Room, known as 'Market House' and an adjoining cottage known as 'Limber Cottage' (78), which date from the late 18th century. The front of the Tea Room is faced with watershot stonework. The nearby little building (79), has been nicely repointed and restored and again probably dates from the 18th century.

Opposite are three interesting properties namely Troutbeck Cottage, Troutbeck House and Beckside (80). Troutbeck Cottage appears to date at least from the 18th century and may at one time have been a barn, since there is evidence of what has once been a wider opening at ground floor level. The adjoining Troutbeck House that has Victorian windows and a very lofty entrance doorway again may be quite old. Looking carefully at the stonework in my opinion it was once a lower building which has been raised in height in the 19th century using watershot stonework, with new windows inserted. Beckside, with its Victorian frontage is again, I think, an older building altered in the 19th century.

Adjoining is Fern House (81), which again was originally a smaller house probably dating from the 18th century, which has been extended and much altered in the mid 19th century. The original gable end of the older house can be picked out in the stonework when viewed from the grounds of the Village Hall. The Village Hall (82), dates from 1926 with later extensions which have been added over the years. Of particular interest is the large Art Nouveau styled window in the south-west gable. The rear portion of Greta (83), dates from the latter part of the 17th century, the front part being added on later and much altered in the 18th and 19th centuries.

Now cross Townfoot Bridge and turn left into the road running on the south side of Kettlewell Beck.

The Smithy (84), appears to date from the early part of the 18th century. Opposite is a late 17th century barn (85), converted into two dwelling houses known as 'Plover Cottage' and 'Curlew Cottage'. This building may at one time have been separate from the adjoining Low Hall, since the stone quoins stop short of the next building but they may, of course, have been joined further back.

Low Hall which is now the Over & Under Shop (86), is an interesting building dating back to the 17th century. It has some rather nice 18th century windows fronting on to the road, with nice moulded stone surrounds. Note the interesting stone quoins to the north elevation, especially the very tall vertical ones at the north-west corner of the building. Inside there is a 17th century doorway which has once been on the outside and, so the building has in my opinion been extended southwards, possibly in the late 18th or early 19th centuries. There is also an 18th century stone fireplace in the ground floor shop portion of the building. The south elevation is very Victorian in character having a datestone over the main entrance inscribed 'T.1849.T'. Home Croft (87), was built about 1987.

Coach House (88), dates from the mid to late 18th century and has now been converted into cottages. Across the road is a block comprising two properties namely Green End Cottage and Victoria Cottage (89). Victoria Cottage has a nice 17th century doorway with a delightful moulded detail and the two dwellings probably date from this period, although they have been much altered over the years.

Alva Cottage (90), dates from the late 17th century. There are two windows from this period in the east gable which have long since lost their mullions, together with remnants of windows from this period on the south elevation. Almost adjoining is Maypole Barn (91), a fine 18th century building converted into a dwelling in the 1980s. Note the War Memorial and Village Stocks opposite in the nicely laid out Garden of Remembrance. Adjoining are two properties, namely Fellside and the former Police Station, now known as 'Valley View' (92), which are Edwardian dating from the early part of the 20th century.

Little Beck (93), has its origins in the 17th century. Note the Maypole (94), having a nice weather vane with the date '1898'. Knocklong and Maypole Cottage (95), appear to date from the 18th century, Maypole Cottage having been converted from a barn.

Now walk eastwards along the fairly wide section of road known as 'The Green'.

Spring Cottage (96), is a lovely late 17th century building with some nice 18th century three light mullioned windows, one at ground floor level and one at first floor level, both having moulded stone surrounds. The house opposite (97), dates from the 18th century with evidence of mullioned windows from this period. The adjoining property, Manningham House (98), has been refronted but probably dates back to the 18th century. The three cottages namely Pollys Cottage, Calton Cottage and Woodbine Cottage (99), appear to date from the late 17th century having been very much altered in the 18th century and more recent times.

Manor Cottage (100), dates from the 17th and 18th centuries. The Kings Head (101), dates from the 17th century with 18th century two and three light mullioned windows inserted in the front elevation. It possesses a fine 17th century fireplace, the arch having one of the largest spans to be found in the part of Upper Wharfedale covered by this book.

The large barn opposite (102), dates from the latter part of the 17th century having a fine flight of stone steps and some 18th century and later openings. Bridge House (103), appears to date from the 18th century and Lych Gate House (104), was built in the 1980s. Over the high wall to the

Kettlewell Church

right is The Manor House (105), a late 17th century building which was extensively altered in the Georgian period, having a fine semi-circular headed staircase window on its north elevation together with a nicely detailed entrance and windows with moulded surrounds to the south elevation.

Note the fine Lynch Gate as you enter the Churchyard.

The first church on this site was probably built by or under the patronage of the Percys, probably in the time of Henry I, but nothing remains from this time except the Font. This is of interest, carrying the three boars' heads of the Percy badge, a plain cylindrical form raised upon four short pillars. This Church was served until the 16th century by the Canons of Coverham Abbey, and after that by a Vicar. The old structure was pulled down in 1819 and a new Church to the designs of Thomas Anderton was erected in 1820. Today the Tower

which has 18th century characteristics survives, but the remainder of the building was rebuilt between 1882 and 1885 to the designs of TH & F Healey, being relatively simple and restrained for what was generally a very flamboyant period of Victorian architecture. There is, however, in my opinion some striking stained glass. The fine East Window was erected to the memory of Charles Godfrey Haggas Cutcliffe-Hyne, a Lieutenant in the Irish Guards who at the age of eighteen, in 1916, 'Gave his life for This England'. Another stained glass window was moved here from the Methodist Church when it closed and the western window on the south side of the Nave is of interest. This depicts St Francis and St Hubert and is in memory of Major John Holdsworth MC of Scargill who was killed in 1945 aged twenty four years.

Now retrace your steps back to the National Park car park.

When I walk the few yards from our home emerging through the little archway leading from The Woggan into Main Street on a fine day, I at once feel that I am on holiday seeing people sitting having coffee outside The Dales Kitchen, or as I walk down the street getting a glimpse of the lovely old Ashfield House tucked away in Summers Fold and then the many visitors sitting outside our four ancient hostelries usually drinking Black Sheep, Theakston's, John Smith's or Tetley's! As I enter The Square my childhood memories once more really come alive as I see again the delightful old pump, the great bulk of Grassington House hiding away in a corner, the former white painted cottages which now form the Upper Wharfedale Museum, the picturesque Georgian doorway leading into Peter Walbank's shop and, of course, the Black Horse shyly peeping into The Square from behind the building which is now the Grassington Pharmacy.

I hope that you have enjoyed reading this little book as much as I have enjoyed writing it, and if you have been able to do some, or all, of the walks you may have learnt something about the fascinating history of this very beautiful corner of the Yorkshire Dales. Not only is the scenery breathtaking causing visitors from all corners of the world to instantly fall in love with it, but most of the buildings we have seen and admired were not built yesterday! A very large proportion were built nearly three hundred and fifty years ago and some, including a few of the churches, go back many centuries.

As we approach the start of the Third Millennium, which hopefully many of those reading this book will see, it is worth reflecting upon the fact that when the clock strikes midnight on the 31st December 1999 it is not just a point in time that will be recorded at Greenwich and elsewhere, but much more importantly it will mark two thousand years since the birth of Jesus Christ, which will be celebrated in the many lovely churches and chapels which I have tried to describe and nowhere more so than in Linton Church, which is so dear to many people of the Grassington area such that it might well be called the 'Little Cathedral of Upper Wharfedale'.

Norman arches to
North aisle of
Linton Church

Bibliography

Beaumont H M: Sir William Milner

Bogg E: Higher Wharfedale

Brooks S D: A History of Grassington

Brooks S D; The Parish and People of Linton in Craven

Crowther J: Rambles Round Grassington

Evans P: Thesis on Conservation of Historic Buildings

Gill M C: The Wharfedale Mines

Gower T: Discover Grassington and Upper Wharfedale

Houghton F W: Upper Wharfedale

I WAS GLAD: Welcome to Scargill House, Kettlewell

Joy D: Yorkshire Dales Review No. 60 Autumn 1997

Kennedy P: The Struggle of a Minority – A Short History of Catholicism in Craven

Lodge E: A Wharfedale Village – A detailed study of the History of Burnsall and Thorpe-sub-Montem

Loughlin J & M: St Margaret Clitherow's Church, Threshfield

Mee A: Yorkshire West Riding

Musgrove F: The North of England – A History from Roman Times to the Present

Pevsner N: The Buildings of England – Yorkshire West Riding

Pontefract E and Hartley M: Wharfedale

Raistrick A: Buildings in the Yorkshire Dales

Raistrick A: Green Tracks on the Pennines

Raistrick A: Kettlewell – A history of the village since pre-Norman times

Raistrick A: Old Yorkshire Dales

Raistrick E: Village Schools – An Upper Wharfedale History

Raistrick E: What to see in Grassington, Linton and Threshfield

Royal Commission on the Historical Monuments of England – Fold Farmhouse, Kettlewell

Speakman C: Yorkshire Dales Review No. 61 Winter 1997

Speight H: Upper Wharfedale

Taylor J: Littondale Life

Upper Wharfedale Field Society – Vernacular Buildings Study Group – Reports upon the following buildings – Conistone: Chapel House, Old Hall, Renshaw's Farmhouse; Grassington: 11 Hardy Grange, 13 Hardy Grange, Lady Well Cottage, 53 Main Street, Scaw Ghyll, The Nook Chapel Street, The Old Manse, Town Head Farmhouse; Hawkswick: Strand House; Hebden: Chapel Garth; Kettlewell: Fold Farmhouse, Methodist Chapel, Old Hall; Kilnsey: Old Hall; Linton: Beckside, Fountaine Cottage, The Grange, Manor House Farm, Nook Farm, Sedber Barn, White Abbey; Thorpe: Village Profile; Threshfield: Park Grange Farm, School, Toft House Farm.

Walton J: Homesteads of the Yorkshire Dales

Whitaker T D: The History and Antiquities of the Deanery of Craven in the County of York – Volume 2

Wright C E: History and Description of the Church of St Michael and All Angels Linton in Craven

Wright J E: The Church of St Peter, Hebden in the beautiful Yorkshire Dales

Wright J E: The Parish Church of St Michael and All Angels Linton in Craven North Yorkshire

Index

Notes